# READ JAPANESE KANJI TODAY

**The Easy Way to Learn 400 Basic Kanji**

Len Walsh

TUTTLE Publishing

Tokyo | Rutland, Vermont | Singapore

# ACKNOWLEDGMENTS

I am indebted to Professors Takahashi Makoto, Uehara Akira, and Liu Kang-Shih for their assistance in preparing this manuscript, and to Boye De Mente and Frank Hudachek for their invaluable editorial suggestions. I also wish to thank the Asia House for the research grant that made this book possible.

Published by Tuttle Publishing, an imprint of Periplus Editions (HK) Ltd.

**www.tuttlepublishing.com**

Copyright © 2009, 2017 by Len Walsh

ISBN 978-4-8053-1432-6

**Distributed by**

**North America, Latin America & Europe**
Tuttle Publishing
364 Innovation Drive
North Clarendon, VT 05759-9436 U.S.A.
Tel: 1 (802) 773-8930; Fax: 1 (802) 773-6993
info@tuttlepublishing.com
www.tuttlepublishing.com

**Japan**
Tuttle Publishing
Yaekari Building, 3rd Floor, 5-4-12 Osaki,
Shinagawa-ku, Tokyo 141 0032
Tel: (81) 3 5437-0171
Fax: (81) 3 5437-0755
sales@tuttle.co.jp
www.tuttle.co.jp

**Asia Pacific**
Berkeley Books Pte. Ltd.
61 Tai Seng Avenue #02-12 Singapore 534167
Tel: (65) 6280-1330; Fax: (65) 6280-6290
inquiries@periplus.com.sg
www.periplus.com

First edition
20 19 18 17    10 9 8 7 6 5 4 3 2 1    1703MP

Printed in Singapore

## ABOUT TUTTLE
## "Books to Span the East and West"

Our core mission at Tuttle Publishing is to create books which bring people together one page at a time. Tuttle was founded in 1832 in the small New England town of Rutland, Vermont (USA). Our fundamental values remain as strong today as they were then—to publish best-in-class books informing the English-speaking world about the countries and peoples of Asia. The world has become a smaller place today and Asia's economic, cultural and political influence has expanded, yet the need for meaningful dialogue and information about this diverse region has never been greater. Since 1948, Tuttle has been a leader in publishing books on the cultures, arts, cuisines, languages and literatures of Asia. Our authors and photographers have won numerous awards and Tuttle has published thousands of books on subjects ranging from martial arts to paper crafts. We welcome you to explore the wealth of information available on Asia at **www.tuttlepublishing.com**.

# Contents

# INTRODUCTION

## What Is Japanese Writing?

The Japanese write their language with ideograms they borrowed from China nearly two thousand years ago. Some two thousand years before that, the ancient Chinese had formed these ideograms, sometimes called pictographs or characters, and known in Japanese as "kanji" 漢字 (literally translated as "Chinese letters"), from pictures of objects and actions they observed around them.

To the Chinese, the sun had looked like this ☀, so this became their written word for **sun**. This pictograph was gradually squared off and simplified, first to ⊙ then to ⊖ and finally to 日, to give it balance and an idealized shape, and to make it easier to read and write. This is still the way the word **sun** is written in both China and Japan today.

The ancient Chinese first drew a pictograph of a tree like this 🌲. Over centuries it was gradually simplified and stylized and proportioned to fit into a uniform square for easy writing and recognition. It was squared off, first to 米 and finally to 木, which became the written word for **tree**.

To form the word for **root** or **origin**, the Chinese just drew in more roots at the bottom of the tree 本 to emphasize that portion of the picture. Over time, they squared and simplified this pictograph to 本, which is still today the written word for **root** or **origin**.

When the characters, the kanji, for **sun** 日 and for **origin** 本 are used together in a compound word, that is, a word made up of more than one kanji, they form the word 日本, which is how you write the word **Japan** in Japanese.

When the individual pictograph for **sun** 日 and the one for **tree** 木 are combined to make one new composite kanji 東, it shows the sun at sunrise rising up behind a tree, and becomes the pictograph for **east**.

The Chinese drew a pictograph of the stone lantern that guarded each ancient Chinese capital 髙 then gradually, over centuries, squared it off and simplified it to a stylized form, first 帛 and finally 京, which is now the written word for **capital**. These two kanji, 東 and 京, put together into a compound word 東京, form the written word **Tokyo**, eastern-capital, the capital of Japan.

Kanji may look mysterious and impenetrable at first approach, but as these examples show, they are not difficult at all to decode and understand. The kanji characters are not just random strokes: each one is a picture or a composite of several pictures and has a meaning based on the content of the pictures.

4

The Japanese written language contains a number of kanji, but not as many as Westerners often assume. To graduate from grammar school a student must know about 1,000 characters. At this point the student is considered literate. A high school graduate should know about 2,000 kanji, which is about the number used in daily newspapers. To read college textbooks, a student will need to know about 3,000. In a good dictionary, there may be about 6,000 characters.

These thousands of kanji, however, are all built up from less than 300 separate elements, or pictographs, many of which are seldom used. Once you learn the most frequently used elements you will know not only a number of the common kanji (some of the elements stand alone as kanji themselves), but you also will be able to learn hundreds of other kanji simply by combining the elements in different ways.

For example, you already know the kanji for **tree** 木. The kanji for a **person** is a pictograph of a person standing up 人. When the element for person is combined with other elements to make a new kanji, it is often squared off to イ, for better balance and aesthetic appearance in the new pictograph. When you combine the element for **tree** and the element for **person** you form a new kanji 休, a pictograph of a person resting against a tree. The meaning of this new kanji is **to rest**.

The Chinese also combined the element for **person** イ with the element for **root** 本 into a new composite kanji, a pictograph showing "the root of a human." The meaning of this new kanji 体 is **the human body**.

Another example is the kanji meaning **old** 古. It is formed by combining the element 十, which by itself is a separate kanji meaning **ten** (it is a pictograph of two crossed hands 廾 having ten fingers), and the element 口, which also is a separate kanji by itself, meaning **mouth** (obviously a pictograph of a mouth). The new kanji 古, literally ten mouths, figuratively ten generations, means **old**.

In kanji that are formed from combinations of elements, of which some are themselves stand-alone kanji and some are not, there are generally two to four elements, occasionally five or more. When combining elements, the Chinese placed each separate element either at the left, right, top, bottom or center of the kanji square in which the characters are written, wherever it looked the best.

For example, the kanji for **tree** 木, when used as an element in other composite kanji, is sometimes placed on the left side of the new kanji, as in 村, sometimes on the right, as in 休, sometimes on the top, as in 杏, and sometimes on the bottom, as in 集. A few elements form a frame 囗 or a partial frame 冂 around the kanji square. The kanji 困, meaning **to be in trouble**, is an example of the element for tree 木 being circumscribed by a **frame** 囗.

Naturally, some kanji are used with greater frequency than others. The objective of this book is to teach you to recognize and understand the basic meaning of more than 400 of the most common and useful characters after only a few hours study. Through associations with Japanese proper names like **Ginza, Tokyo, Osaka, Honda, Nissan, Hitachi,** and **Mr. Yamamoto,** and with Japanese words you already know, like **kimono, geisha,** and **typhoon,** you will also be able to remember the pronunciations of many of these 400 characters with very little effort.

For full comprehension of the Japanese language, spoken or written, knowledge of grammar is of course absolutely necessary. There are already many excellent textbooks on Japanese grammar and other aspects of the Japanese language available to anyone who has the time and desire to learn Japanese. This book is limited therefore to teaching only how to read and understand the Japanese kanji and how the kanji are used in Japanese.

In the 1960s, when the first edition of this book was issued, kanji were taught through rote memory, whether to Japanese school children in their own school systems or to foreigners interested in the language. The number of strokes in each kanji, the order in which the strokes were written, and penmanship were stressed. Students were required to write each new kanji enough times so that its shape stuck in their memory.

There was no attempt, except in scholarly research papers, to show how the kanji were first formed as pictures by the Chinese and then developed into ideographs, or how to explain the structure of each kanji is built up from a few parts, each part with its own distinctive meaning.

Now, there are several books in English which teach kanji through mnemonic systems based on the meaning of the pictographs and symbols that the Chinese drew when they invented kanji. There are now also many books written in Japanese for Japanese primary-school children suggesting to the children that they learn kanji the easy way, through the mnemonic of the pictographs on which the Chinese based the kanji, although the traditional rote-memory method is still preferred in the Japanese school system.

One Japanese scholar, for example, wrote in the preface to his Primary School Pictograph Kanji Dictionary: "There are many children who do not like the study of kanji. There are also many children who say the only way to pass the kanji tests is by rote memory. Haven't you all had the experience of being able to memorize the kanji only by writing each character over and over again? This naturally turns you away from the kanji. But there are many kanji that look like pictures and many parts of kanji repeated in different characters. Looking at kanji this way will make the study of kanji much more friendly. This dictionary clearly and simply explains how kanji were developed and how they were constructed, and will make your study of kanji much easier."

It is possible, of course, to learn the kanji through rote memory, but at great expense in time and effort. The shortcut is to learn the meanings of the interchangeable parts rather than simply try to memorize a square full of lines. The character for the word **listen** 聞 becomes much less formidable when you see that 門 is a picture of a **gate** 門, and that 耳 is a picture of an **ear** 耳 eavesdropping at the gate.

READ JAPANESE KANJI TODAY uses this time-saver—the principle that each kanji is composed of interchangeable parts and that if you remember the meaning of the parts it will help you remember the meaning of the whole. Each part was originally a picture drawn by the Chinese to represent an actual object or action, just as in western culture the Egyptians did the same to draw their hieroglyphics. To memorize the kanji all you need to do is look behind the pictographs and see what the Chinese used as models.

Looking behind the pictographs into antiquity to see what scenes the Chinese actually drew at first, and how these pictographs evolved over the centuries, is often very difficult. Chinese, Japanese, and Western scholars have been successful in tracing the history of many kanji, but for other kanji there are still differences of opinion on what the original pictograph was, what its original meaning was, and how both pictograph and meaning evolved.

This book is not a history, and my objective is just to show you the easiest way to understand and memorize the kanji and their meanings. Where there are disputes between the scholars on the origin or evolution of a kanji, I have selected the version which best helped me remember the kanji. If you, the reader, can discover a better mnemonic, by all means use it.

## How The Characters Were Constructed

The earliest writing in both the East and the West was done with pictographs. To write the "word" for **cow** or **mountain** or **eye**, both the Chinese and those in early western cultures drew a picture of a **cow**, a **mountain**, or an **eye**. To the Chinese these pictures were 牛, 山, and 目. To the early Westerners—Sumerians, Phoenicians and Egyptians—they were 𓃾, 𓈙, and 𓁹.

To write words which stood for ideas or actions or feelings—words that pictures of single objects or actions could not express—the Chinese combined several pictographs to depict a scene which acted out the meaning of the word. They combined, as we saw above, pictures of the **sun** 日 and a **tree** 木 in a scene to show the sun rising up behind the **tree** 東. They used this scene to stand for the word **east**—the direction you face when you see the sun rising up behind a tree.

In other examples, two pictographs of trees were put side by side 林 to stand for the word **woods**, and three pictographs of trees were put together 森 to stand for the word **forest**.

At the point where the Chinese ran out of concrete objects to draw, symbolism became essential. Without symbols, scenes representing complex thoughts would have grown to the size of panoramas. The kanji for these complex pictographs would then have too many elements and lines, generally called strokes, to be written in one square and still be readable.

Some Chinese characters have over 60 strokes, but the Chinese found out early on that kanji having more than 25 or 30 strokes were difficult to read and write. They continually abbreviated many of the kanji, reducing the number of strokes in some elements and eliminating other elements entirely. They are still abbreviating the kanji to this day. Some, but not all, of the Chinese abbreviations have been adopted by the Japanese.

Symbols are images that a society agrees represent something else. Any symbol can represent anything, as long as everyone agrees that this is so, like red and green traffic lights. The Chinese agreed on symbols for their written language. They decided, for example, that the symbol ⟂ would represent the word for **up**. It started out as ⊥, and is now written 上. **Down** began as the reverse ⟂, and is now written 下.

To stand for the words power or authority, rather than devise a scene showing perhaps a general backed by his army, or a father disciplining his children, the Chinese simply used the symbol of a hand holding a stick 彐 to symbolize this meaning. (The Egyptians used a pictograph of a whip to symbolize the same thing.)

As a kanji by itself, the hand holding a stick was first drawn by the Chinese as 彐, gradually stylized as 父, then 父, and now is written 父, meaning **father**. When the hand holding a stick is used as one element in a composite kanji, it is usually further stylized to 攵 or 尹.

In the same way, **pleasure** was symbolized by a drum and cymbals 樂 in Chinese, and by a man jumping with joy 𓀃 in Egyptian hieroglyphics.

Another technique the Chinese used to form new kanji was to add what they called an "indicative" to an existing kanji to call attention to a part of the picture that highlights the meaning of the new character. For example, the pictograph for **sword** was drawn 刀 by the Chinese, and eventually squared to 刀. Then the Chinese added an indicative, a dot ヽ on the edge of the blade, and made the pictograph of a new kanji 刃, written in final form 刃, meaning **blade**.

Another example of an indicative is the addition of a line signifying "roots" to the bottom of the kanji for tree 木 to form the new kanji 本, meaning root or **origin**, as we saw above.

8

Placing the "indicative" in different sections of the pictograph will change the aspect that is emphasized, and thus the meaning of the new kanji. For example, adding an indicative to a **tree** 木 down around the roots, as noted above, gives the meaning **root** 本. Adding the same line as an indicative among the branches of the tree 未 emphasizes that the tree is still growing and producing new branches, and gives the new kanji the meaning of **still growing** or **immature** or **not yet**. Adding instead a slightly longer line closer to the top of the **tree** 末 emphasizes the top of the tree and makes a new kanji meaning **tip** or **end** or **extremity**.

To remember the meanings of the kanji as they are used in Japanese, there is no need to remember whether an element is a pictograph, a symbol, an indicative, or an ideograph, or indeed to trace the permutations of the original Chinese drawing of a specific kanji down to its form today. That is best left to the scholars, who themselves still find different theories about the origins. Rather, your objective is to memorize the meaning of the present-day **kanji** by using your own understanding of what the pictures in the ideograph meant to the Chinese who first drew it.

For example, the kanji 口, as described above, means **mouth**. When a line is drawn through the middle of the **mouth** it forms the new kanji 中 meaning **center** or **middle**. Some scholars say this form is an indicative, the added line in the center emphasizing center. Other scholars say it is a picture of a flagpole with another pole drawn through its center. Some say it is a pictograph of an arrow piercing the center of a target. Others say it is a board with a line through the center or a box with a line down the middle.

At this stage of your study, it is important only to remember that 中 means **center** or **middle**. Whatever symbolic connection you make between 中 and **center** that helps you to remember the connection between them is the mnemonic that you should use.

I have given my interpretation, based on a composite of opinions among Chinese, Japanese and Western scholars, of the meanings of the pictures in each kanji. The purpose is to help you remember the 400+ kanji in this book. If you find an interpretation of the pictures which better helps you to remember the kanji, then that is the interpretation you should use.

There came a time when the early nations of the Western world decided to give up pictographic writing for something simpler. They began to use a phonetic system in which a specific picture stood for a certain sound instead of standing for a certain meaning. Their scholars arbitrarily selected some pictures to stand for the sounds they used in their language and abandoned all the other pictures. One of the phonetic systems thus developed was, of course, the forefather of the English alphabet.

The pictograph the Egyptians selected for the sound of **A** was **cow** ⊔, by this time written ⴻ. The meaning **cow** was dropped. The picture ⴻ stood for the pronunciation **A** and nothing else. Through many hundred years of change, ⴻ came gradually to be written ⅄, which became the English letter **A**. (The Chinese pictograph for **cow**, on the other hand, basically has not changed at all, and still means **cow**.)

The Egyptian pictograph for **eye** ⬯ came to be our letter **O**, and the Egyptian pictograph for **mountain** ⌒ became our letter **S**. In fact, all 26 letters of the our alphabet are, in one way or another, direct descendants of this early picture writing of the West. The Chinese, on the other hand, just went on with the characters. They did at one time start the rudiments of a phonetic system but abandoned it.

The simple Chinese pictographs can be grouped into a few major categories. Most pictographs were drawn from objects the Chinese saw around them. Many were drawings of human beings in different shapes and postures, and of parts of the human body. Natural objects such as trees, plants, rocks, the sun, birds, and other animals were another major source. Weapons, which in that era meant only hand-held weapons like bows and arrows, knives, axes, spears, and lances, also were a source. Other important categories were houses and buildings, kitchen utensils, and clothing.

After the Chinese had invented all the characters they needed at the time, their next step was to standardize the kanji into a form easy to read and write. Over a period of about 2,000 years, they did this by simplifying and re-proportioning the pictures so they would all be about the same size, fit into the same-sized square, and be uniformly written throughout the country.

This was done by squaring circles, straightening some lines and eliminating others, and abbreviating or eliminating the more complicated portions of the picture. The shapes of some were changed slightly to make them more aesthetic or to make them easier and quicker to write. In fact, when the characters first took on their modern form they were called "clerical script" and were the form followed by the government bureaucrats in their record-keeping.

Some of the changes differed according to where in the square the element would be put. For example, the pictograph **fire** 🔥 became the kanji 火. When added as an element at the top of a composite kanji, **fire** 火 is generally written ⍍, for example 炎, and when added at the bottom is generally written ⺣, for example 黒.

When the kanji for **person** 人 is added at the left of a composite kanji, it is generally written 亻, as in 休, a person next to a tree, meaning **to rest**. When a **person** is added at the top of a composite kanji, it is generally written ⼇, as in the character 亡, meaning **die**. (The picture ∟ means corner.) The composite character was originally written 𠃊, "a person being hidden in a corner, no longer seen," then squared to 𠄌, and finally to 亡.

The process of combining pictographs into new kanji, then stylizing and simplifying them, made the final characters a little more abstract and less pictorially representative than the original pictures, of course, but the form of the original picture is still clearly visible and with just a little imagination on your part the pictures and scenes depicted in the kanji will come alive.

## How Japan Borrowed Characters From China

Until the third century A.D., scholars say, the Japanese had no written language at all. How their society, already well-developed by that time, was able to get along without a script is very difficult to imagine. I suspect that somewhere along the line an archeologist will discover evidence of native writing or a form of borrowed script that existed in Japan before it borrowed characters from China. But until that time, what the scholars say must be accepted.

In any case, the Japanese had a spoken language, and when they saw that their neighbor, China, had both a spoken and a well-developed written language, they decided to borrow the Chinese writing system. The Japanese took the written Chinese characters and attached them to the Japanese spoken words of corresponding meaning. Where the Japanese had no equivalent word, they borrowed the Chinese meaning and pronunciation as well as the written character. They called these characters **kanji**, a compound word composed from two separate kanji, **kan** 漢, meaning **China**, and **ji** 字, meaning **letter**.

While the Japanese could use these imported Chinese characters to write the basic roots of Japanese words, they could not use the characters to write grammatical word endings because Japanese grammar and morphology were so different from Chinese. In Chinese, there were no grammatical endings to show what part of speech a word is (corresponding in English to endings such as **-tion**, **-ish**, **-ed**, **-ful**, and to such auxiliary words as **had been**, **will be**, **could**, and **would**), whereas in Japanese there were.

At first, the Japanese tried to use the Chinese characters to write both the word root and the grammatical ending. But after a few hundred years they concluded that this did not work too well, so they decided to abbreviate some of the Chinese characters into a phonetic system, similar to what some early Western cultures had done to form an alphabet from their pictographs.

The Japanese then used Chinese characters to write the roots of the words and wrote the grammatical endings, where grammar was needed, in the phonetic system they had just developed. They called the phonetic letters **kana**.

The Japanese actually have two separate sets of **kana**, one called **katakana** and one called **hiragana**. The pronunciation of each set is identical to the other. The function of each set is also identical to the other, although each set of kana is used in different situations.

The Japanese written language is now composed, therefore, of word roots (the kanji) and grammatical endings (the kana.) The word root remains the same no matter what part of speech the word is. The same kanji is used as the word root whether the word is a noun, adjective, or verb, and some words, particularly nouns, just need the root. Then, where grammatical endings are needed, different **kana** are added to show the grammar or the part of speech.

This works basically the same as in English, where, for example, **beaut** would be the word root. The root alone is usually a noun. Adding **-ify** makes **beautify**, the verb. Adding **-iful** makes **beautiful**, the adjective, and adding **-ifully** makes **beautifully**, the adverb. The Japanese use kanji for the root **beaut** and use **kana** for the grammatical endings **-ify**, **-iful**, and **-ifully**.

Some Japanese words were formed with only one kanji, plus the grammatical ending where needed, and some with two kanji. Words of one kanji usually represent a more elementary thought than words of two kanji. Some words may contain three or even four kanji, but this is comparatively rare. One example is the English word **democracy**, which translates in Japanese to a four-kanji word 民主主義 **MINSHUSHUGI**.

Any of the kanji, with a few exceptions, can be used either as a word by itself or together with other kanji to form compound words. A kanji can theoretically form a compound with any other kanji, although of course not all the possible compounds are actually in use. As the Japanese need new words, they can coin them by combining two appropriate kanji into a new compound.

The pronunciation of a kanji when it is used as a word by itself is usually different from its pronunciation in compounds. A kanji will generally keep the same pronunciation in any compound in which it appears, although there are many exceptions. One reason for the different pronunciations is that sometimes the same kanji was borrowed from different regions of China at different times.

For example, the kanji 京, meaning capital, is pronounced **MIYAKO** when it is used by itself. In the compound word 東京 **TOKYO**, the capital city of Japan, it is pronounced **KYŌ**. In the compound word 京阪 **KEIHAN**, the abbreviation for the Kyoto-Osaka region, it is pronounced **KEI**.

It is quite easy to distinguish the kanji from the kana. The kana are written with at most four separate lines, or strokes, and usually with only two or three. The kanji, on the other hand, except for the word **one**, which is just one horizontal line 一, and one other exception, have a minimum of two strokes and often many more.

Examples of **katakana**:  アイウエオカキクケコ

Examples of **hiragana**:  あいうえおかきくけこ

Examples of **kanji**:  漢雨運罪競線歯聞街

**Kana** will appear at the end of many words to give them grammatical context. A typical written Japanese sentence will have a mix of kanji and kana, and look like this:

私の友達は金曜日に東京を発ちます。

The difference in written form between the kanji and the **kana** should be easily recognizable. Japanese does not leave spaces between separate words. The grammatical endings in **kana** usually show where each word ends.

Japanese books and newspapers, being in sentence form, are written with both kanji and **kana**. The language a visitor to Japan will see in the streets—shop names, advertisements, prices, street names, traffic signs, tickets, bills, receipts, train station names, family names—not generally in sentence form, are most often written with kanji only.

The **kana** are not difficult and both sets can be learned in a few days. It is just a matter of memorizing them as you memorized the alphabet as a child and will not take much more effort. For those readers interested in learning the **kana**, a chart and additional description are included as *Appendix A*.

The stories of the origin and development of each pictorial element in each kanji character were taken mainly from the compendium SHUO WEN CHIE TSU, published in China about 1,800 years ago.

For many of the kanji, the SHUO WEN lists more than one theory of their origin. This is understandable since more than 2,000 years passed between the first invention of the kanji and their compilation in the SHUO WEN lexicon. During that time, there were many changes in the form of the characters and their pronunciation, and many new interpretations of the history of each kanji. After the SHUO WEN, etymologists, including scholars from Japan, have discovered what they believe to be still other interpretations of the origin of some of the characters.

Whether the explanations of the origins given in the SHUO WEN CHIE TSU or by later scholars are correct is not important here since this book is not a text in etymology but rather a simplified method for learning the kanji. Where there is a difference of opinion between scholars, READ JAPANESE KANJI TODAY uses the interpretation which, I hope, is best mnemonically for English-speaking readers.

## Japanese Pronunciation

Japanese pronunciation is comparatively straightforward. The vowels are pronounced as in Italian—the **A** as in car, the **E** as in bed, the **I** as in medium, the **O** as in go, and the **U** as in Luke—and the consonants as in English. Sometimes in Japanese the vowels are long and sometimes they are short. Long vowels when written in roman letters will have a line drawn over the top of the letter. In Japanese, long vowels are handled by the **kana**.

When speaking in Japanese, just drag the long vowels out for twice the time as the short. This is often a difficult thing to do, but it is a very important distinction to make—a **SHOKI** 書記 is a secretary and **SHŌKI** 笑気 is laughing gas; a **SHŌJO** 少女 is a young girl and a **SHŌJŌ** 猩猩 is an orangutan. For practical purposes, there is no difference in the pronunciation of these sets of words except that some vowels are long and some are short.

In certain cases consonants are doubled, that is a single **K** becomes **KK** or a single **P** becomes **PP**. The double consonant is pronounced by holding it slightly longer than a single consonant. Like the long and short vowels, this is an important distinction to make but one quite easy to effect, and the reader will master it with just a little practice.

Another important note in pronouncing Japanese words is that the syllables are about equally stressed, whereas in English multi-syllabic words usually have one syllable stressed heavily. The Japanese say **YO–KO–HA–MA**, giving each syllable equal weight and length, since there are no long vowels in this word. Some English-speakers say **YO–ko–HA–ma**, accenting the first and third syllable, and some say **yo–ko–HA–ma**, heavily accenting the third syllable.

When foreigners pronounce Japanese with this heavy extra stress on certain syllables, some of the other syllables are drowned out for Japanese listeners. The first Americans to come to Japan told the Japanese they were **a–ME–ri–cans**. The Japanese couldn't hear the **A** sound and thought the visitors said they were **Merikens**. This is why the Japanese named the wheat flour the Americans brought with them **merikenko**, the Japanese word for flour being **ko**.

# How To Write The Kanji

Japanese school-children spend untold hours each year in practice kanji-writing. They do this to reinforce the kanji in their memory, to drill the correct order in which each kanji stroke is drawn, and to develop the proper style of penmanship.

For English-speaking visitors who will not be in Japan that long, the reason to practice writing the kanji is only to reinforce the meaning of the kanji in their memory. Each kanji is a work of calligraphic art, but it would take years of practice before a non-native could write the kanji at that level. Very few will ever be able to write Japanese in the cursive style. If a non-native can write each kanji so it can be clearly read by native Japanese, then what can be expected in a reasonable length of time will have been achieved.

In writing kanji, the order of each stroke and the direction of the pen during the stroke follow specific, rigid rules. The rules were developed by the Chinese to produce a uniform, idealized, artistically balanced script, particularly in cursive writing or writing with a brush. The rules follow logical precepts that make it easy to write the characters in printed-script, and also in the cursive script where each stroke blends into the next without lifting pen or brush from paper. When writing fast or jotting down informal notes, however, Japanese and Chinese adults often ignore the rules and follow shortcuts.

For your own purposes, I suggest that you follow the rules of stroke order as closely possible without excessive concern for minor alterations. The important goal is to get all the strokes into the right position and in the right proportion inside the square so a native speaker can correctly read the kanji that you write. Art and penmanship can follow later.

You should practice-write each kanji as many times as it takes you to memorize the pictograph. The quickest way to learn the kanji is by relating the meanings of the pictographs in each kanji to the word the kanji represents, not by memorizing the stroke order by rote repetition. You will eventually master stroke order, but it will take a lot longer. At this early stage, your time is better spent impressing each picture into memory.

In writing practice you should draw the kanji as a set of pictographs. Each kanji should fit into the same-size square, and each element, that is, each sub-pictograph, should be placed in the same portion of the square as it is in the model that you are copying. There are general rules of stroke order, and the reader should follow these general rules as closely as possible without being obsessive. Each general rule has exceptions, and there are exceptions to the exceptions.

Only a simplified version of the general rules of stroke order and some of the exceptions are given here. This should be enough to allow you to memorize the

400+ kanji in this book in a week or two, which is the book's objective. As you proceed to further study of the kanji, you will find many excellent texts in English which provide material for your next step.

The first general rule of stroke order is to begin at the top left point in the square and proceed to the bottom right point in the square. The first exception is that when the right top point is higher than the left top point, as it is in **hand** 手, pronounced **TE**, the first stroke starts from the right top point and is drawn to the left ╱㇄ .

Other important rules are (and remember that there are exceptions to each):

1. Draw from top left point to bottom right point.
2. Horizontal strokes are written left to right.
3. Horizontal strokes are written before vertical.
4. Vertical strokes are written top to bottom.
5. If there is a complete element in the left-hand side of the square, it is drawn in full before the right-hand side is started.
6. If there is a complete element in the top part of the square, it is drawn in full before the bottom part is started.
7. An outer frame is drawn first, except that the bottom line goes in last, after the strokes inside the square are drawn.
8. Central vertical strokes are drawn before the left and right diagonal strokes.
9. Diagonal lines on the left side precede diagonal lines on the right side.
10. Horizontal or vertical lines that cut through a kanji are written last.

In learning to recognize each kanji and its meaning, the rules of stroke order and the art of writing kanji are only marginally helpful. In English, for example, to write the word "book" you could as easily start at the right bottom of the letter **k** and continue leftward until you reach the left side of the letter **b**. As long as the finished word looks like *book*, your writing will be understood by anyone who reads it. The fact that you violated all the conventions of writing script does not detract from your ability to make your writing understood, although your writing may not win an award for penmanship. In the same way, when writing kanji, a few contraventions of stroke order will not compromise your ability to be understood, as long as you have the picture right and all the strokes in the right place.

## How To Use This Book

READ JAPANESE KANJI TODAY provides a pictorial mnemonic method for learning kanji. Each kanji character is presented with its pictorial origin, its modern meaning, its main pronunciations, and examples of how it is used. The examples were selected from common applications that visitors to Japan will see frequently as they travel about the country, such as on signs, in newspapers, in magazine ads, on product packaging, and so forth.

The pronunciations given in the text for each kanji are limited to the most common ones, generally the pronunciations needed to read the kanji that are usually seen by visitors to Japan.

The **kana** endings, which show the grammar of the words, are generally omitted in the examples in this book so the reader can focus on remembering the kanji. The grammatical endings of some of the words are given in roman letters, however, so the reader can see the pronunciation of the base form of the word. For example, the pronunciation for the kanji 聞, **to hear** in the verb form, is given in this book in roman letters as **KIKU**, whereas the kanji 聞 actually represents only **KI**, the root sound of the word. The **KU** sound, which is the grammatical ending representing the infinitive form of the verb, must be written in kana.

The infinitive form of the verb is the one most often used in English-Japanese dictionaries, so it is shown in this book in roman letters to make it easier for you to look up these words in a dictionary later.

The main portion of the book is organized into 10 sections consisting of roughly 40 kanji each. You should proceed through the book from beginning to end, rather than jumping from place to place, since the elements and kanji are arranged so that those introduced earlier in the book become the building blocks for those in the later pages.

Each section contains approximately the number of kanji that you could readily learn in a day. Thus, if you follow this prescription, you should be able to learn the 400+ kanji in this book in a period of 10 days. However, there is no particular reason why you need to complete a section in a single day. You should feel free to read or re-read the book for 5 minutes or 5 hours at a stretch according to your mood and convenience.

The *Afterword* following Section 10 provides some advice for continuing with your kanji studies. *Appendix B* features a *Kanji Summary Table* that includes all of the kanji introduced in this book. The kanji are listed in the order they are presented in the book, and a page reference, common readings, and English meanings are included for each. *Appendix C* is an alphabetical index of the English meanings for all of the kanji introduced in the book.

You will learn the meaning of the kanji most quickly by focusing on the pictographs and what the Chinese meant them to represent, then linking each pictograph or combination of elements, through whatever mnemonic you are comfortable with, to current Japanese usage.

# SECTION ONE

## Kanji List

| | | | | | |
|---|---|---|---|---|---|
| 1 日 | 2 木 | 3 本 | 4 未 | 5 末 | 6 東 |
| 7 京 | 8 田 | 9 力 | 10 男 | 11 女 | 12 妹 |
| 13 母 | 14 人 | 15 毎 | 16 休 | 17 体 | 18 子 |
| 19 好 | 20 大 | 21 天 | 22 王 | 23 全 | 24 太 |
| 25 小 | 26 少 | 27 立 | 28 一 | 29 二 | 30 三 |
| 31 五 | 32 四 | 33 十 | 34 世 | 35 協 | 36 九 |
| 37 八 | 38 六 | | | | |

| 1 日 4 strokes | ON READINGS: **NICHI, JITSU**<br>KUN READINGS: **hi, bi, ka**<br><br>*sun, a day* | 休日 **kyūjitsu** *holiday, day off*<br>日曜日 **Nichiyōbi** *Sunday*<br>二日 **futsuka** *second day of the month*<br>日なた **hinata** *a sunny place* |
|---|---|---|

丨 冂 日 日

The ancient Chinese saw the sun like this ☼, so that is how they wrote the word for **sun**. They later found it took too long to write the rays, so they shortened the pictograph to ⊙. When they simplified the character to its final form, to make it even easier to write and at the same time look aesthetically acceptable to the Chinese eye, they squared the circle and changed the dot into a line 日.

The basic meaning of 日 is **sun**. The Chinese saw that the passage of the sun across the sky took one day, so they extended 日 also to mean **one day**. This kanji, as do most, has several pronunciations. When 日 forms a word by itself, it is generally pronounced **HI, BI, KA**. When it is put together with other kanji in a compound word it is pronounced **NICHI** or **JITSU**. [The different pronunciations for the same kanji are indicated by KUN readings (based on native Japanese sounds), and by ON readings (based on Chinese-originated sounds).]

| 2 木 4 strokes | ON READING: **MOKU**<br>KUN READING: **ki**<br><br>*tree, wood* | 木製 **mokusei** *wooden*<br>木曜日 **Mokuyōbi** *Thursday*<br>木材 **mokuzai** *wood, timber*<br>植木 **ueki** *plant* |
|---|---|---|

一 十 才 木

The Chinese pictograph for **tree** was 𣎼. It was gradually simplified to 朱, and then to 朩. Squared off to final form it was written 木. The horizontal line represents all the branches, the vertical line the trunk, and the diagonal lines the roots. The meaning of 木 is **tree** or **wood**. When it forms a word by itself it is generally pronounced **KI**, and when it is combined with other kanji in a compound word it is generally pronounced **MOKU**.

| 3 本 5 strokes | ON READING: **HON** KUN READING: **moto** *origin, source, book* | 日本語 **Nihongo** *Japanese (language)* 日本 **Nippon, Nihon** *Japan* 本日 **honjitsu** *today* 本当 **hontō** *truth* |
| --- | --- | --- |
| | 一　十　才　木　本 | |

To form the character for **root**, the Chinese just drew in more roots at the bottom of the tree 本 to emphasize that part. Eventually, they squared off all the added roots to one straight line ― , and the final form of the kanji became 本. In addition to the meaning **root**, the Chinese extended the meaning to the root of things, the **origin** or **source**. They extended 本 later to mean **book** as well, which they felt to be the root or source of knowledge. It is pronounced either **HON** or **MOTO**, both as a word by itself and in compound words.

The compound word 日本, formed by putting the kanji for **sun** 日 together with the kanji for **root** or **origin** 本, means **origin of the sun**. It is pronounced **NIHON** or **NIPPON**, which is what the Japanese call their country. 日本 would normally be pronounced **NICHI-HON**, but for euphony the Japanese use **NI-HON** or **NIPPON**.

| 4 未 5 strokes | ON READING: **MI** KUN READING: **ma(da)** *immature, not yet there* | 未来 **mirai** *future* 未知 **michi** *unknown* 未成年 **miseinen** *a minor (children)* 未完成 **mikansei** *uncompleted* |
| --- | --- | --- |
| | 一　二　キ　オ　未 | |

On the pictograph for **tree** the Chinese drew in more branches to make a new kanji that would indicate the tree was still growing and had not yet matured. To draw the final form, they combined all the new branches into one short straight line ― and drew it in among the other branches 未. This new kanji 未 means **immature** or **not yet there.** It is pronounced **MA-DA** when used by itself, where **DA** is written in kana. 未 is pronounced **MI** in compound words.

| 5 | ON READING: **MATSU** | 週末 **shūmatsu** *weekend* |
|---|---|---|
| 末 | KUN READING: **sue** | 月末 **getsumatsu** *end of month* |
| | *the end, extremity, tip* | 場末 **basue** *outskirt* |
| 5 strokes | | 末っ子 **suekko** *the youngest child* |

一　二　十　才　末

The Chinese later capped the pictograph for **tree** 🌳 with one line at the top —
and made another new character 末, meaning **the end, as far as you can go,
the extremity, the tip.** When used as a word by itself it is pronounced **SUE**, and
when combined with other kanji in a compound word it is pronounced **MATSU**.

This kanji 末 looks very much like the kanji 未, meaning **immature** or **not
yet there**, described above. The difference is that in the kanji meaning **extremity**
末, the line capping the growth of the tree is longer than the line representing
the normal branches, while in the kanji meaning **immature** 未, the line representing the fluffing out of leaves and branches is shorter than the line representing the normal branches.

| 6 | ON READING: **TŌ** | 東京 **tokyō** *Tokyo* |
|---|---|---|
| 東 | KUN READING: **higashi** | 東口 **higashi-guchi** *east exit* |
| | *east* | 東洋 **tōyō** *the East, oriental* |
| 8 strokes | | 関東 **kantō** *Kanto district* |

一　厂　冂　冃　日　車　東　東

A picture of the sun at sunrise rising up behind a tree 🌲 was the scene the
Chinese picked to stand for **east**. In this new kanji, they drew the **tree** 木 and
the **sun** 日 in the same way they did when they were used as separate kanji, but
in the new composite kanji they put the sun behind the tree to show that it was
sunrise. The final form of **east** was written 東. When this kanji forms a word
itself it is pronounced **HIGASHI**. Where 東 appears with another kanji to form
a compound word, as in **TŌKYŌ**, it is pronounced **TŌ**.

| 7 京 | ON READINGS: **KYŌ, KEI** | 京都 **kyōto** *Kyoto* |
| | | 上京する **jokyō suru** *go to Tokyo* |
| | *capital* | 帰京する **kikyō suru** *back in Tokyo* |
| | | 京風 **kyōfū** *Kyoto style* |
| 8 strokes | ` 亠 广 古 古 亨 京 京 | |

The **KYŌ** in **TŌKYŌ** was originally a pictograph of a stone lantern 髙. These lanterns stood at the gates of the Chinese Emperor's Palace, later at the gates of the Imperial City, and came therefore to symbolize the nation's **capital**. The Chinese drew the early pictograph 床. Now it is written 京. It is not used as a word by itself. In compound words with other kanji it is pronounced **KYŌ** or **KEI**. 東京 **TŌKYŌ**, east-capital, means **eastern capital**.

| 8 田 | ON READING: **DEN** KUN READING: **ta, (da)** | 油田 **yuden** *oilfield* |
| | | 田畑 **tahata** *fields (for farming)* |
| | *rice-field, rice-paddy* | 田植え **taue** *rice planting* |
| | | 田園 **den-en** *rustic, rural* |
| 5 strokes | l 冂 冊 冊 田 | |

The Chinese, who farmed the world's first rice-paddies about 12,000 years ago, drew a picture of the paddies 昍, later simplified to 壨, and then to the final form 田. This kanji means **rice-field** or **rice-paddy**. When used with other kanji in compound words it is pronounced **DEN**. When used by itself, or in proper names, 田 is usually pronounced **TA** or **DA**, whichever sounds better. The well-known Honda Corporation writes its name 本田, **original-field**.

| 9 力 | ON READINGS: **RIKI, RYOKU** KUN READING: **chikara** | 努力 **doryoku** *effort* |
| | | 馬力 **bariki** *horsepower* |
| | *strength, power* | 力仕事 **chikara shigoto** *heavy work* |
| | | 力持ち **chikara mochi** *mighty person* |
| 2 strokes | フ 力 | |

A strong hand bearing down on things 手 represented the idea of strength or power. Drawing in all the fingers took too much time, so the Chinese abstracted the form of the hand and drew it ⌒. Squaring this to fit the kanji square, they wrote the final form 力, meaning **strength** or **power**. When used as a word by itself it is pronounced **CHIKARA**, and when it is used in compound words it is pronounced **RYOKU** or **RIKI**.

| 10 男 7 strokes | ON READINGS: **DAN, NAN** KUN READING: **otoko** *man, male* | 男性 **dansei** *man, male* 長男 **chōnan** *eldest son, oldest son* 男子 **danshi** *boy, man* 男らしい **otoko-rashi'i** *masculine* |
|---|---|---|
| | 丨 冂 冂 冊 田 甲 男 | |

The Chinese added **power** 力 to a **field** 田 and formed the new kanji 男, meaning **man** or **male**. This signifies the male half of the human species "man" and not the species itself. When this character is used as a word by itself it is pronounced **OTOKO**, and when it is used in compound words it is pronounced **DAN** or **NAN**. 男 appears on all the doors where only males should enter.

| 11 女 3 strokes | ON READINGS: **JO, NYO, NYŌ** KUN READINGS: **onna, me** *woman* | 少女 **shōjo** *young girl* 女房 **nyōbō** *(my) wife* 女の子 **onna-no-ko** *girl* 女神 **megami** *Goddess* |
|---|---|---|
| | く 女 女 | |

A **woman** the Chinese pictured as a pregnant lady, seated with her arms outstretched 𡥀. This was later written 𠨰 and finally 女. It is pronounced **ONNA** or **ME** when it is used to form a word itself, and **JO, NYO** and **NYŌ** when it is used in compound words. 女 appears on all the doors where only females enter.

| 12<br><br>妹<br><br>8 strokes | ON READING: **MAI**<br>KUN READING: **imōto**<br><br>*younger sister* | 姉妹 **shimai** *sisters*<br>妹さん **imōto-san** *(someone's) sister*<br>弟妹 **teimai** *brothers and sisters* |
| --- | --- | --- |
| | く　夕　女　女　妅　妷　妹　妹 | |

The Chinese put together the kanji for **woman** 女 with the kanji for **immature** 未 to make a new kanji 妹, meaning **younger sister**. Used as a word by itself it is pronounced **IMŌTO**. In compound words 妹 is pronounced **MAI**.

| 13<br><br>母<br><br>5 strokes | ON READING: **BO**<br>KUN READING: **haha**<br><br>*mother* | 父母 **fubo** *father and mother*<br>祖母 **sobo** *grand mother*<br>母親 **hahaoya** *mother*<br>お母さん **okāsan** *mother* |
| --- | --- | --- |
| | ㇈　口　口　呂　母 | |

**Mother** to the Chinese was a woman 女 with her breasts drawn in. To the character for **woman** 女 they added breasts 女, and topped her with a hat to shade her eyes 毋. The final form of this character is 母. Used as a kanji by itself it is generally pronounced (with the addition of several kana to indicate words of respect) **OKĀSAN**. This is the most popular spoken-Japanese word for **mother**, but to be understood it must be pronounced with a distinctly long **Ā**, as in お母さん **O-KA-A-SAN**, to distinguish it from **OKASAN**, which means **Mr. Oka**. 母 can also be pronounced **HAHA** when it forms a word by itself. When used with other kanji in compound words it is pronounced **BO**.

| 14<br><br>人<br><br>2 strokes | ON READINGS: **NIN, JIN**<br>KUN READING: **hito**<br><br>*person* | 成人 **seijin** *adult (human)*<br>人間 **ningen** *human beings*<br>人形 **ningyō** *doll*<br>人々 **hitobito** *people* |
| --- | --- | --- |
| | ノ　人 | |

Person, which refers to the species "human being," means either man or woman. The Chinese pictured **person** as the human form in general 𠆢. In final form they drew it 人. It is pronounced **HITO** when it makes a word itself, and pronounced

NIN or JIN in compound words. A **Japanese person** is a 日本人, pronounced **NIHONJIN** or **NIPPONJIN**. A **person from America** is an **AMERIKAJIN**. There are no kanji for the word "America" so the **AMERIKA** in **AMERIKAJIN** is written in phonetic (kana) letters, and the written word looks like this アメリカ人.

| 15 | ON READINGS: **MAI, GOTO** | 毎度 **maido** *everytime, always* <br> 毎日 **mainichi** *every day* <br> 毎回 **maikai** *every time, each time* <br> 毎週 **maishū** *every week* |
|---|---|---|
| 毎 | *every* | |
| 6 strokes | ノ　ー　ケ　匇　匇　毎 | |

Since every **person** 人 had a **mother** 母, the Chinese combined these two kanji into a new composite kanji 毎 with the meaning **every**. They wanted to add the pictograph for **person** 人 to the pictograph for **mother** 母 in the most aesthetic way so that the new kanji would be easy to read and write and would fit proportionately within the kanji square. Putting 人 and 母 side by side would make the new kanji too wide, and putting one above the other would make it too high. Instead, they decided to modify slightly the shape of one of the elements, in this case the element for **person** 人, to ⌐, and wrote the new kanji for **every** 毎.

毎 is rarely used as a word by itself. In compound words, where two or more kanji form a word, 毎 is pronounced **MAI** or **GOTO**, depending mainly on whether it is the first or second kanji in the compound. For example, the compound word 毎日, **every day**, which incidentally is the name of a leading Japanese daily newspaper, is pronounced **MAINICHI**. The compound word 日毎 uses the same two kanji but in reverse order. It also means **daily**, but in a more formal sense, with an emphasis on each-and-every-day. 日毎 is pronounced **HI-GOTO**.

| 16 | ON READING: **KYŪ** | 定休日 **teikyūbi** *regular holiday* |
|----|---|---|
| 休 | KUN READING: **yasu(mu)** | 夏休み **natsuyasumi** *summer holiday* |
| | | 昼休み **hiruyasumi** *lunch break* |
| | *to take a break, to take a holiday, to rest* | 休み時間 **yasumijikan** *recess time* |
| 6 strokes | ノ イ 仁 什 休 休 | |

The Chinese pictograph for **resting** was a **person** 人 beside a **tree** 木. They first put it together as 人木. Then, as with the kanji 毎 **MAI**, above, they decided that the **person** 人 had to change its shape to blend with the other element in the kanji square. In the composite kanji **every** 毎, the element for **mother** 母 was rather short and wide, so the element for **person** 人 was added at the top of the square instead of beside the **mother** 母. In the kanji for **resting**, the element for **tree** 木 was tall and thin, so the element for **person** 人 had to be added at the left-hand side of the square instead of at the top. The Chinese changed the shape of **person** to fit the left-hand side and drew it 亻. They wrote the new kanji 休. It means **rest**, or **take a break**, or **take a holiday**. Used as a word by itself it is pronounced **YASU-MU** (with kana at the end to show the grammar). Used in compound words it is pronounced **KYŪ**. A 休日 **KYŪJITSU**, rest-day, is a **holiday** or a **day off**.

| 17 | ON READINGS: **TAI, TEI** | 体育館 **tai'ikukan** *gymnasium, gym* |
|----|---|---|
| 体 | KUN READING: **karada** | 体重 **taijū** *body weight* |
| | | 体形 **taikei** *body shape* |
| | *body* | 体裁 **teisai** *appearance, presentation* |
| 7 strokes | ノ イ 仁 什 休 休 体 | |

The Chinese combined the kanji 本, meaning **root** or **origin**, with the kanji 人, meaning **person**, into a new composite kanji symbolizing the root of a person 体, meaning **the human body**. The shape of **person** 人 was changed, as it was in the kanji 休 meaning **rest**, to fit into the left-hand side of the kanji square. When 体 is used as a word by itself it is pronounced **KARADA**. When used in compound words it is pronounced **TAI** or **TEI**. 体 could also mean the body of an animal, so the technical term 人体 **JINTAI**, human-body, is often used to indicate specifically the **human body**.

| 18 | ON READINGS: **SHI, SU** | 子孫 **sison** *descendant, offspring* |
|---|---|---|
| | KUN READING: **ko** | 様子 **yōsu** *appearance, complexion* |
| 子 | *child* | 親子 **oyako** *parent and child, family* |
| | | 子供 **kodomo** *child* |
| 3 strokes | ㇇　了　子 | |

For the character for **child**, the Chinese drew a picture of a swaddled baby 옷. It soon was drawn 孚, then squared off to the final form 子. It is pronounced **KO** when used as a kanji by itself, or used in proper names, and **SHI** and **SU** when used in compound words. An 男 の 子 **OTOKO-no-KO**, male-child, is a **boy**, and an 女 の 子 **ONNA-no-KO**, woman-child, is a **girl**. In both these examples, **no** is a grammatical particle and is written in kana. 男 **OTOKO**, 女 **ONNA**, and 子 **KO** are all essentially used as stand-alone kanji, words by themselves (linked by the grammatical particle **no** の, indicating the possessive tense) and are not compound words.

OTOKO-no-KO 男 の 子 can be written 男子 without the particle **no**, but in this case it becomes a compound word and is pronounced **DANSHI**. It still means **boy**. In the same way, **ONNA-no-KO** 女 の 子, when written without the particle **no**, 女子, is pronounced **JOSHI** and means **girl**. The forms **JOSHI** and **DANSHI** are used more in writing, and **OTOKO-no-KO** and **ONNA-no-KO** are used more in speech.

| 19 | ON READING: **KŌ**<br><br>KUN READINGS: **su(ku),**<br>**kono(mu)** | 良好 **ryōkō** *goodness*<br>好み **konomi** *taste, choice*<br>好き嫌い **suki-kirai** *likes and* |
| :-- | :-- | :-- |
| 好 | *love, like, goodness* | *dislikes*<br>お好み焼き **okonomiyaki**<br>*Japanese pancake with tidbit* |
| 6 strokes | く　夕　女　女゚　奵　好 | |

A woman 女 and a 子 child together signified love and goodness to the Chinese. They combined these two separate pictographs, each a kanji on its own, into one new composite kanji written 好, meaning **love**, **like**, or **goodness**. It is pronounced **SU-KU** or **KONO-MU** when it is used as a word by itself (the kanji 好 is the **SU** or the **KO** part; the rest has to be written in kana, expressing the grammatical endings). Used in compound words, 好 is pronounced **KŌ**. A 好男子 **KŌDANSHI**, good-man-child, is a **handsome young man**.

| 20 | ON READINGS: **DAI, TAI**<br>KUN READINGS: **ō, ō(ki'i)** | 大小 **daishō** *small and large, size*<br>大衆 **taishū** *masses, the public* |
| :-- | :-- | :-- |
| 大 | *big, large* | 大通り **ōdōri** *avenue*<br>大きさ **ōkisa** *size, measurement* |
| 3 strokes | 一　ナ　大 | |

A man standing with his arms stretched out as far as he can manage 大 was what the Chinese saw as "big." Their early writings show it drawn as 大. Now it is drawn 大 and means **big** or **large**. When used by itself it is pronounced **Ō-KI'I** (like many Japanese words when used by themselves, it needs grammatical endings which must be written in kana; the kanji 大 only provides the **Ō** sound; the **KI** sound and the **I** sound—two separate sounds needing two separate kana—have to be written in kana). When used in compound words, 大 is pronounced **DAI** or **TAI**. 大日本 **DAI-NIHON** (or **DAI-NIPPON**) means **Greater Japan**. 大田 **ŌTA**, **big-field**, is the name of a ward in Tokyo. 大好き **DAISUKI**, big-like, means **like very much**, **be extremely fond of**.

| 21 | ON READING: **TEN** | 天然 **ten-nen** *natural* |
|---|---|---|
| | KUN READINGS: **ama, ame** | 天才 **tensai** *genius* |
| 天 | *heaven, sky* | 天の川 **ama-no-gawa** *the Milky Way*<br>天気 **tenki** *weather* |
| 4 strokes | 一 二 チ 天 | |

Above the kanji meaning **big** 大, which is a picture of a person with his arms outstretched, the Chinese added a barrier line ⁻ to signify that above a person is **heaven** with man in his place below. The final form of the new composite kanji is 天, meaning **heaven** or **sky**. When it forms a word by itself it is pronounced **AMA** or **AME**. Used with other kanji in compound words it is pronounced **TEN**. 天体 **TENTAI**, heaven-body, means **heavenly bodies**, like the sun and the moon. A 天子 **TENSHI**, heaven-child, means the **ruler of a nation**.

| 22 | ON READING: **Ō** | 王子 **ōji** *prince* |
|---|---|---|
| | | 王女 **ōjo** *princess* |
| 王 | *king* | 国王 **kokuō** *king*<br>王国 **ōkoku** *kingdom* |
| 4 strokes | 一 丁 干 王 | |

Below the line for heaven ⁻ the Chinese added horizontal lines for man — and earth ＿ and unified them with a connecting vertical line │ symbolizing the king or ruler. They drew the kanji 王, meaning **king**. Used either by itself or in compound words it is pronounced **Ō**. A 女王, **JO-Ō**, woman-king, is a **queen**. An 王子, **ŌJI**, king-child, is a **prince**.

| 23 | ON READING: **ZEN**<br>KUN READINGS: **sube(te),**<br>**matta(ku)** | 安全 **anzen** *safety, safe*<br>完全 **kanzen** *integrity, completeness*<br>全部 **zenbu** *whole*<br>全員 **zen-in** *everyone*<br>全ての **subete no** *all, every* |
|---|---|---|
| 全 | *the whole, complete;*<br>*completely, totally* | |
| 6 strokes | ノ 八 ハ 仐 全 全 | |

The Chinese put a cover ⌒ over heaven, man, earth, and ruler 王 to symbolize everything, the whole, completely. They wrote the final kanji 全, meaning
**the whole** or **complete**. Used as a word by itself it is pronounced **SUBE-TE** or
**MATTA-KU** (with the grammatical ending **KU**, indicating it is an adverb, written
with a kana), an expressive word meaning **completely**, **entirely**, **perfectly**, **totally**,
**absolutely**, or just the opposite: **not at all**, **not in the least**. In compound words it
is pronounced **ZEN**. 全体 **ZENTAI**, whole-body, means **all**, the **whole**, **generally**. 全力 **ZEN-RYOKU**, whole-strength, means **with all your might**.

| 24 | ON READINGS: **TAI, TA**<br>KUN READINGS: **futo(i),**<br>**futo(ru)** | 太陽 **taiyō** *sun*<br>丸太 **maruta** *log*<br>太字 **futoji** *bold*<br>図太い **zubutoi** *strong nerves, crusted* |
|---|---|---|
| 太 | *fat, very big* | |
| 4 strokes | 一 ナ 大 太 | |

The Chinese doubled 大 **big** and made it 夻, meaning **very big**. Then, instead
of writing two **bigs**, one atop the other, they just used a ditto mark 丶 at the
bottom of the first "**big**" and made the final kanji 太. It means **fat** or **very big**. It
is pronounced **FUTO-I** or **FUTO-RU** when it forms a word by itself. When it is
used in compound words, 太 is pronounced **TAI** or **TA**.

| 25 | ON READING: **SHŌ**<br>KUN READINGS: **chi'i(sai),**<br>**ko, o** | 小学校 **shōgakkō** *elementary school*<br>小さい **chi'isai** *small*<br>小切手 **kogite** *check*<br>小川 **ogawa** *stream* |
|---|---|---|
| 小 | *small* | |
| 3 strokes | 亅 小 小 | |

The same man standing, this time with his arms pulled in toward his sides 朳

signified smallness. The Chinese drew it first 朿, and then in final form 小. It means **small**, in the sense of size. Used by itself it is pronounced **CHI'I-SAI** (an adjective, needing two kana, **SA** and **I** to write **CHI'I-SAI**, since the kanji 小 itself only represents **CHI'I**) or **O**. In compounds it is pronounced **KO** or **SHŌ**.

| 26 少 4 strokes | ON READING: **SHŌ** KUN READINGS: **suko(shi), suku(nai)** *few, little* | 少年 **shōnen** *young boy* 多少 **tashō** *some* 少ない **sukunai** *few* 少し **sukoshi** *a little* |
|---|---|---|
| | ) 丿 小 少 | |

To symbolize "small" in the sense of quantity, meaning **few**, the Chinese drew a bottom ╱ under 小**small** to indicate that that was it, nothing more. The final form was 少, meaning **a few** or **a little**. Used by itself it is pronounced **SUKO-SHI** or **SUKU-NAI**. Used in compound words with other kanji 少 is pronounced **SHŌ**.

| 27 立 5 strokes | ON READINGS: **RITSU, RYŪ** KUN READINGS: **ta(tsu), ta(teru), tachi** *to stand, to rise up* | 独立 **dokuritsu** *independence* 建立 **konryū** *construction* 立場 **tachiba** *stance, position* 組立て **kumitate** *setup, assembly* |
|---|---|---|
| | ﹡ 亠 广 立 立 | |

The Chinese represented just plain "**standing**" by a person standing, this time not in the abstract but on the ground 产. They first squared it off to 立, and finally wrote it 立. It means **to stand** or **to rise up**. As a word by itself it is pronounced **TA-TSU** (the intransitive verb form, meaning stand up yourself), **TA-TERU** (the transitive verb form, meaning stand or raise something else up), or **TACHI**. Used in proper names it is generally pronounced **TACHI**. Used in compound words 立 is pronounced **RITSU** or **RYŪ**. The well-known electrical equipment manufacturer **HITACHI**, for example, is written 日立, **sun-rise**.

| 28 | ON READING: **ICHI** | 一月 **ichi-gatsu** *January* |
| | KUN READINGS: **hito,** | 一人 **hitori** *unit (person), one person* |
| | **hito(tsu)** | 一つ **hitotsu** *one (piece)* |
| —— | *one* | 一日 **ichinichi, tsuitachi** *one day,* |
| | | *first day of the month* |
| 1 stroke | —— | |

The Chinese wrote the number **one** with one flat horizontal line 一. They found it hard to simplify this pictograph, so never changed its shape. It is pronounced **ICHI** either in compound words or by itself. It can also be pronounced **HITO-TSU** (with a kana, since the kanji 一 only provides the **HITO** sound) either in compound words or by itself.

| 29 | ON READING: **NI** | 二月 **nigatsu** *February* |
| | KUN READINGS: **futa,** | 二人 **futari** *two people* |
| | **futa(tsu)** | 二つ **futatsu** *two (pieces)* |
| 二 | *two* | 二日 **futuka** *two days, second day of* |
| | | *the month* |
| 2 strokes | 一 二 | |

The number **two** followed the same pattern and was written 二. It is pronounced **NI**, either in compound words or by itself. It can also be pronounced **FUTA-TSU** (again with a kana, since the kanji 二 only provides the **FUTA** sound) in compound words or by itself.

| 30 | ON READING: **SAN** | 三分 **sanpun** *three minutes* |
| | KUN READINGS: **mi, mit(tsu)** | 三人 **san-nin** *three people* |
| 三 | *three* | 三つ **mittsu** *three (pieces)* |
| | | 三月 **sangatsu** *March* |
| 3 strokes | 一 二 三 | |

The number **three** was done the same, and was written 三. It is pronounced **SAN** either in compound words or by itself. 三 can also be pronounced **MI** or **MIT-TSU** (with a kana) in compound words or by itself.

| 31 | ON READING: **GO** | 五分 **gofun; gobu** *five minutes* |
|---|---|---|
| 五 | KUN READING: **itsu(tsu)** | 五人 **go-nin** *three people* |
| | *five* | 五つ **itsutsu** *five (pieces)* |
| 4 strokes | 一　丁　五　五 | 五月 **gogatsu** *May* |

The number **five** started out the same, with five flat horizontal lines ☰. The Chinese found that there were too many horizontal lines to write clearly in a small space and, further, there was no way to draw them cursively with a brush in one continuous line without lifting the brush from the paper, so they took two of the lines and made them vertical 丹. Then they opened up the upper corner for aesthetic balance and wrote it 五. It is pronounced **GO** either in compound words or by itself. It can also be pronounced **ITSU-TSU** (with a kana) in compound words or by itself.

| 32 | ON READING: **SHI** | 四月 **shigatsu** *April* |
|---|---|---|
| 四 | KUN READINGS: **yo, yon, yot(tsu)** | 四人 **yonin** *four people* |
| | | 四時 **yoji** *four o'clock* |
| | *four* | 四つ **yottsu** *four (pieces)* |
| 5 strokes | 丨　冂　冂　四　四 | |

The number **four** was pictured as four fingers balled into a fist 🖐. The Chinese first simplified it a bit to ⊞, and then in final form as 四. It is pronounced **SHI** either in compound words or by itself. 四 can also be pronounced **YO, YON** or **YOT-TSU** (with a kana) in compound words or by itself.

| 33 | ON READING: **JŪ** | 十円 **jūen** *ten yen* |
| | KUN READINGS: **tō, to** | 十月 **jūgatsu** *October* |
| 十 | | 十分 **jippn, juppun** *ten minutes* |
| | *ten* | 十日 **tōka** *ten days, tenth day of the* |
| | | *month* |
| 2 strokes | 一 十 | |

The number **ten** was pictured as the ten fingers of two crossed hands 🖐. The fingers took too long to write so the Chinese simplified the final form to just the cross 十. It is pronounced **JŪ** either in compound words or by itself. 十 also can be pronounced **TŌ** or **TO**, either in compound words or by itself. In compound words it is also sometimes pronounced **JIT** or **JUT**.

| 34 | ON READINGS: **SE, SEI** | 世紀 **sekai** *century* |
| | KUN READING: **yo** | 世界 **sekai** *world* |
| 世 | | 出世 **shusse** *success in career* |
| | *generation* | 世の中 **yo-no-naka** *public, society* |
| 5 strokes | 一 十 卅 卅 世 | |

The Chinese connected three tens 卅 and underlined them with a one 一 to emphasize that thirty years was one life-span, one generation. They simplified it first to 卋 then squared it off to the final form 世, meaning a **generation**. Used as a word by itself it is pronounced **YO**. In compound words it is pronounced **SE** or **SEI**. A 二世 **NISEI**, two-generation, is a **Nisei**, a second-generation American, born in the USA, of Japanese parentage. An 一世 **ISSEI** (**ICHISEI** pronounced euphonically), one-generation, is an **Issei**, a first-generation Japanese who emigrated to the United States.

| 35 | ON READING: **KYŌ** | 協会 **kyōkai** *association* |
| | | 協調 **kyōchō** *cooperation* |
| 協 | *to unite, to join in cooperation* | 協定 **kyōtei** *agreement* |
| | | 協同体 **kyōdōtai** *collaboration* |
| 8 strokes | 一 十 十⁷ 十ᵏ 忖 忉 協 協 | |

The Chinese tripled power 力力力 then multiplied by **ten** 十 to form the new composite kanji 協, many-strengths-together, meaning **to unite**, **to join together in cooperation**. 協 is not used as a word by itself. Used with other kanji in compound words it is pronounced **KYŌ**. The compound word 協力 **KYŌRYOKU**, unite-strength, means **cooperation**.

| 36 | ON READINGS: **KYŪ, KU** | 九人 **kyūnin** *nine people* |
| | KUN READING: **kokono(tsu)** | 九月 **kugatsu** *September* |
| 九 | *nine* | 九日 **kokonoka** *nine days, nineth day of the month* |
| | | 九つ **kokonotsu** *nine (pieces)* |
| 2 strokes | ノ 九 | |

For number **nine**, the Chinese started with the number **ten** 十 and dropped one off 十↓ to get down to number **nine**. They first wrote it as 九 and finally squared it off to 九. (To "square off" a pictograph means to line up and re-proportion the components to make it aesthetically pleasing and easy to read and write; in **nine** 九, the squaring off is done by rounding). It is pronounced **KYŪ** or **KU** either in compounds or when used by itself. It can also be pronounced **KOKONO-TSU** (with kana), either in compound words or by itself.

| 37 | ON READING: **HACHI** | 八日 **yōka** *eight days, eighth day of* |
| | KUN READINGS: **ya, yat(tsu), yō** | *the the month* |
| | | 八月 **hachigatsu** *August* |
| 八 | *eight* | 八百屋 **yao-ya** *greengrocery* |
| | | 八つ **yattsu** *eight (pieces)* |
| 2 strokes | ノ 八 | |

To symbolize the act of splitting or dividing, the Chinese drew a straight verti-cal line **|**, then divided it in two **| |** . It was stylized as **/ \** and came to be the kanji for the number **eight** 八 (but also retaining the concept of "divide") since **eight** is one vertical line divided up. It is pronounced **HACHI** either in compound words or by itself. It can also be pronounced **YA, YAT-TSU** or **YŌ** in special cases. 八 appears in many other kanji as an element that brings to the composite kanji the meaning of "divide."

| 38 | ON READING: **ROKU** | 六月 **rokugatsu** *June* |
| | KUN READINGS: **mu, mui, mut(tsu)** | 六分 **roppun** *six minutes* |
| | | 六つ **muttsu** *six (pieces)* |
| 六 | *six* | 六日 **muika** *six days, sixth day of the* |
| | | *month* |
| 4 strokes | 丶 亠 宀 六 | |

The Chinese drew a pictograph of the element for **eight** 八 and the element for **two** 二 escaping through the top to symbolize eight minus two, the number six. They wrote the final form of the kanji 六, meaning **six**. Used as word by itself it is pronounced **MUT-TSU**. In compound words 六 is pronounced **ROKU, MU,** or **MUI**.

# SECTION TWO

| | | | | | |
|---|---|---|---|---|---|
| 39 刀 | 40 刃 | 41 分 | 42 七 | 43 切 | 44 川 |
| 45 州 | 46 水 | 47 海 | 48 氷 | 49 入 | 50 口 |
| 51 中 | 52 仲 | 53 介 | 54 界 | 55 央 | 56 映 |
| 57 画 | 58 古 | 59 品 | 60 区 | 61 町 | 62 丁 |
| 63 言 | 64 信 | 65 己 | 66 記 | 67 計 | 68 舌 |
| 69 話 | 70 活 | 71 語 | 72 英 | 73 上 | 74 下 |
| 75 山 | 76 火 | 77 炎 | 78 谷 | | |

| 39 | ON READING: **TŌ** | 刀剣 **tōken** *sword* |
|---|---|---|
| | KUN READING: **katana** | 短刀 **tantō** *dagger* |
| 刀 | *sword* | 名刀 **maitō** *noted sword, masterpiece of sword* |
| | | 日本刀 **Nihontō** *Japanese swords* |
| 2 strokes | フ　刀 | |

To form the kanji for a **sword** the Chinese drew a sword as ⅁ then squared it off to 刀. As a kanji by itself it is pronounced **KATANA**. Combined with other kanji in compound words, it is usually pronounced **TŌ**.

When 刀 is used as an element in a new kanji and appears in the left-hand or right-hand portion of the new kanji's square, it is often abbreviated to ⎟. When it appears at the top or the bottom of the new kanji's square it remains 刀, although its proportions may change to fit the square. A 小刀, **SHŌTŌ** or **KOGATANA**, is a **short sword** or **knife** and a 大刀, **DAITŌ**, is a **long sword**.

| 40 | ON READING: **JIN** | 自刃 **jijin** *suicide* |
|---|---|---|
| | KUN READING: **ha** | 刃物 **hamono** *knife, edged tool* |
| 刃 | *blade* | 両刃 **ryōba** *double edge* |
| | | 刃先 **hasaki** *cutting edge, blade edge* |
| 3 strokes | フ　刀　刃 | |

The Chinese started with the **sword** 刀 then, onto the blade, added a mark ＼ to emphasize the meaning **blade**. They wrote the new kanji in final form like this 刃, meaning **blade**. Used as a word by itself it is pronounced **HA**. Used in compound words 刃 is pronounced **JIN**.

| 41 | ON READINGS: **BUN, BU, FUN (PUN)**<br><br>KUN READINGS: **wa(keru), wa(karu)** | 自分 **jibun** *self*<br>分別 **funbetsu; bunbetsu** *sense; separated, sorted*<br>分数 **bunsū** *fraction*<br>三十分 **sanjippun, sanjuppun** *thirty minutes*<br>五分の一 **gobun-no-ichi** *one fifth* |
|---|---|---|
| 分 | *to cut and divide, to understand; piece, a part, share; minute* | |
| 4 strokes | ノ 八 分 分 | |

When 刀 **sword** is added as an element to the element for **eight** 八 (used in its meaning of **divide**) it forms the new kanji 分 meaning **cut and divide**. This kanji, 分, has many other meanings, but all subsume the idea of cut and divide. Used by itself, 分 is pronounced **WA-KARU** (intransitive) or **WA-KERU** (transitive). In compound words it is pronounced **BUN, FUN** or **BU**. The common word in Japanese for **understand** is 分 **WA-KARU** (to cut and divide knowledge into bite-size bits so it can be absorbed).

Many Japanese words, particularly those in common language as spoken for millennia, have many exceptions to the rules of definition and pronunciation. For example, 分, a very common character, in compounds means **a piece** or **part** or **division, after something has been cut and divided**. 一分 **IPPUN** (changed from **ICHIFUN** for euphony), means **one minute**, a division of an hour. The same kanji written in the same way 一分 also has the specialized meaning of **one-tenth**, in which case it is pronounced **ICHIBU**. The compound word 十分, **JIPPUN**, ten-minutes, means ten minutes. The same two characters in the same order in another compound word 十分 are pronounced **JŪBUN**, ten-parts-out-of-ten, which means **enough, sufficient, adequate**.

分子 **BUNSHI**, piece-child, means **molecule**. Pronounced exactly the same way, 分子 also means **the numerator** of a fraction. (**The denominator** of a fraction is 分母 **BUNBO**, mother-part.)

| 42 七 2 strokes | ON READING: **SHICHI** KUN READINGS: **nana, nana(tsu), nano** *seven* | 七月 **shichigatsu** *July* 七五三 **shichi-go-san** *The Seven-Five-Three Festival* 七つ **nanatsu** *seven (pieces)* 七日 **nanoka** *seven days, seventh day of the month* |
| --- | --- | --- |
| | 一 七 | |

The Chinese took the Asian glyph for number **seven** 十, turned it upside down 七 and used it as the character for **seven**. It is pronounced **SHICHI** either in compound words or by itself. 七 can also be pronounced **NANA, NANA-TSU** (with kana) or **NANO** either in compound words or as a word by itself.

| 43 切 4 strokes | ON READING: **SETSU** KUN READING: **ki(ru)** *to cut* | 親切 **shinsetsu** *kindness* 大切 **taisetsu** *importance* 切手 **kitte** *stamp* 切符 **kippu** *ticket* |
| --- | --- | --- |
| | 一 七 切 切 | |

Then they added 七 seven to 刀 sword to get enough cutting power and made a new composite kanji 切, meaning **cut**. Used by itself it is pronounced **KI-RU**. In combination with other kanji it is pronounced **SETSU**.

| 44 川 3 strokes | ON READING: **SEN** KUN READING: **kawa (gawa)** *river* | 河川 **kasen** *river* 川岸 **kawagishi** *riverbank* 川上 **kawakami** *upstream, up the river* 川下り **kawakudari** *river-rafting* |
| --- | --- | --- |
| | 丿 川 川 | |

From a view of a flowing river 川 the Chinese drew the pictograph for **river** 川. In final form they straightened it to 川. Used by itself it is pronounced **KAWA**, sometimes changed to **GAWA** for euphony. In compound words it is pronounced **SEN**. It is often used in family and geographical names, where it is generally pronounced **KAWA**. Examples are 立川 **TACHIKAWA**, Rising-river and 小川 **OGAWA**, Small-river.

40

| 45 州 6 strokes | ON READING: **SHŪ** KUN READING: **su** sandbank; state, province | 欧州 **ōshū** *Europe* 八重州 **Yaesu** *Yaesu district* 中州 **nakasu** *towhead, sandbar* 州知事 **shūchiji** *state governor* |
|---|---|---|

丿　丿　少　州　州　州

The Chinese added sandbanks to the river 〜〜 to indicate a bit of land surrounded by water. They drew the kanji in final form as 州. It retains the meaning of **sandbank**, and has the extended meanings of **land surrounded by water** and a **separate political state**. It is pronounced **SU** when used by itself, and **SHŪ** when used in compound words. 本州 **HONSHŪ**, main-state, is the name of the main island of Japan. 九州 **KYŪSHŪ**, nine-states, is the southern-most of the main islands of Japan. It took its name from the island's nine ancient provinces.

| 46 水 4 strokes | ON READING: **SUI** KUN READING: **mizu** water | 水分 **suibun** *moisture* 水泳 **suiei** *swimming* 水色 **mizuiro** *aqua blue* 水玉 **mizutama** *polka dot* |
|---|---|---|

亅　汀　オ　水

The Chinese saw that if you squeeze a river 水 you get water. They drew the pictograph for **water** therefore first as 水 and finally 水. Used as a kanji by itself 水 is pronounced **MIZU**. Used with other kanji in compound words it is generally pronounced **SUI**, as in 水分 **SUIBUN**, water-portion, meaning **moisture**. In what looks to be an exception to the pronunciation rules, 大水 big-water, meaning **flood**, is pronounced **ŌMIZU**, but in this case 水 **water** is actually a word by itself modified by 大 **big**, and is not part of a compound word.

When **water** 水 is used as an element to form other kanji, it changes shape considerably, to fit and balance the kanji square. The change proceeds from 〜〜 to 〜 then 氵, and finally 氵. This element is used very frequently and appears in most kanji that refer in some way to water or liquids.

| 47 | ON READING: **KAI**<br>KUN READING: **umi** | 海岸 **kaigan** *coast*<br>海水浴 **kaisuiyoku** *bathing* |
|---|---|---|
| 海<br><br>9 strokes | *ocean* | 海辺 **umibe** *seaside*<br>海鳥 **umidori** *seabird* |

| 丶 | ﾆ | 氵 | 汁 | 沪 | 汴 | 洵 | 海 | 海 |
|---|---|---|---|---|---|---|---|---|

The Chinese added the element for **water**, modified to 氵, to the element for every 毎 to symbolize "water, water everywhere." They wrote the final form 海, meaning **ocean**. Used as a word by itself it is pronounced **UMI**. In compound words it is pronounced **KAI**. The 日本海 **NIHONKAI**, Japan-ocean, is the **Japan Sea**. 海女 **AMA** (This word has a special pronunciation for each of the kanji; It looks like it should be pronounced **KAIJŌ**, but the correct pronunciation of the two kanji when used together, and only in this case, is **AMA**) refers to the women who dive to the ocean bottom to harvest ocean products like pearls or fish or seaweed.

| 48 | ON READING: **HYŌ**<br>KUN READINGS: **kōri, hi** | 氷河 **hyōga** *glacier*<br>氷山 **hyōzan** *iceberg* |
|---|---|---|
| 氷<br><br>5 strokes | *ice* | 氷雨 **hisame** *a sleety rain*<br>かき氷 **kakigōri** *shaved ice* |

| 丨 | 刁 | 刃 | 氺 | 氷 |
|---|---|---|---|---|

To turn **water** 水 into **ice**, the Chinese just aimed the point of an ice-pick 丶 at the top of the water frozen into ice, and drew the new kanji 氷. It is pronounced **KŌRI** or **HI** when it is used as a kanji by itself. In compound words it is pronounced **HYŌ**. 氷水 **KŌRIMIZU** is **ice-water** (two separate words, not a compound word), as you would order ice water in a restaurant.

| 49 入 | ON READING: **NYŪ** KUN READINGS: **i(reru), hai(ru)** | 入学 **nyūgaku** *entry (school)* 入力 **nyūryoku** *entry (data)* 入る **hairu** *to enter, to go in* 入れ歯 **ireba** *false teeth* 入場券 **nyūjōken** *admission ticket* |
| --- | --- | --- |
| | *to insert, to put in, to enter, to go in* | |
| 2 strokes | ノ 入 | |

To symbolize the meaning **enter**, the Chinese drew a pictograph of a smaller river flowing into a larger 𣲘. In final form the rivers became lines, written 入. This kanji means **enter** or **insert**. Used as a word by itself as a transitive verb it is pronounced **I-RERU** and means **insert** or **put in**. Used as a word by itself as an intransitive verb it is pronounced **HAI-RU** and means **enter** or **go in**. Used with other kanji in compound words it is pronounced **NYŪ** and can mean either **enter** or **insert**.

| 50 口 | ON READINGS: **KŌ, KU** KUN READING: **kuchi (guchi)** | 人口 **jinkō** *population* 口調 **kuchō** *accent, tone* 早口言葉 **hayakuchi kotoba** *tongue twister* 出口 **iriguchi** *exit* |
| --- | --- | --- |
| | *mouth, opening* | |
| 3 strokes | 丨 冂 口 | |

**Mouth** or **opening** 👄 was first pictured by the Chinese as ⊔. Then, with little alteration, its final form became 口. Used as a word by itself it is pronounced **KUCHI** (sometimes **GUCHI** for euphony). Used with other kanji to form a compound word it is usually pronounced **KŌ** or **KU**.

At the entrance to public places like train stations, hotels, big buildings, or department stores there will often be a sign 入口 **IRIGUCHI**, enter-opening, meaning **entrance**. Other entrances may have their own descriptive name, as for example those places that have an **east entrance** will have a sign 東口 **HI-GASHIGUCHI**, east-entrance.

| 51 中 4 strokes | ON READING: **CHŪ (JŪ)** <br> KUN READING: **naka** <br><br> *middle, inside* | 中央 **chūō** *midst, middle, center* <br> 中学校 **chūgakkō** *junior high school* <br> 背中 **senaka** *back (of body)* <br> 真ん中 **man-naka** *midst, center* |
|---|---|---|
| | 、　　冂　　口　　中 | |

A **mouth** or **opening** 口 with a line through the middle 中 means **middle** or **inside**. Some scholars say the Chinese drew the pictograph as a picture of an arrow striking the middle of a target, and others say it is a box or board with a line down the middle. In any case, whatever the origin of the pictograph, the line got in the middle and the meaning of the kanji 中 is **middle** or **inside**. Used by itself as a word it is pronounced **NAKA**. Used in compound words it is pronounced **CHŪ** (sometimes **JŪ** for euphony).

中東 **CHŪTŌ**, middle-east, is the **Middle East**. 日本中 **NIHONJŪ** (**NIHONCHU** pronounced euphonically), Japan-inside, means **throughout Japan**. 中立 **CHŪRITSU**, middle-stand, means **neutrality**. 一日中 **ICHINICHIJŪ**, one-day-middle, means **all day long**.

| 52 仲 6 strokes | ON READING: **CHŪ** <br> KUN READING: **naka** <br><br> *relationship* | 仲秋の **chūshū no** *harvest* <br> 仲間 **nakama** *company, peer* <br> 仲良し **nakayoshi** *a good friend* |
|---|---|---|
| | ノ　　亻　　化　　仁　　仲　　仲 | |

They combined the element for **person** 人 with the element for **middle** 中 into a new kanji to symbolize a person in the middle, the one who stands between two sides. The Chinese wrote the new kanji 仲, meaning **relationship**. Used as a word by itself, which is not common, it is pronounced **NAKA**. Used in compound words it is pronounced **CHŪ**. Used in a compound word with the kanji for person 人, it has a special pronunciation and so does the kanji for **person**. 仲人, meaning a **go-between** or a **match-maker**, is pronounced **NAKŌDO**.

| 53 | ON READING: **KAI** | 仲介 **chūkai** *agency* |
| | | 紹介 **shōkai** *introduction* |
| 介 | *to mediate* | お節介 **osekkai** *meddlesome* |
| | | 介護 **kaigo** *nursing care* |
| 4 strokes | ノ　入　介　介 | |

The Chinese drew a pictograph of a **person** 人 cased in armor│　│, first as │人│, then simplified to 疒, symbolizing the idea of being between things. They wrote the final form 介, meaning **to mediate**. Used either as a word by itself or in a compound word it is pronounced **KAI**. 介入 **KAINYŪ**, mediate-enter, means **intervention**. 仲介 **CHŪKAI**, relation-mediate, means an **intermediary**, **to mediate**, or **through the good offices of**.

| 54 | ON READING: **KAI** | 境界 **kyōkai** *border, barrier, boundary* |
| | | 限界 **genkai** *limit* |
| 界 | *boundary* | 社交界 **shakōkai** *social circles* |
| | | 世界地図 **shikaichizu** *world atlas* |
| 9 strokes | 丶　冂　冂　冊　田　尹　界　界　界 | |

The element for **between** 介 (from a pictograph of a person cased in armor) was added to the element for **rice-paddy** 田 to symbolize the line between rice-paddies, or the **boundary**. The Chinese wrote the new composite kanji 界, meaning **boundary**. Used either as a word by itself or in compound words it is pronounced **KAI**. 世界 **SEKAI**, generation-boundary, means the **world**.

45

| 55 央 5 strokes | ON READING: **Ō** | 中央分離帯 **chūō-bunritai** *median* |
| | *the exact middle* | 中央道 **Chūōdō** *Chūō Expressway* |
| | ヽ 冂 冂 央 央 | |

As described above, the mouth with a line through the middle 中 means **middle**, with the connotation "inside." The Chinese invented another kanji to mean **middle** with the connotation "center," that is, **the exact middle**. They drew a circle ◯ around the center of a man with arms outstretched 大 and formed the pictograph 查. They later squared the circle 查, then let the man's arms be the bottom of the square forming the final kanji 央. It is not used as a word by itself. In compound words it is pronounced **Ō** and means **the exact middle**.

The compound word 中央, **CHŪ-Ō**, middle-center, is a common word meaning **central**. 中央口 **CHŪ-Ō-GUCHI**, means **central-entrance**.

| 56 映 9 strokes | ON READING: **EI** KUN READINGS: **utsu(ru), utsu(ru), ha(eru)** | 反映 **han-ei** *reflection* 映像 **eizō** *image, projection* |
| | *to reflect, to stand out; reflection* | 映す **utsusu** *to reflect, to mirror* 夕映え **yūbae** *the setting sun* |
| | 丨 冂 丬 日 日 日 日 映 映 | |

The Chinese focused **sunlight** 日 on the **center** 央 of an object to get a **reflection**. They combined the two elements into a composite kanji 映, meaning **reflect** or **reflect an image** as in photography, xerography, a movie, or a mirror. Used as a word by itself it is pronounced **UTSU-SU** (transitive), **UTSU-RU** (intransitive) or **HA-ERU** (intransitive). In compound words it is pronounced **EI**.

| 57 画 8 strokes | ON READINGS: **GA, KAKU** | 画家 **gaka** *painter* 図画 **zuga** *graphic* |
| | *picture, painting, drawing* | 計画 **keikaku** *plan* 区画 **kukaku** *compartment* |
| | 一 厂 厂 币 币 币 画 画 | |

They drew a frame or boundary 囗 around a field 田 to form the pictograph 囲,

which in its final form became 画, meaning **picture**, **painting**, or **drawing**. It later also came to mean a **kanji stroke**. 画 is not used as a character by itself. In compound words, 画 is pronounced **GA** or **KAKU**.

A 日本画 **NIHONGA** is a Japanese painting, distinguished from a Western-style oil painting. An 映画 **EIGA**, reflection-picture, is **a movie.**

| 58 | ON READING: **KO** | 中古 **chūko** *secondhand, used* |
|---|---|---|
| | KUN READING: **furu(i)** | 古典 **koten** *classic(al)* |
| 古 | | 古着 **furugi** *used clothing* |
| | *old (thing; not used for people)* | 使い古し **tsukaifurushi** *worn-out, used* |
| 5 strokes | 一 十 十 古 古 | |

The character for mouth 口 is used sometimes to mean a **person**, similar to the English-language usage in the phrase "too many mouths to feed." In the kanji 古, the mouth 口 stands for a whole generation of people. The **ten** 十 on top of **mouth** 口 means ten-generations, which the Chinese interpret to mean **old**. When used as a word by itself it is pronounced **FURU-I**. In compound words it is pronounced **KO**. A 古本 **FURUHON**, old-book, is a **previously-owned book**.

| 59 | ON READING: **HIN** | 作品 **sakuhin** *a piece of work, production* |
|---|---|---|
| | KUN READING: **shina** | 上品 **jōhin** *elegance* |
| 品 | | 品物 **shinamono** *article, item* |
| | *goods, things* | 手品師 **tejinashi** *magician* |
| 9 strokes | 丶 冂 口 口 口 口 品 品 品 | |

Three **mouths** or **openings** 口 口 口, here referring to the openings of boxes, were piled up 品 to indicate many boxes. The Chinese used this kanji to mean **goods** or **things**. As a kanji by itself it is pronounced **SHINA**. Used with other kanji in compound words it is pronounced **HIN**. The compound word 中古品 **CHŪKOHIN**, middle-old-things, means **second-hand goods**.

| 60 | ON READING: **KU** | 区別 **kubetsu** *separation* |
|----|---------------------|------------------------------|
| 区 | | 区分 **kubun** *division, distribution* |
| | *ward, district, section* | 地区 **chiku** *area, district, division* |
| | | 区立 **kuritsu** *ward (municipal)* |
| 4 strokes | 一　ブ　又　区 | |

Three mouths □ □ □ inside a boundary ⎿ forms the pictograph 㡱, symbol-izing many mouths inside a boundary. It means **ward** or **district** or **section**, almost always in reference to a geographical division.

The Chinese recently abbreviated 㡱 to 区 to make it easier to write in cursive style. Instead of using nine lines to draw three boxes inside the boundary, they substituted an ✕. The Japanese have almost universally adopted this abbrevia-tion, but on some older maps the character will still be seen as 㡱.

区 is not used as a word itself. In compound words it is pronounced **KU**. Three of the wards in Tokyo are 品川区 **SHINAGAWAKU**, Shinagawa Ward, 中央区 **CHŪŌKU**, Chuo Ward, and 大田区 **ŌTAKU**, Ota Ward.

| 61 | ON READING: **CHŌ** | 町会 **chōkai** *neighborhood* |
|----|---------------------|-------------------------------|
| | KUN READING: **machi** | *association* |
| 町 | | 市町村 **shichōson** *municipal* |
| | *town, section of a ward* | 町外れ **machihazure** *outskirt* |
| | | 町内 **chōnai** *intramural, community* |
| 7 strokes | 丨　冂　冂　冊　田　田　町 | |

A geographical division smaller than a 区 is a 町. This kanji is formed from a pictograph of a field 田 with a sign 𠮷 in front, giving the field a name. 町 means a **town** or a **section of a ward**. Used as a kanji by itself or in geographical names it is pronounced **MACHI**. Combined with other kanji in compound words it is pronounced **CHŌ**.

| 62 | ON READINGS: **CHŌ, TEI** | 包丁 **hōchō** *kitchen knife* |
|---|---|---|
| 丁 | *unit of measure, counter of things (tofu, etc.), block* | 丁度 **chōdo** *just, exactly, only*<br>丁ねい **teinei** *courtesy, politeness* |
| 2 strokes | 一 丁 | |

The sign 丁 alone also forms a character. It is a **unit of measure**, a **counter of things**. It is not used as a word by itself. With other kanji in compound words it is pronounced **CHŌ** or **TEI**. Blocks of houses inside a town or ward are counted in 丁 **CHŌ**, as are certain foods like blocks of bean-curd and bowls or plates of certain foods, like noodles. Counting bowls of noodles becomes 一丁 **ITCHŌ** (**ICHI-CHŌ** pronounced euphonically), 二丁 **NICHŌ**, 三丁 **SANCHŌ**.

| 63 | ON READINGS: **GEN, GON**<br>KUN READINGS: **i(u), koto** | 名言 **meigen** *word of wisdom*<br>伝言 **dengon** *message* |
|---|---|---|
| 言 | *to say, to speak* | 言い訳 **i'iwake** *excuse, apology*<br>言葉 **kotoba** *word, tongue* |
| 7 strokes | 丶 一 二 三 言 言 言 | |

A mouth 口 speaking its lines 三 forms the character 言 which means **to say** or **to speak**. Used as a kanji by itself it is pronounced **I-U** (which sounds like **YU**) or **KOTO**. Used in compound words it is pronounced **GEN** or **GON**.

| 64 | ON READING: **SHIN** | 信用 **shinyō** *confidence, trust*<br>通信 **tsūshin** *correspondence* |
|---|---|---|
| 信 | *to believe, to trust* | 信号 **shingō** *signal*<br>信じる **shinjiru** *to believe, to trust* |
| 9 strokes | ノ 亻 亻 亻 亻 信 信 信 信 | |

The Chinese put a person's "**sayings**" 言 together with the person 人 to form a new kanji 信 meaning believe or trust. It is not used as a word by itself. It is pronounced **SHIN** in compound words, and is a common character in the financial world since it is used to mean the **Trust** in "Savings & Trust" used in the names of banking institutions.

| 65 | ON READINGS: **KO, KI** | 自己 **jiko** *self* |
|---|---|---|
| | KUN READING: **onore** | 自己紹介 **jikoshōkai** |
| 己 | *self; from start to finish* | *self-introduction*<br>利己的 **rikoteki** *selfish, egoistic*<br>知己 **chiki** *friend, acquaintance* |
| 3 strokes | ﹃ コ 己 | |

The Chinese drew a picture of a convoluted thread 乙 to signify "**from one end to the other**." They squared it off in final form to 己. It is not often used as a stand-alone kanji, either by itself or in compound words, but it does appear as an element in a number of other kanji, generally bringing the meaning **from beginning to end**. In one example of its use as a stand-alone kanji, though rarely seen or heard, 己 is pronounced **ONORE**, meaning **I myself, completely me from start to finish**. In compound words it is pronounced **KO** or **KI** and means **self**.

| 66 | ON READING: **KI** | 記号 **kigō** *sign, code* |
|---|---|---|
| | KUN READING: **shiru(su)** | 伝記 **denki** *biography* |
| 記 | *to say it, to write it, to chronicle it* | 記す **shirusu** *to write, to mark down*<br>記事 **kiji** *article, report* |
| 10 strokes | 丶 亠 亖 言 言 言 言 訁 訁 記 | |

The element for say 言 was combined with the element meaning from beginning to end 己 to make the new composite kanji 記, meaning **say it** (or **write it**) **from beginning to end**, or **chronicle it**. Used as a kanji by itself it is pronounced **SHIRU-SU**. With other kanji in compound words it is pronounced **KI**. A 日記 **NIKKI**, day-chronicle, is a **diary**. 記入 **KINYŪ**, write-enter, means **make an entry** or **fill out a form**.

| 67 | ON READING: **KEI** | 計算 **keisan** *accounting, calculation* |
|---|---|---|
| | KUN READING: **haka(ru)** | 体重計 **taijūkei** *weight scale* |
| 計 | *counting, measuring* | 時計 **tokei** *clock*<br>計量 **keiryō** *measurement* |
| 9 strokes | 丶 亠 亖 言 言 言 訁 計 | |

**Speaking** 言 in **tens** 十 means **counting** or **measuring** 計. This character appears over the cashier's counter in restaurants or stores, where it means **counting**. It is also used on all types of measuring instruments from thermometers to computers, where it means **measuring**. On instruments, the other kanji appearing with 計 indicates what it measures, and the kanji 計 can sometimes be translated as **meter**. Used as a kanji by itself 計 is pronounced **HAKA-RU**. Used in compound words it is pronounced **KEI**. A 小計 **SHŌKEI**, small-total, is a **sub-total**.

| 68 | ON READING: **ZETSU** | 毒舌 **dokuzetsu** *evil tongue* |
| | KUN READING: **shita** | 猫舌 **nekojita** *sensitive tongue* |
| 舌 | *tongue* | 舌打ち **shitauchi** *clicking* |
| | | 舌触り **shitazawari** *texture (of food)* |
| 6 strokes | 一　二　千　千　舌　舌 | |

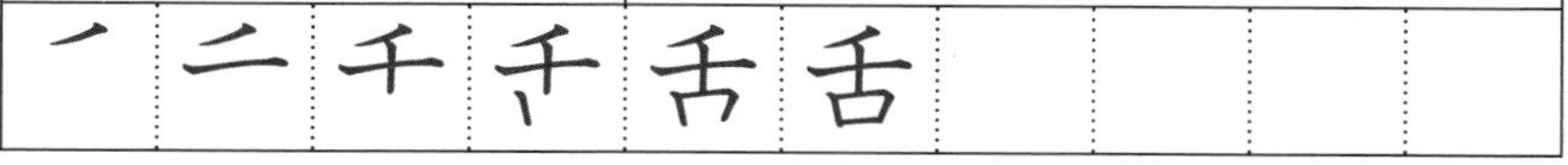

A **mouth** 口 with a tongue 𠃊 sticking out, drawn slightly forked 舌, means **tongue**. Used as a kanji by itself 舌 is pronounced **SHITA**. With other kanji in compound words it is pronounced **ZETSU**.

| 69 | ON READING: **WA** | 手話 **shuwa** *sign language* |
| | KUN READINGS: **hanashi,** | 会話 **kaiwa** *conversation* |
| | **hana(su)** | 話し合い **hanashiai** *discussion* |
| 話 | *to talk* | 昔話 **mukashi-banashi** *folk tale* |
| | �丶　�　�　言　言　言　言　訁　訁　訃 | |
| 13 strokes | 訐　話　話 | |

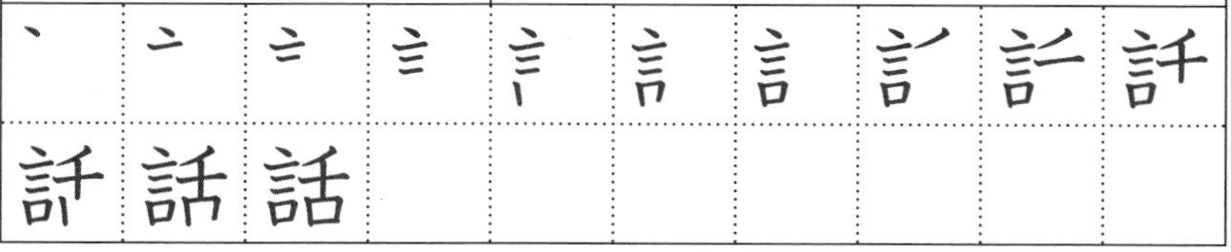

The Chinese understood that "to talk" requires more eloquence than "to say," so they added **tongue** 舌 to **say** 言 to make 話 **talk**. The difference between **say** 言 and **talk** 話 in Japanese is about the same as in English. To say is to express, as in " 'this is delicious', she said." To talk is to communicate, as in "talk on the telephone." 話 is pronounced **HANASHI** (noun) or **HANA-SU** (verb) when used as a word by itself. In compound words it is pronounced **WA**.

| 70 活 9 strokes | ON READING: **KATSU** | 活動 **katsudō** *action, movement* 活発な **kappatsu na** *active* 生活 **seikatsu** *life* 活躍 **katsuyaku** *good showing* |
| | *life, activity* | |
| | ` 丶 冫 氵 汀 汗 汗 活 活 | |

A moist tongue was a sign of life in China, so the Chinese combined the kanji for **water** 水, modified to シ, and the kanji for **tongue** 舌 to make a new kanji meaning **life** or **activity** 活. It is not used as a kanji by itself. With other kanji in compound words 活 is pronounced **KATSU**. The name of a major Japanese entertainment group is 日活 **NIKKATSU**, Sun-Life.

| 71 語 14 strokes | ON READING: **GO** KUN READING: **kata(ru)** | 語学 **gogaku** *language* 外国語 **gaikokugo** *foreign language* 物語 **monogatari** *story, tale* 語る **kataru** *to talk, to tell* |
| | *word, language* | |
| | ` 亠 主 言 言 言 訂 訂 語 | |
| | 語 語 語 語 | |

The Chinese drew the pictograph for **word** or **language** by combining the element for **say** or **speak** 言 with the idea of **many people**. They had already used **ten mouths** 古 to mean **ten generations**, or old, so for the idea of "**many people**" they settled for **five mouths** 吾 and drew the final kanji 語, meaning **word** or **language**. Used as a word by itself it is pronounced **KATA-RU**. With other kanji in compound words it is pronounced **GO**. 日本語 **NIHONGO** means the Japanese language.

| 72 | ON READING: **EI** | 英雄 **eiyū** *hero* |
|----|----|----|
| **英** | *brilliant, superior, talented; England* | 英国 **Eikoku** *England*<br>英米 **eibei** *Anglo-America*<br>英検 **eiken** *English proficiency (test)* |
| 8 strokes | 一　十　艹　艹　芐　苎　英　英 | |

The Chinese pictograph of plants was drawn at first as 屮 屮. It was later drawn ⁺⁺ and finally ⁺⁺. It never became a kanji on its own but it is used as an element in many other kanji, where it brings the meaning **plant**. It usually appears at the top of a kanji. For example, the Chinese combined **plant** ⁺⁺ and **center** 央 into the new kanji 英, center-of-the-plant, signifying the most beautiful flower that grows at the center of a plant, meaning a **very beautiful flower**. In Chinese it still has this meaning, but in Japanese it has come to mean **brilliant, superior, talented**. 英 is not used as a kanji by itself. In compound words it is pronounced **EI**. The Chinese long ago selected 英 to be the kanji meaning England. 英語 **EIGO**, England-language, means **the English language**.

| 73 | ON READING: **JŌ**<br>KUN READINGS: **ue, uwa, nobo(ru), a(garu), a(geru), kami** | 地上 **chijō** *above ground; the ground*<br>上着 **uwagi** *coat, jacket*<br>風上 **kazakami** *upwind, windward*<br>売り上げ **uriage** *sales, performance* |
|----|----|----|
| **上** | *up, over, on top of; to climb up, to rise up* | |
| 3 strokes | 丨　卜　上 | |

For **up** and **down**, the Chinese began with dots above and below a centerline, ∸ and ⊤. To make them easier to write and to recognize, they expanded the dots to vertical lines ⊥ and ⊤, and added handles.

上 means **up** or **over** or **on top of**. Used as a verb it can mean **climb up** or **rise up** (intransitive), and **put up** or **raise up** (transitive). When used as a kanji by itself, 上 is pronounced **UE** or **UWA** as an adverb, and **NOBO-RU** or **AGA-RU** or **AGE-RU** as a verb. When used in compound words it is pronounced **JŌ** or **KAMI**.

| 74 | ON READING: **KA, GE**<br><br>KUN READINGS: **shita, shimo, o(riru) sa(garu), kuda(ru), kuda(saru), moto** | 下流 **karyū** *downstream*<br>上下 **jōge** *tops and bottoms*<br>下見 **shitami** *preview*<br>風下 **kazashimo** *leeward*<br>足下 **ashimoto** *foot, step* |
|---|---|---|
| 下 | *down, under, below; to climb down, to drop down, to give down* | |
| 3 strokes | 一　丁　下 | |

下 means **down** or **under** or **below**. Used as a verb it can mean **climb down** or **drop down** or **give down** (this is the provenance of the polite, often-used Japanese word **KUDA-SAI**, please give down to me). When used as a kanji by itself, 下 is pronounced **SHITA** or **SHIMO** as an adverb, and **O-RIRU, SA-GARU, KUDA-RU** or **KUDA-SARU** as a verb. When used in compound words it is pronounced **KA, GE** or **MOTO**.

Some compound words using 上 and 下 are:

上映中 **JŌ-EICHŪ**, upon-screen-middle. This word appears on movie-posters at all theaters, and means **Now Playing**.

下町 **SHITAMACHI**, down-town, meaning **downtown**.

川上 **KAWAKAMI**, up-river, meaning **upstream**.

川下 **KAWASHIMO**, down-river, meaning **downstream**.

下水 **GESUI**, down-water, meaning **sewage**.

下り **KUDARI**, (with kana; 下 provides only the sound **KUDA**), descending, meaning **out-bound**, pertaining to trains and subways.

上り **NOBORI**, (with kana; 上 provides the sound **NOBO**), meaning **in-bound**, pertaining to trains and subways.

| 75 山 3 strokes | ON READING: **SAN**<br>KUN READING: **yama**<br><br>*mountain* | 富士山 **fujisan** *Mt. Fuji*<br>登山 **tozan** *mountain climbing*<br>山登り **yamanobori** *hill climbing*<br>山形 **Yamagata** *Yamagata Prefecture* |
|---|---|---|
|  | 丨　山　山 | |

The character for **mountain** was taken from a picture of a range of mountains with three peaks. The Chinese first drew it ⋀⋀. Then each peak became a line, and the final character for **mountain** became 山. As a word by itself, and in most proper names, it is pronounced **YAMA**. In compound words it is pronounced **SAN**. A 氷山 **HYŌZAN** (SAN euphonized), ice-mountain, is an **iceberg**. Like many words of nature, 山 is a favorite character for Japanese family names:

| 山下 | **YAMASHITA** | Below-the-mountain |
|---|---|---|
| 山川 | **YAMAKAWA** | Mountain-stream |
| 大山 | **ŌYAMA** | Big-mountain |
| 山本 | **YAMAMOTO** | Original-mountain |

| 76 火 4 strokes | ON READING: **KA**<br>KUN READING: **hi**<br><br>*fire* | 火口 **kakō** *crater*<br>火事 **kaji** *fire*<br>火花 **hibana** *spark*<br>花火 **hanabi** *firework* |
|---|---|---|
|  | 丶　丷　少　火 | |

The character for fire is a picture of a flame 🔥. It was first drawn 火, then 火. The final form was simplified to 火, meaning **fire**. Used as a word by itself it is pronounced **HI**. In compound words it is pronounced **KA**. A 火山 **KAZAN** (**KASAN** pronounced euphonically), fire-mountain, is a **volcano**.

| 77 | ON READING: **EN** | 炎上 **enjō** *burn, flame* |
| | KUN READING: **hono-o** | 肺炎 **haien** *pneumonia* |
| 炎 | *flame* | 炎症 **enshō** *inflammation* |
| | | 炎天下 **entenka** *in the hot sun* |
| 8 strokes | ` ヽ ゛ ⺍ 火 炏 炏 炎 炎 | |

The Chinese doubled the **fire** 火火, placing one atop the other 炎, to draw the character for **flame**, implying very hot. Used as a word by itself it is pronounced **HONO-O**. In compound words 炎 is pronounced **EN**. 火炎 **KA-EN**, fire-flame, means **blaze**. 炎天 **ENTEN**, flame-sky, means **scorching weather**.

| 78 | ON READING: **KOKU** | 谷川 **tanigawa** *mountain stream* |
| | KUN READINGS: **tani, ya** | 渓谷 **keikoku** *gorge, valley* |
| 谷 | *valley, gorge* | 谷間 **tanima** *valley, cleavage* |
| | | 渋谷 **Shibuya** *Sibuya district (in Tokyo)* |
| 7 strokes | ` ハ 公 公 谷 谷 谷 | |

To draw the pictograph for **valley**, the Chinese started with a mountain range 仌, then cut it apart 八 and drew in the opening 口 leading to the valley. The final form was 谷, meaning **valley** or **gorge**. Used as a word by itself or in proper names, 谷 is pronounced **TANI** or **YA**. In compound words it is pronounced **KOKU**.

# SECTION THREE

## Kanji List

| | | | | | |
|---|---|---|---|---|---|
| 79 穴 | 80 工 | 81 空 | 82 石 | 83 由 | 84 油 |
| 85 井 | 86 月 | 87 夕 | 88 外 | 89 名 | 90 多 |
| 91 期 | 92 棋 | 93 碁 | 94 明 | 95 光 | 96 早 |
| 97 草 | 98 朝 | 99 土 | 100 出 | 101 生 | 102 星 |
| 103 者 | 104 圧 | 105 里 | 106 黒 | 107 玉 | 108 宝 |
| 109 国 | 110 内 | 111 理 | 112 米 | 113 斗 | 114 料 |
| 115 無 | 116 科 | 117 年 | | | |

| 79 | ON READING: **KETSU** | 墓穴 **boketsu, haka-ana** *grave* |
|---|---|---|
| 穴 | KUN READING: **ana** | 風穴 **kaza-ana, fūketsu** *crack; cold air duct* |
| | *hole, open space* | 穴場 **anaba** *a best-kept secret spot* |
| 5 strokes | 丶 丶 宀 灾 穴 | 落とし穴 **otoshiana** *gimmick* |

The Chinese drew a pictograph for **roof** ↑↑, then simplified it to ⌒. It is not used as a kanji by itself, but frequently appears as an element symbolizing a roof or a cover.

Early houses were a roof over a hole or open space cut into the ground, so the Chinese pictograph to symbolize a **hole** or **open space** was the element for **cut** or **divide** (also used for number **eight**) 八 placed under the element for **roof** ⌒. The new kanji was drawn 穴 and means **hole** or **empty space**. Used as a word by itself it is pronounced **ANA**. In compound words 穴 is pronounced **KETSU**.

| 80 | ON READINGS: **KŌ, KU** | 工場 **kōjō, kōba** *factory, plant* |
|---|---|---|
| 工 | | 加工 **kakō** *processing* |
| | *to fabricate, to make* | 細工 **saiku** *workmanship* |
| 3 strokes | 一 丁 工 | 工夫 **kufū** *artifice, devise* |

A pictograph of a workman's ruler was used to symbolize the concept **fabricate** or **make**. The Chinese changed it slightly in final form and wrote the kanji 工. It is not used as a word by itself. When used as a kanji in compound words it is pronounced **KŌ** or **KU**. A 大工 **DAIKU**, big-maker, is a **carpenter**. 人工 **JINKŌ**, man-made, means **man-made** or **artificial**.

| 81 | ON READING: **KŪ** | 空港 **kūkō** *airport* |
| | KUN READINGS: **sora, kara, a(ku)** | 青空 **aozora** *blue sky* |
| 空 | | 空手 **Karate** *Karate* |
| | *sky; empty, vacant* | 空き巣 **akisu** *thief* |
| 8 strokes | ` 丶　丷　宀　穴　空　空　空　空 ` |

The Chinese put together the element for **hole** or **empty space** 穴 with the element for **fabricate** or **make** 工 and made a new composite kanji 空, meaning **sky**, the biggest empty space of all. It also means **empty** or **vacant**. Used as a word by itself 空 is pronounced **SORA**, **KARA**, or **A-KU**. Used with other kanji in compound words it is pronounced **KŪ**. 空中 **KŪCHŪ**, sky-middle, means **mid-air**.

| 82 | ON READINGS: **SEKI, SHAKU** | 宝石 **hōseki** *gem, jewel* |
| | | 石庭 **sekitei** *stone garden* |
| 石 | KUN READING: **ishi** | 磁石 **jishaku** *magnet* |
| | *stone* | 石川 **Ishikawa** *Ishikawa Prefecture* |
| 5 strokes | 一　厂　不　石　石 |

A mountain cliff 𠂆 with a stone ◯ below was the Chinese pictograph for **stone**. They first wrote it /◯, then /◯, and in final form 石. Used as a word by itself or in family names it is pronounced **ISHI**. In compound words 石 is pronounced **SEKI** or **SHAKU**. A 小石 **KO-ISHI**, small-stone, is a **pebble**.

| 83 | ON READINGS: **YU, YŪ** | 由来 **yurai** *origin, derivation* |
| | | 経由 **keiyu** *(to go) through* |
| 由 | *the path out, the way, the means* | 自由 **jiyū** *freedom, liberty* |
| | | 理由 **riyū** *reason* |
| 5 strokes | 丨　冂　巾　由　由 |

Starting with the pictograph of a rice-paddy 田, the Chinese extended one line outside the boundary and drew a new kanji 由 meaning **the path out** or **the way** or **the means**. It is not often used as a word by itself. Used in compound words 由 is pronounced **YU** or **YŪ**.

| 84 油 8 strokes | ON READING: **YU** <br> KUN READING: **abura** <br><br> *oil* | 油性 **yusei** *oiliness* <br> しょう油 **shōyu** *soy sauce* <br> 軽油 **keiyu** *gas oil* <br> 油絵 **aburae** *oil painting* |
|---|---|---|

`　丶　　丶　　氵　　氵　　汩　　沺　　油　　油`

The Chinese character for **oil**, either animal, vegetable, or mineral, contained the element for **the path out** 由, to extract the oil, and the element for **water** or **liquid** 氵, to make sure the oil flows. They drew the kanji in final form as 油. Used as a word by itself it is pronounced **ABURA**. In compound words it is pronounced **YU**. 石油, **SEKIYU**, stone-oil, means **petroleum** (also stone-oil in Latin). A 油田, **YUDEN**, oil-field, is an **oil field**.

| 85 井 4 strokes | ON READINGS: **SEI, SHŌ** <br> KUN READING: **i** <br><br> *well, frame* | 市井の **shisei no** *ordinary* <br> 井戸 **ido** *(water) well* <br> 井げた **igeta** *frame* |
|---|---|---|

`　一　　二　　井　　井`

The Chinese drew a pictograph of the frame around the well-top on which to rest your water pail 井. (The dot in the center is the water pail inside the well.) They simplified it to 井, which looks just like a tic-tac-toe frame. In final form they made it more aesthetic 井. It means either **well** or **frame**. It is not used as a word by itself. As a kanji in compound words it is pronounced **I**, **SEI**, or **SHŌ**. A 油井, **YUSEI**, oil-well, is an **oil well**. The 天井 **TENJŌ**, sky-frame, is the ceiling, as in the **ceiling** of a room.

| 86 月 4 strokes | ON READINGS: **GETSU, GATSU** <br> KUN READING: **tsuki** <br><br> *moon, month* | 月曜日 **Getsuyōbi** *Monday* <br> 正月 **shōgatsu** *New Year, January* <br> 月見 **tsukimi** *moon viewing* <br> 三日月 **mikazuki** *crescent* |
|---|---|---|

`　丿　　冂　　月　　月`

A picture of a quarter-moon 月 became the character for **moon**. The Chinese wrote it first like this 月, then squared it off and gave it balance 月. Used as a word by itself it is pronounced **TSUKI**. In compound words it is pronounced **GETSU** or **GATSU**. Like **sun** 日, **moon** 月 is also used to measure time as well as to signify itself. A **sun** 日 is a day and a **moon** 月 is a month.

The names of the months are formed from the numbers 1 through 12 combined in a compound word with 月 **moon**, pronounced **GA-TSU**. For example, 一月, **ICHI-GATSU**, is **January**, 二月, **NI-GATSU**, is **Febru-ary**, and 十月, **JŪ-GATSU**, is **October**.

| 87 | ON READING: **SEKI** | 一朝一夕 **itchō-isseki** *in a day* |
| | KUN READING: **yū** | 夕方 **yūgata** *(early) evening* |
| 夕 | *evening* | 夕べ **yūbe** *evening* |
| | | 夕焼け **yūyake** *sunset* |
| 3 strokes | ノ ク 夕 | |

A picture of the full moon rising from behind a mountain in early evening ⌒⌒ formed the character for **evening**. The Chinese first drew it as 𝄇 then abstracted it to 夕. In compound words it is pronounced **YŪ** or **SEKI**. 夕 is not used as a word by itself. 夕日 **YŪHI** or **SEKIJITSU**, evening-sun, is the **setting sun**. A 夕立, **YŪDACHI**, evening-rising, is **an unexpected rain shower which starts up in early evening**.

| 88 | ON READINGS: **GAI, GE** | 海外 **kaigai** *abroad, overseas* |
| | KUN READINGS: **soto, hoka,** | 外科 **geka** *surgery* |
| | **hazu(su)** | 外税 **sotozei** *tax-exclusive (price)* |
| 外 | *other, outside of* | その外 **sonohoka** *else, other* |
| | | 外す **hazusu** *to take off, to leave (one's seat)* |
| 5 strokes | ノ ク 夕 夗 外 | |

The character for **evening** 夕 combined with the divining rod ⼘, used by sha-mans and necromancers who worked at night to bring their customers news from the spirit world, made the composite kanji 外, meaning **other** or **outside of**. Used as a word by itself 外 is pronounced **SOTO, HOKA**, or **HAZU-SU**. In compound words it is pronounced **GAI** or **GE**. A 外人 **GAIJIN**, other-person, is a **foreigner**.

| 89 名 6 strokes | ON READINGS: **MEI, MYŌ** KUN READING: **na** *name* | 氏名 **shimei** *full name* 有名 **yūmei** *famous* 名字 **myōji** *family name* 名前 **namae** *name* |
|---|---|---|

ノ　ク　タ　夕　名　名

The Chinese drew a pictograph of the answer to a sentry's query, shouted in the dark, "Who goes there?" The answer had better be your name, or you risked an arrow in the chest. In this pictograph, the Chinese combined the element for **evening** 夕 with the element for **mouth** 口 to form the kanji 名. It means **a name**. Used as a word by itself, 名 is pronounced **NA**. In compound words it is pronounced **MEI** or **MYŌ**. A 名人 **MEIJIN**, name-person, is a **recognized expert** or **master**. A 名画 **MEIGA**, name-picture, is a **masterpiece**, said of paintings and sometimes movies.

| 90 多 6 strokes | ON READING: **TA** KUN READING: **ō(i)** *many* | 多種多様 **tashutayō** *wide variety* 多数決 **tasūketsu** *majority vote* 多い **ōi** *large, many, much* 多々 **tata** *many, much* |
|---|---|---|

ノ　ク　タ　夕　多　多

They added the pictograph for **evening** 夕 to another pictograph for **evening** 夕 to make a new kanji 多, many evenings. They dropped the idea of evenings and used the kanji to mean just **many**. It is pronounced **Ō-I** when used as a word by itself. In compound words it is pronounced **TA**. 多分, **TABUN**, many-parts, means **maybe, possibly, probably**. 多少 **TASHŌ**, many-few, means **to some extent**.

| 91 | ON READINGS: **KI, GO** | 期間 **kikan** *period* |
|---|---|---|
| | | 期待 **kitai** *hope, expectation* |
| 期 | *period of time, term; periodic* | 予期 **yoki** *anticipation* |
| | | 最期 **saigo** *fate, death* |

| 一 | 十 | 廿 | 甘 | 甘 | 甘 | 其 | 其 | 其 | 期 | 期 |
|---|---|---|---|---|---|---|---|---|---|---|

**12 strokes**  期 期

The Chinese drew a pictograph of the screen of wood or reed that farmers used to separate their grain from chaff 甘, then squared it off to 其. This is not used as a kanji by itself but it is an element in many other kanji.

For example, the screen is used at harvest time, the date determined by the passing of the moons, so the Chinese combined the element for screen 其 and the character for moon 月 and formed the new kanji 期. This character means **period of time**, or **term** or **periodic**. It is not used as a word by itself. In compound words it is pronounced **KI** or **GO**. 期末 **KIMATSU**, term-end, means the **end of the term**.

| 92 | ON READINGS: **KI, GI** | 棋士 **kishi** *Go or Japanese chess player* |
|---|---|---|
| 棋 | *Japanese chess* | 将棋 **shōgi** *Japanese chess* |

| 一 | 十 | 才 | 木 | 木 | 杧 | 栁 | 枻 | 桾 | 棋 |
|---|---|---|---|---|---|---|---|---|---|

**12 strokes**  棋 棋

The **screen** to filter grain 其 was used by farmers after harvest time as a board for board-games. The first was Oriental chess, played with wooden pieces. The Chinese combined the element for **screen** 其 with the element for **wood** 木 (to represent the wooden game pieces) to make a new composite kanji for the game. They first put the element for **wood** at the bottom of the board 棊. Soon they saw it wouldn't fit, so they put it at the side of the board instead, drawing the kanji in final form 棋. It is pronounced **KI** or **GI**, and means the game of **Japanese chess** called **SHŌGI**.

| 93 **碁** 13 strokes | ON READING: **GO**<br><br>*Go (game)* | 囲碁 **igo** *game of Go* |
|---|---|---|

一 十 廿 甘 甘 其 其 其 其 其

碁 碁 碁

The second game was **GO**, a strategic board game sometimes called "encirclement chess." It is played with small stones instead of wooden pieces placed upon the board, so the Chinese replaced the element for **wood** 木 with the element for **stone** 石. They put the stone at the bottom of the board and drew the final kanji 碁. It is pronounced **GO**. A 碁石 **GŌ-ISHI**, Go-stone, is a **stone piece used in the game of Go**.

| 94 **明** 8 strokes | ON READINGS: **MEI, MYŌ**<br>KUN READINGS: **a(kari),**<br>**aka(rui), aki(raka),**<br>**a(keru), a(ku)**<br><br>*bright* | 説明 **setsumei** *explanation*<br>光明 **kōmyō** *brightness, rosy future*<br>明るい **akarui** *bright, light, cheerful*<br>明かり **akari** *light*<br>夜明け **yoake** *dawn*<br>明くる日 **akuruhi** *yesterday* |
|---|---|---|

｜ 冂 月 日 日) 明 明 明

The Chinese put together the character for **sun** 日 and the character for **moon** 月 to form a new kanji 明 meaning **bright**. It is pronounced **A-KARI, AKA-RUI, AKI-RAKA, A-KERU** or **A-KU.** when used as a word by itself. In compound words it is pronounced **MEI** or **MYŌ**. 明日 **MYŌ-NICHI**, next-brightening-of-the-sun, is a literary word for **tomorrow**. This same compound word 明日 also has the very special pronunciations of **ASU** or **ASHITA**, which are more common ways of saying **tomorrow**.

| 95 | ON READING: **KŌ** | 光線 **kōsen** *beam, ray* |
|---|---|---|
| 光 | KUN READINGS: **hikari, hika(ru)** | 観光 **kankō** *sightseeing* |
| | | 光り **hikari** *light* |
| | *light; to shine, to sparkle* | 七光り **nanahikari** *coat tail, influence* |
| 6 strokes | 丿　丶丿　丷丶　业　屵　光 | |

The Chinese saw the sun as ⟡, then removed the rays and wrote ⊙ for sun. They took the rays and pulled them all together ✳ to form the pictograph for **rays**. In final form they squared and balanced off the rays and drew the kanji 光. It means **rays** of light, either natural rays of the sun or stars, or reflected rays from any polished surface. 光 also means **to shine** or **sparkle**. Used as a word by itself it is pronounced **HIKARI** or **HIKA-RU**. In compound words it is pronounced **KŌ**. The name of a popular resort town near Tokyo is 日光 **NIKKŌ** (**NICHIKO** pronounced euphonically), Sun-shine.

| 96 | ON READING: **SŌ, SA** | 早朝 **sōchō** *early morning* |
|---|---|---|
| 早 | KUN READINGS: **haya(i), haya(maru)** | 早速 **sassoku** *immediately* |
| | | 素早い **subayai** *quick, rapid* |
| | *early, fast, quick* | 早送り **hayaokuri** *fast-forward* |
| 6 strokes | 丨　冂　冃　日　旦　早 | |

A picture of the sun at dawn rising over a field of flowers ⚘ symbolized the idea **early** to the Chinese. To keep it simple, they drew the pictograph with the sun and just one flower ⚘. The **sun** had already been squared to 日. The flower was squared to 十, and the final character became 早. It means **early**, **fast**, or **quick**. Used as a word by itself it is pronounced **HAYA-I** or **HAYA-MARU**. In compound words it is pronounced **SŌ** or **SA**. The common phrase for "**Good morning**," literally "**It is early**," is written using 早 along with kana to give the grammar. 早口 **HAYAKUCHI**, fast-mouth, means **fast talker** or **talk fast**.

| 97 草 9 strokes | ON READING: **SŌ** KUN READING: **kusa** *grass* | 雑草 **zassō** *weed* 牧草 **bokusō** *feed crop, grass* 草花 **kusabana** *flowers* 草刈り **kusakari** *mowing* |
|---|---|---|

一　十　艹　艹　芢　芦　苩　荁　草

The element for plants ⁺⁺ was added to the element for **fast** 早 to form the new composite kanji 草, meaning **grass**, a fast growing plant. Used as a word by itself it is pronounced **KUSA**. In compound words, 草 is pronounced **SŌ**.

| 98 朝 12 strokes | ON READING: **CHŌ** KUN READING: **asa** *morning* | 朝食 **chōshoku** *breakfast* 朝刊 **chōkan** *morning paper* 毎朝 **maiasa** *every morning* 今朝 **kesa** *this morning* |
|---|---|---|

一　十　十　古　古　古　直　卓　朝　朝
朝　朝

For the word **morning**, the Chinese wanted to combine a pictograph of the sun rising at dawn over a field of flowers 𦰌 with the pictograph for **moon** 月 which had just been out all night and was ready to retire. They had already used the pictograph for the sun over a field of flowers, however, written 早 to mean **early**, so they had to add another flower ⼲ above the sun 日 to differentiate morning from early. Then they added the element for **moon** 月 and formed the kanji for **morning** 朝. Used as a word by itself it is pronounced **ASA**. In compound words it is pronounced **CHŌ**. 朝日, **ASAHI**, morning-sun, meaning **morning sun**, is a very popular name for business firms in Japan.

| 99 | ON READINGS: **DO, TO** | 国土 **kokudo** *national land, country* |
|---|---|---|
| | KUN READING: **tsuchi** | 土地 **tochi** *ground, land* |
| 土 | *earth, soil* | 土曜日 **Doyōbi** *Saturday* |
| | | 赤土 **akatsuchi** *red soil* |
| 3 strokes | 一 十 土 | |

A flower sprouting from the earth ⚓ symbolizes **earth**. The Chinese squared the flower 十 and formed the kanji 土. It means **earth** or **soil**. As a word by itself 土 is pronounced **TSUCHI**. In compound words it is pronounced **DO** or **TO**. 土木 **DOBOKU** (changed from **DOMOKU** for euphony), soil-and-wood, means **civil engineering**. It is often used in the name of construction companies in the civil engineering field.

| 100 | ON READING: **SHUTSU** | 出場する **shutujō suru** *to come in/ on/out* |
|---|---|---|
| | KUN READINGS: **de(ru), da(su)** | 提出 **teishutsu** *submission, induction* |
| 出 | *to come out, to go out, to take out, to send out, to depart* | 外出 **gaishutsu** *going out* |
| | | 飛び出す **tobidasu** *to dive, to pop up, to start out* |
| 5 strokes | 丨 屮 屮 出 出 | |

When the earth supports a flower coming out in full bloom ⚓, the emphasis in meaning changes from "**the earth**" to "**the act of coming out.**" The Chinese first drew the pictograph ⚓, and finally squared it off to 出. It means **come out**, **go out**, **take out**, **send out**, or **depart**, and is the opposite in meaning of 入 which means **come in**, **go in**, **put in**, **send in**, or **enter**. When used as a word by itself, 出 is pronounced **DE-RU** or **DA-SU**. Used with other kanji in compound words it is pronounced **SHUTSU**.

Each railroad or subway wicket, as well as most public-building doors, will have the two directions pointed out with signs: 出口 **DEGUCHI** for **exit**, and 入口 **IRIGUCHI** for **entrance**.

| 101 | ON READINGS: **SEI, SHŌ**<br>KUN READINGS: **i(kiru),**<br>**u(mu), u(mareru), o(u),**<br>**ha(eru), ki, nama** | 先生 **sensei** *teacher*<br>一生 **isshō** *whole life*<br>生い立ち **oitachi** *(personal)*<br>*background* |
|---|---|---|
| 生<br><br>5 strokes | *to live, to be born, to give*<br>*birth; life; raw, uncooked* | 生地 **kiji** *fabric, dough*<br>生もの **namamono** *fresh food* |
| | ノ　ー　十　牛　生 | |

When the flower is pictured at its peak of growth ready to give birth to another cycle of life 坐, the emphasis in meaning shifts again—to **birth**. The
Chinese first drew this pictograph as 屮 and later 生. In the final form they
squared it off to 生. This character has many meanings, though these all
evolve quite naturally from the basic meaning indicated by the picture—giving
birth. It means **to live**, **to be born**, **to give birth**, **life**, and has many other con-
notations. It also has many pronunciations. The most common pronunciations
when 生 is used as a word by itself are **I-KIRU**, **U-MU**, **U-MARERU**, **O-U**,
**HA-ERU**, **KI** and **NAMA**. In compound words it is usually pronounced **SEI**
or **SHŌ**.

Pronounced **NAMA**, 生 means "**born, but not processed further**," that is,
**raw** or **uncooked**. It is seen on signs in many beer halls, where it means **draft
beer**. 生水 **NAMAMIZU**, unprocessed-water, means **unpotable water**. 人生,
**JINSEI**, person-born, means **human life**.

| 102 | ON READINGS: **SEI, SHŌ**<br>KUN READING: **hoshi** | 星座 **seiza** *asterism*<br>流れ星 **nagareboshi** *shooting star* |
|---|---|---|
| 星<br><br>9 strokes | *star* | 惑星 **wakusei** *planet*<br>黒星 **kuroboshi** *black mark; failure* |
| | 丶　丷　冂　冎　日　尸　臼　星　犀　星 | |

The Chinese put together the element for **sun** 日 and the element for **life** 生
to form a new kanji symbolizing a living-sun or **star** 星. Used by itself it is
pronounced **HOSHI**. In compound words it is pronounced **SEI** or **SHŌ**. 明星
**MYŌJŌ**, (**MYŌSHŌ** pronounced euphonically), bright-star, is **Venus**. 火星
**KASEI**, fire-star, is **Mars**.

| 103 | ON READING: **SHA** <br> KUN READING: **mono** | 医者 **isha** *doctor* <br> 芸者 **Geisha** *Geisha* <br> 若者 **wakamono** *the young, youth* <br> 変わり者 **kawarimono** *eccentric person* |
|---|---|---|
| 者 <br> 8 strokes | *person* | 一 十 土 少 者 者 者 者 |

土 **TSUCHI**, **earth**, is used as an element in many other kanji, where it brings the idea of earth. The Chinese put the element for **earth** 土 together with the element for **sun** 日, then joined the two with a connecting line ╱ to symbolize those who do the work to hold the world together. This formed the kanji 者, which means **person** in the sense of a specific person known by what they do or what they are, such as a doctor, journalist, novelist, scholar, sick person, young person, pedestrian, and so on. 者 is pronounced **MONO** when it is a word by itself. In compound words it is pronounced **SHA**. A 記者 **KISHA**, write-down-person, is a **journalist** or **reporter**.

| 104 | ON READING: **ATSU** | 重圧 **jūatsu** *pressure* <br> 気圧 **kiatsu** *atmospheric pressure* <br> 指圧 **shiatsu** *finger pressure* <br> 電圧 **den-atsu** *voltage* |
|---|---|---|
| 圧 <br> 5 strokes | *pressure* | 一 厂 厈 厈 圧 |

The Chinese put together a pictograph of a mountain cliff ⌒ packed with earth 土 to symbolize the **pressure** this exerts on all below. The new composite kanji was written 圧, and means **pressure**, of any type. It is pronounced **ATSU**, either by itself or in a compound word. The formal compound word for **pressure** in general is 圧力 **ATSURYOKU**, pressure-power. 水圧 **SUI-ATSU**, water-pressure, means **hydraulic pressure.**

| 105 | ON READING: **RI** | 一里塚 **ichirizuka** *milestone* |
| 里 | KUN READING: **sato** | 万里 **banri** *long distance* |
| | *village* | 里親 **sato-oya** *foster parent* |
| | | 山里 **yamazato** *mountain village* |

| | ＼ | 冂 | 冃 | 日 | 甲 | 甲 | 里 | | |
| 7 strokes | | | | | | | | | |

The elements for **rice-paddy** 田 and for **earth** 土 (indicating an earthen rampart around the paddy) formed the character for **village** 里. When used as a word by itself it is pronounced **RI**. In compound words it is pronounced **SATO**. 古里 **FURUSATO**, old-village, is a person's **home village**, usually referring to the nostalgia of one's home-town, far away from city life.

| 106 | ON READING: **KOKU** | 黒板 **kokuban** *blackboard* |
| 黒 | KUN READING: **kuro(i)** | 暗黒 **ankoku** *blackness* |
| | *black* | 白黒 **shirokuro** *black and white* |
| | | 腹黒い **haraguroi** *black-hearted* |

| | ＼ | 冂 | 冃 | 日 | 甲 | 甲 | 里 | 里 | 黒 | 黒 |
| | 黒 | | | | | | | | | |
| 11 strokes | | | | | | | | | | |

The elements for **rice-paddy** 田 and for **earth** 土, with the addition of the element for **fire** 火 to symbolize the torching of the rice stalks into blackened charred remains after the harvest, were put together to form the kanji 黒, meaning **black**. When the kanji for **fire** 火 is used as an element to build other kanji, it changes shape to fit into the segment of the square where it is placed. At the bottom of the square, 火 usually changes shape to 灬. Used as a word by itself, 黒 is pronounced **KURO** as a noun or **KURO-I** as an adjective. In compound words it is pronounced **KOKU**.

| 107 | ON READING: **GYOKU** | 玉座 **gyokuza** *throne* |
| 玉 | KUN READING: **tama** | 玉子焼き **tamagoyaki** *rolled egg* |
| | *jewel, ball* | ビー玉 **bīdama** *marble* |
| | | 目玉焼き **medamayaki** *sunny-side up (egg)* |

| | 一 | 丁 | 干 | 王 | 玉 | | | | |
| 5 strokes | | | | | | | | | |

The Chinese drew a picture of a string of beads of jade 􀀁 to symbolize a **jewel**. They first wrote it 􀀁 and finally 王. Then they added a dot ` for the ditto mark to indicate that the jewels continued all around the string, making the final form 玉, meaning a **jewel** or a **ball**. 玉 is pronounced **TAMA** when used as a word by itself. With other kanji in compound words it is pronounced **GYOKU**.

| 108 |  | 国宝 **kokuhō** *national treasure* |
|---|---|---|
| 宝 | ON READING: **HŌ** <br> KUN READING: **takara** | 宝庫 **hōko** *reservoir, gold mine* <br> 宝物 **takaramono** *treasure* |
|  | *treasure* | 子宝 **kodakara** *child, healthy baby* |
| 8 strokes | ' ｀ 宀 宀 宁 宇 宝 宝 | |

A **jewel** 玉 stored for safety under a protective roof 宀 symbolized a **treasure**. The composite kanji was written 宝, meaning **treasure**. As a word by itself it is pronounced **TAKARA**. Used in compound words it is pronounced **HŌ**. A 宝石 **HŌSEKI**, treasure-stone, is a **precious jewel**.

| 109 |  | 国語 **kokugo** *national language* |
|---|---|---|
| 国 | ON READING: **KOKU** <br> KUN READING: **kuni** | 天国 **tengoku** *heaven* <br> 島国 **shimaguni** *island nation* |
|  | *country, state* | 雪国 **yukiguni** *snow country* |
| 8 strokes | 丨 冂 冂 冃 冃 国 国 国 | |

The Chinese put a four-sided enclosure 囗 around the element for **jewel** 玉 to form the new kanji meaning **country** or **state** 国. Used as a word by itself it is pronounced **KUNI**. In compound words it is pronounced **KOKU**. 外国 **GAIKOKU**, other-country, means **overseas**. A 外国人 **GAIKOKUJIN**, overseas-person, is a **foreigner**. 四国 **SHIKOKU**, four States, is the name of one of the main islands of Japan. 日本国 **NIHONKOKU**, Japan-country, is the country of **Japan**. A 国宝 **KOKUHŌ**, country-treasure, is a **National Treasure**. 国立 **KOKURITSU**, country-stand, means **nationally operated**.

| 110 | ON READING: **NAI** | 内容 **naiyō** *content* |
|---|---|---|
| 内 | KUN READING: **uchi** | 家内 **kanai** *wife* |
| | *inside* | 内側 **uchigawa** *inside, interior* |
| | | 内気な **uchiki na** *shy* |
| 4 strokes | 丨 冂 内 内 | |

A three-sided enclosure 冂 signifies a cover or a roof rather than a boundary. 冂 is neither a kanji nor an element but just the part of a pictograph that suggests a building. The Chinese put the element for **person** 人 inside a three-sided enclosure 冂 to write the kanji 内 , meaning **inside**. Used as a word by itself it is pronounced **UCHI**. Used in compound words 内 is pronounced **NAI**. 国内 **KOKUNAI**, country-inside, means **domestic** or **internal**, pertaining to a country's affairs.

| 111 | ON READING: **RI** | 理科 **rika** *science* |
|---|---|---|
| 理 | | 理由 **riyū** *cause, reason* |
| | *to manage, to supervise; reason, rationality* | 整理する **seiri suru** *to organize, to coordinate* |
| | | 心理学 **shinrigaku** *psychology* |
| 11 strokes | 一 丁 干 王 玌 玥 玥 玥 理 理 理 | |

The Chinese combined the kanji meaning **jewel** 宝 , modified to fit the square aesthetically by tilting it slightly and dropping the dot 王 , with the kanji meaning **village** 里 to make a new kanji 理 , symbolizing the man in the village who held the jewel, the boss, the man who ran the village. 理 came to mean **manage** or **supervise** by being smarter than the rest, using reason, the power of the mind. It also came to mean **reason** or **rationality**. It is not used as a word by itself. In compound words it is pronounced **RI**.

| 112 | ON READINGS: **BEI, MAI** | 欧米 **Ōbei** *Europe and the U.S.* |
|---|---|---|
| 米 | KUN READING: **kome** | 新米 **shinmai** *newcomer, beginner* |
| | *rice* | 白米 **hakumai** *white rice* |
| 6 strokes | | 米粒 **kometsubu** *a rice grain* |

| ` | ` ` | `⺌` | 半 | 米 | 米 | | | |
|---|---|---|---|---|---|---|---|---|

When the rice plants have flowered, the grains are harvested and the stalks are cut. The stalks are bundled, tied and stacked and look like this 米. The Chinese drew a pictograph of the bundled stacks 米, and later squared it off to 米, meaning **rice**. This refers to uncooked rice, harvested and packaged but not yet ready to eat. Used as a kanji by itself it is pronounced **KOME**. In compound words it is pronounced **BEI** or **MAI**. 米国, **BEIKOKU**, rice-country, means **America**.

| 113 | ON READING: **TO** | 北斗七星 **Hokuto shichisei** *Triones* |
|---|---|---|
| 斗 | | 一斗 **itto** *18.039 liter* |
| | *ladle, unit of measure (liquid, etc.)* | |
| 4 strokes | | |

| ` | ⺀ | ⻌ | 斗 | | | | | |
|---|---|---|---|---|---|---|---|---|

To form the kanji for **ladle** or **measure** the Chinese drew a pictograph of a ladle or a scoop 斗. They first drew it as 斗, then simplified it to 斗, and finally squared it off to 斗. It is rarely used as a kanji by itself (when it is, it is pronounced **TO**). It usually appears as an element in other kanji.

| 114 | ON READING: **RYŌ** | 料金 **ryōkin** *charge, fee* |
| | | 材料 **zairyō** *material, ingredient* |
| 料 | *charge, rate, fee, materials measured* | 手数料 **tesūryō** *handling charge* |
| | | 送料 **sōryō** *postage, shipping cost* |
| 10 strokes | `丶` `丷` `丷` `半` `米` `米` `米` `米` `料` `料` | |

The Chinese then put together the element for **rice** 米 and the element for **measure** 斗 and formed the new kanji 料, meaning **materials measured** and **set out to be used in performing a task**, as in, for example, cooking. The meaning was extended to cover also the **payment for performing the task**. 料 is not used as a kanji by itself. In compound words it is pronounced **RYŌ**. 料理 **RYŌRI**, materials-management, means **cook**.

| 115 | ON READINGS: **MU, BU** KUN READING: **na(i)** | 無名の **mumei no** *anonymous, unknown* |
| | | 無意味 **muimi** *meaningless* |
| 無 | *to cease to exist; none, no* | 無事 **buji** *no damage, safety* |
| | | 皆無 **kaimu** *nothing* |
| | `丿` `⺈` `⺁` `午` `缶` `缶` `無` `無` `無` `無` | |
| 12 strokes | `無` `無` | |

When the rice grains have been cleaned from the stalks, the stalks are gathered and bundled and readied for burning to clear the ground. The Chinese pictograph for the tied and bundled stalks was 𣎸. They squared it off to 無. Then to the bottom of the bundle they added fire 火, modified to ⺗ to fit the square, and drew a new kanji 無, meaning **cease to exist**, **none**, or **no**. Used as a word by itself it is pronounced **NA-I**. In compound words it is pronounced **MU** or **BU**. 無料 **MURYŌ**, no-payment, means **free of charge**. 無理 **MURI**, not-reasonable, means **unreasonable** or **unjustifiable**. 無理 is a common way of saying "you are asking too much."

| 116 | ON READING: **KA** | 科学 **kagaku** *science* |
| | | 教科書 **kyōkasho** *textbook* |
| 科 | *category, department, branch* | 学科 **gakka** *department, subject (in school)* |
| 9 strokes | ´  二  千  壬  禾  禾  禾  科  科 | |

The pictograph for a stalk of grain growing in the field was drawn ◔人. It was later stylized as 米, and finally 禾. It is not a kanji by itself but is used as an element in other kanji, where it brings the meaning **grain**.

The Chinese put the element for **grain** 禾 together with the element for **ladle** or **measure** 斗, for example, and formed the new kanji 科, symbolizing **ladling out the grains into categories**. 科 means a **category**, a **department**, or a **branch**. It does not form a word by itself. In compound words it is pronounced **KA**.

In hospitals and universities the 外科 **GEKA**, outside-category, is the **surgery department**, and the 内科 **NAIKA**, inside-category, is the **internal medicine department**.

| 117 | ON READING: **NEN** | 年れい **nenrei** *age* |
| | KUN READING: **toshi** | 少年 **shōnen** *young boy* |
| 年 | *year, age* | 年上の **toshiue no** *senior, elder* |
| 6 strokes | ´  ー  二  午  年  年 | |

To form the kanji meaning **year** or **age** the Chinese combined the element for **a stalk of grain growing in the field** 禾 with the element for **person** 人 to represent the annual production of grain, sown and harvested by the villagers. The element for person was placed at the top of the kanji square and changed its shape to ⌐ to fit. The element for the **stalk of grain** was placed in the center of the kanji square, and changed its shape from 禾 to 朱 to 牛 to 井. The final form of the composite kanji became 年. It is pronounced **TOSHI** when used as a word by itself, and pronounced **NEN** in compound words.

三年 **SAN-NEN**, three-year, means **three years**. 五年生 **GO-NENSEI**, five-year-student, means a **fifth-grader**. 生年月日, **SEINEN-GAPPI (SEINEN-GATSU-HI** pronounced euphonically), born-year-month-day, means **date of birth**, and appears on most application forms that ask your **age**. 年中無休 **NEN-JŪMUKYŪ**, year-throughout-no-rest, means **open all year-round**.

# SECTION FOUR

## Kanji List

| | | | | | |
|---|---|---|---|---|---|
| 118 白 | 119 食 | 120 欠 | 121 飲 | 122 数 | 123 林 |
| 124 森 | 125 果 | 126 汁 | 127 菓 | 128 茶 | 129 手 |
| 130 友 | 131 左 | 132 右 | 133 肉 | 134 焼 | 135 有 |
| 136 寸 | 137 村 | 138 守 | 139 寺 | 140 竹 | 141 等 |
| 142 詩 | 143 時 | 144 持 | 145 主 | 146 住 | 147 付 |
| 148 府 | 149 受 | 150 争 | 151 甲 | 152 押 | 153 単 |
| 154 戦 | 155 共 | 156 交 | 157 校 | 158 学 | 159 文 |

| 118 | ON READINGS: **HAKU, BYAKU**<br><br>KUN READINGS: **shiro, shiro(i), shira**<br><br>*white* | 白髪 **shiraga** *gray hair*<br>白衣 **kōhaku** *white coat*<br>白夜 **byakuya** *the midnight sun*<br>真っ白 **masshiro** *pure white*<br>白ける **shirakeru** *uncomfortable* |
|---|---|---|
| 白<br><br>5 strokes | ノ イ 冇 冇 白 | |

The Chinese drew a pictograph of a single grain of rice 🌢 to symbolize the color **white**. They modified it first to 🌢, then squared it off to 白. When used as a word by itself it is pronounced **SHIRO, SHIRO-I** or **SHIRA**. In compound words it is pronounced **HAKU** or **BYAKU**. A 白人 **HAKUJIN**, whiteperson, is a **Caucasian**.

| 119 | ON READINGS: **SHOKU, JIKI**<br><br>KUN READINGS: **tabe(ru), ku(u)**<br><br>*to eat* | 食事 **shokuji** *meal*<br>断食 **danjiki** *fast, non-eating*<br>給食 **kyūshoku** *feeding service*<br>食べ物 **tabemono** *food*<br>大食い **ōgui** *gourmand* |
|---|---|---|
| 食<br><br>9 strokes | ノ 人 个 今 今 夸 食 食 食 | |

The element for a grain of rice 白 cooking over the element for fire 火 under the protective cover of a roof 𠆢 formed the kanji for **eat**. The element for fire 火 was modified to 𣱼 and then to 𧘇 to fit the square. The final kanji was written 食. As a word by itself it is pronounced **TAB-ERU** or **KU-U**. In compound words it is pronounced **SHOKU** or **JIKI**. 夕食 **YŪSHOKU**, eveningmeal, means **dinner**. 食品 **SHOKUHIN**, food-goods, means **foodstuffs**. 食人 **SHOKUJIN**, eat-people, is **cannibalism**.

| 120 | ON READING: **KETSU** | 欠乏 **ketsubō** *deficiency, starved* |
| | KUN READINGS: **ka(ku), ka(keru)** | 欠席 **kesseki** *absence* |
| 欠 | | 欠片 **kakera** *crumb, fragment* |
| | *lack, absence; to lack, to decline* | 欠ける **kakeru** *to lack, to decline* |
| 4 strokes | ノ　ト　ケ　欠 | |

A pictograph of an open mouth ﾋ was added to the element for **person** 人 to symbolize the idea of **a lack** that needs fulfilling. The open mouth was simplified to ﾄ, and the final form of the new kanji was written 欠, meaning **a lack** or **absence**. Used as a word by itself it is pronounced **KA-KU** or **KA-KERU**. In compound words it is pronounced **KETSU**. 出欠 **SHUKKETSU** (**SHUTSUKE-TSU** pronounced euphonically), attend-absent, means **taking attendance**.

| 121 | ON READING: **IN** | 飲食店 **inshokuten** *restaurant* |
| | KUN READING: **no(mu)** | 飲酒運転 **inshu-unten** *drink-driving* |
| 飲 | *to drink* | 飲む **nomu** *to drink* |
| | | 飲み物 **nomimono** *beverage* |
| | ノ　入　今　今　今　自　食　飠　飲 | |
| 12 strokes | 飲　飲 | |

The Chinese combined the element for **lack** 欠 (a person with an open mouth waiting for the lack to be fulfilled) with the element for **eat** 食, symbolizing that the person needs more than eating and wants a drink. The element **eat** was modified slightly to 飠 for better proportion in the kanji square, and the new kanji was written 飲, meaning **drink**. Used as a word by itself, generally as a verb, it is pronounced **NO-MU**. In compound words it is pronounced **IN**. 飲水 **NOMIMIZU**, drink-water, means **drinking water**. 飲料 **INRYŌ**, drink-materials, means **beverages**.

| 122 | ON READING: **SŪ** | 数字 **sūji** *digit, figure, number* |
|---|---|---|
| | KUN READINGS: **kazu, kazo(eru)** | 人数 **ninzū** *headcount* |
| | | 頭数 **atamakazu, tōsū** *headcount;* |
| 数 | *to count; counting, number* | *number of animals* |
| | | 数える **kazoeru** *to count* |
| 13 strokes | ` 丶 丷 丷 半 半 米 类 娄 娄 娄 娄 数 数 数 | |

The element for bundled-stacks of **rice** 米 was put together with the element for **woman** 女, then a pictograph of a hand holding a stick 彐 was added to symbolize a woman using a stick to count stacks of rice. The hand holding the stick was simplified to 攵, and the final kanji was written 数. It means **to count** or **counting** or **number**. Used as a word by itself it is pronounced **KAZU** (as a noun) or **KAZO-ERU** (as a verb). In compound words it is pronounced **SŪ**. 手数料 **TESŪRYŌ**, hand-counting-measure, is **a commission** or **fee "for your trouble."**

| 123 | ON READING: **RIN** | 林業 **ringyō** *forestry* |
|---|---|---|
| | KUN READING: **hayashi** | 山林 **sanrin** *mountain forest* |
| 林 | *woods* | 松林 **matsubayashi** *pine grove* |
| | | 竹林 **chikurin** *bamboo grove* |
| 8 strokes | 一 十 才 木 朾 杜 材 林 | |

A single tree 木 means **tree**. Two of them together 林 means **woods**. Three of them together 森 means a **forest**. (For three, lining them up 林木 would make the square too crowded, so the Chinese put one atop the other two for aesthetics.)

林, used as a word by itself or in family names, is pronounced **HAYASHI**. In compound words it is pronounced **RIN**.

| 124 | ON READING: **SHIN** KUN READING: **mori** forest | 森林 **shinrin** *forest, timbe* 青森 **Aomori** *Aomori Prefecture* 森田 **Morita** *Morita (a Japanese family name)* |

森

12 strokes

一　十　オ　木　木　杢　森　森　森　森
森　森

森, used as a word by itself or in family names, is pronounced **MORI**. In compound words it is pronounced **SHIN**. Both 林 and 森 are popular in family names.

| 125 | ON READING: **KA** KUN READINGS: **ha(te), ha(tasu)** fruit; to carry out; end | 果実 **kajitsu** *fruit* 果肉 **kaniku** *fruity flesh* 結果 **kekka** *result, conclusion* 果たす **hatasu** *to fulfill, to accomplish* |

果

8 strokes

丨　冂　冃　日　旦　旦　果　果

A pictograph of a tree bearing fruit 柴 means **fruit**. The Chinese first simplified fruit to 果 then squared it off to 果. The kanji 果 looks very much like a **tree** 木 **field** 田, but it is not. If thinking of a tree-field helps you remember it, you may call it that, but the pictograph is actually of a tree bearing fruit. 果 means **fruit**. By extension it also means the fruit of your effort, a **result**. In compound words it is pronounced **KA**. Used as a word by itself it is pronounced **HA-TE** or **HA-TASU**.

| 126 | ON READING: **JŪ** KUN READING: **shiru** liquid, juice | 肉汁 **nikujū** *meat juice* 苦汁 **kujū** *bitterness* 汁物 **shirumono** *soup* お汁粉 **oshiruko** *sweet red-bean soup* |

汁

5 strokes

丶　冫　氵　汁　汁

The Chinese combined the element for **water** 水, modified to fit the square 氵, with the element for **ten** 十 to symbolize ten different kinds of liquids, and made the new kanji 汁, meaning **liquid** or **juice**. Used by itself, it is pronounced **SHIRU**. Used in compound words it is pronounced **JŪ**. 果汁 **KAJŪ**, fruit-liquid, is **fruit juice**.

| 127 | ON READING: **KA** | 製菓 **seika** *confectionery production* |
| | | 和菓子 **wagashi** *Japanese-style* |
| 菓 | | *confectionery* |
| | *confection, refreshment, sweets* | 菓子折り **kashiori** *boxed confection* |
| | | 冷菓 **reika** *cold confection* |
| | 一 十 卄 艹 芌 芍 苧 苩 苩 草 草 | |
| 11 strokes | 菓 | |

The earliest confections in China were made from fruit or berries, so the Chinese added the element for **plants** 艹, to stand for sugar and flour, to the element for **fruit** 果 to form a new kanji 菓 meaning **confection**, **refreshment**, or **sweets**. It is pronounced **KA**, either used as a word by itself or in compound words. A 菓子, **KASHI**, little-confection, is a **cake** or **pastry**.

| 128 | ON READINGS: **CHA, SA** | 茶色 **chairo** *brown color* |
| | | 番茶 **bancha** *coarse tea* |
| 茶 | | 紅茶 **kōcha** *red tea* |
| | *tea, brown* | きっ茶店 **kissaten** *coffee shop* |
| | 一 十 卄 ヴ 苂 苂 苐 茶 茶 | |
| 9 strokes | | |

To form the kanji meaning tea, the Chinese combined the element for **plant** 艹 with the element for **tree** 木 to indicate a **bush** 朶, a growth halfway between a plant and a tree, then added leaves ✓ ヽ to indicate the part of the plant that is used to make the **tea**. The final kanji meaning **tea** was drawn 茶. It is pronounced **CHA** or **SA**, either when used by itself or used in compound words. The common word for **tea** is **CHA**, usually preceded by the honorific **O**, which is written in kana, since the kanji 茶 provides only the **CHA** sound. 茶菓 **CHA-KA** (sometimes **CHAGA** for euphony) is a fancy word for **tea and cakes**.

| 129 手 4 strokes | ON READING: **SHU** KUN READINGS: **te, ta** / *hand* | 選手 **senshu** *player* 素手 **sude** *bare hands* 手袋 **tebukuro** *glove* 手繰る **taguru** *to pull* |
| --- | --- | --- |
| | 一 二 三 手 | |

The Chinese used a picture of a hand 手 to be the model for the kanji meaning **hand**. The first pictograph the Chinese drew was 手. It became 手, then 手, and finally the modern kanji 手, meaning **hand**. It is pronounced **TE** or **TA** when used as a word by itself, and **SHU** when used in compound words. 手 also has the special pronunciation **ZU** when used in the compound word 上手 **JŌZU**, upper-hand, which is a very common expression meaning **very skillful**, **great work!**, or **well done**.

| 130 友 4 strokes | ON READING: **YŪ** KUN READING: **tomo** / *friend* | 友情 **yūjō** *friendship, fellowship* 親友 **shinyū** *close friend, best friend* 友達 **tomodachi** *friend* 級友 **kyūyū** *classmate* |
| --- | --- | --- |
| | 一 ナ 方 友 | |

The Chinese drew a picture of two hands reaching out to clasp each other to symbolize the meaning **friend**. They first drew the pictograph omitting a few fingers to save writing time. They later straightened out the lines 友, then squared it off to the final form 友. Used as a word by itself it is pronounced **TOMO**. In compound words it is pronounced **YŪ**. 友人 **YŪJIN**, friend-person, is a formal word for **friend**. 友好 **YŪKŌ**, friend-good, is **friendship** or **friendliness**.

| 131 左 5 strokes | ON READING: **SA** KUN READING: **hidari** / *left* | 左右 **sayū** *left and right* 左折 **sasetsu** *left-hand turn* 左利き **hidarikiki** *left-handed* 左側 **hidarigawa** *left side* |
| --- | --- | --- |
| | 一 ナ 左 左 左 | |

The Chinese combined the element for **hand** 手 (modified to 𠂇 to fit the square) with the element for **carpenter's tool** 工, signifying a carpenter's square or a ruler, and formed the new composite kanji 左. This means **left**, as opposed to right, since the left hand is where a carpenter holds the ruler so he can draw the line with his right. Used as a word by itself 左 is pronounced **HIDARI**. Used in compound words it is pronounced **SA**. 左手 **HIDARITE**, left-hand, means your **left hand**.

| 132 | ON READINGS: **YŪ, U** KUN READING: **migi** | 右折 **usetsu** *right-hand turn* 右左 **migihidari** *right and left* 右腕 **migiude** *right arm, right-hand man* 右側 **migigawa** *right side* |
|---|---|---|
| 右 | *right* | |
| 5 strokes | ノ ナ ナ 右 右 | |

The kanji for right is the same element for **hand** 手 combined with the element for **mouth** 口 signifying the hand you use to eat with. The new kanji is written 右, and means **right**, as opposed to left. Used as a word by itself it is pronounced **MIGI**. Used in compound words 右 is pronounced **YŪ** or **U**. 右手 **MIGITE**, right-hand, means your **right hand**.

| 133 | ON READING: **NIKU** | 肉類 **nikurui** *meat* 食肉 **shokuniku** *fresh, meat* 筋肉 **kin-niku** *muscle* 牛肉 **gyūniku** *beef* |
|---|---|---|
| 肉 | *meat* | |
| 6 strokes | 丨 冂 内 内 肉 肉 | |

The Chinese drew a picture of a slice of meat as ⬭ to form the kanji meaning **meat**. They first drew it 宍, and then in final form 肉. It is pronounced **NIKU** when used either by itself or in compound words. 肉 appears on all the butcher shops in town, and on restaurant menus in the "meat dish" section.

| 134 | ON READING: **SHŌ** KUN READINGS: **ya(ku), ya(keru)** | 焼失 **shōshitsu** *destruction by fire* <br> 全焼 **zenshō** *complete destruction by fire* |
|---|---|---|
| 焼 | *to singe, to burn, to roast* | 焼き物 **yakimono** *pottery* <br> 焼け跡 **yakeato** *burned-out site* |
| 12 strokes | 丶　丷　ㇱ　火　灯　灯　灯　炸　炵　焼 <br> 焼　焼 | |

The Chinese piled three earths 垚 upon a table 兀 to form a barbecue pit then added **fire** 火 and made the kanji 燒, meaning **singe** or **burn** or **roast**. They later abbreviated it further to 焼. When used as a word by itself, generally a verb, it is pronounced **YA-KU** (intransitive) or **YA-KERU** (transitive). In compound words it is pronounced **SHŌ**. 焼肉 **YAKINIKU**, roast-meat, is **a barbecue**. 夕焼け **YŪYA-KE**, evening-burn, is a **sunset**.

| 135 | ON READING: **YŪ, U** KUN READING: **a(ru)** | 有力な **yūryoku na** *dominant, powerful* <br> 有頂天 **uchōten** *exaltation, ecstasy* |
|---|---|---|
| 有 | *to have, to exist* | 有休 **yūkyū** *a paid holiday* <br> 有罪 **yūzai** *guilt* |
| 6 strokes | ノ　ナ　冇　有　有　有 | |

When the kanji for **meat** 肉 is used as an element in other kanji, it changes shape to fit the new kanji square. It changed first from 肉 to 宍 and lastly to 月. Unfortunately, this is written exactly as is 月 **TSUKI**, meaning **moon**.

A pictograph of a reaching hand 屮 holding the element for meat 肉, modified to 月 to fit the square, formed a new composite kanji 有 symbolizing the state of having enough food to exist. 有 means **to have** or **to exist**. Used as a word by itself it is pronounced **A-RU** (a very common verb). In compound words it is pronounced **YŪ** or **U**. 有名, **YŪMEI**, have-name, means **famous**.

| 136 寸<br><br>3 strokes | ON READING: **SUN**<br><br>*unit of measurement, just a tiny bit* | 寸法 **sunpō** *measure, size*<br>一寸先 **issunsaki** *near future*<br>寸前 **sunzen** *(on) the border of, (on) the edge of* |
|---|---|---|

一　寸　寸

A pictograph of a hand Ψ with a dot ＼ to mark the pulse was drawn by the Chinese first as Ψ and then in final form as 寸 to symbolize the distance from the base of the hand to the pulse. It means **3.03 centimeters**, about one inch, which is the average distance from the hand to the pulse.It also means **to take the measure of**, in the sense of measuring physical dimensions. It is pronounced **SUN**, when used either as a word by itself or in compound words. 一寸, **ISSUN** (**ICHI-SUN** pronounced euphonically), one **SUN**, means **3.03 centimeters**. It has also come to mean **just a tiny bit**.

When 寸 **SUN** is used as an element in forming composite kanji, it brings the meaning **to take the measure of**, in the sense of measuring how a society functions, in other words, **to take the measure of, then regulate, society's rules and laws**.

| 137 村<br><br>7 strokes | ON READING: **SON**<br>KUN READING: **mura**<br><br>*village* | 村長 **sonchō** *village mayor*<br>農村 **nōson** *farming village*<br>村役場 **murayakuba** *village office*<br>村八分 **murahachibu** *social ostracism* |
|---|---|---|

一　十　才　木　朾　村　村

To form the kanji for **village**, for example, the Chinese combined this element for **regulate rules and laws** 寸 with the element for **trees** 木 and formed the new kanji 村 to symbolize the forming of a society out of tree-dwellers by regulating laws. 村 means **village**. It is pronounced **MURA** when used as a word by itself, or in proper names. In compound words it is pronounced **SON**.

村 is popular in geographical and family names:

中村 **NAKAMURA**, Middle-village
下村 **SHIMOMURA**, Lower-village
田村 **TAMURA**, Paddy-village
木村 **KIMURA**, Tree-village

| 138 | ON READINGS: **SHU, SU** | 守備 **shubi** *defensive* |
|---|---|---|
| 守 | KUN READINGS: **mamo(ru), mori** | 保守党 **hoshutō** *conservative party* |
| | | 留守 **rusu** *absence* |
| | *to protect, to guard, to defend; amulet* | お守り **omamori** *amulet, charm* |
| 6 strokes | ` ` ` ` ` 宀 宀 守 守 | |

The Chinese put the element for **roof** 宀 over the element for **regulate the laws** 寸 and formed the new kanji 守 meaning **protect** or **guard** or **defend**. It is pronounced **MAMO-RU** when used as a word by itself. In compound words it is pronounced **SHU** or **SU**. It has the special pronunciation **MORI** when it is used in the compound word 子守 **KOMORI**, child-protect, which means **baby-sitter**.

The kanji 守 will be seen, sometimes alone and sometimes alongside one or two other kanji, on the door to guard houses or to the watchman's office in building basements, and on sentry posts.

| 139 | ON READING: **JI** | 寺院 **ji'in** *temple* |
|---|---|---|
| 寺 | KUN READING: **tera** | 金閣寺 **Kinkaku-ji** *Kinkaku-ji temple* |
| | | 寺町 **teramachi** *temple's district* |
| | *temple* | 寺子屋 **terakoya** *small private school* |
| 6 strokes | 一 十 土 丰 寺 寺 | |

The Chinese put the element for **regulate the rules and laws** 寸 with the element for **earth** 土, here indicating "place," to form the new kanji 寺, symbolizing the place where the rules and laws of society are regulated. 寺 means **temple**. Used as a word by itself it is pronounced **TERA**, usually preceded by the honorific **O**, written in kana. In compound words, including most temple names, it is pronounced **JI**. 東大寺 **TŌDAI-JI**, Great-Eastern-Temple, is a well-known temple in the city of Nara.

| 140 | ON READING: **CHIKU** | 竹林 **chikurin** *bamboo grove* |
|---|---|---|
| 竹 | KUN READING: **take** | 竹輪 **chikuwa** *fish sausage* |
| | *bamboo* | 竹やぶ **takeyabu** *bamboo grove* |
| 6 strokes | | 竹笛 **takebue** *bamboo flute* |

ノ　ト　ケ　ケ　竹　竹

A picture of two bamboo shoots 𝔀𝔀 formed the kanji for bamboo. The Chinese simplified the picture first to 个个 and then wrote the kanji in final form as 竹. It is pronounced **TAKE** when used as a word by itself or in a family name like 竹田 **TAKEDA**, Bamboo-field. In compound words it is pronounced **CHIKU**.

Bamboo 竹 is common as an element in other kanji, where it often brings the meaning of written records since early documents were written on bamboo tablets. When used as an element, 竹 basically keeps its shape but the bamboo stems get shortened considerably ⺮.

| 141 | ON READING: **TŌ** | 等分 **tōbun** *dividing equally* |
|---|---|---|
| 等 | KUN READINGS: **hito(shi'i), nado** | 等級 **tōkyū** *grade, class* |
| | | 平等 **byōdō** *equality* |
| | *class, grade; equal, similar; and so on* | 等しい **hitoshi'i** *equal, even* |
| 12 strokes | | |

ノ　ト　ケ　ケ　ケ　竹　竺　竺　笁　笁
等　等

The written records showing the class and value of everything in town were kept for safety in the temple. To signify the meaning **class**, in the sense of value, as in first-class, second-class, and so on, the Chinese added the element for **bamboo** 竹, symbolizing written records, to the element for **temple** 寺 and formed the new kanji 等. Used as a word by itself it is pronounced **HITO-SHI'I**, or **NADO** generally meaning "etcetera," everything else in its class. Used in compound words it is pronounced **TŌ**. 一等, **ITTŌ** (**ICHI-TŌ** pronounced euphonically), first-class, means **first-class**, said of railroad tickets, theater tickets or any other instance of things divided into classes. 二等 **NITŌ**, second-class, means **second-class**. 上等 **JŌTŌ**, up-class, means **high class**.

| 142 詩 13 strokes | ON READING: **SHI** | 詩集 **shishū** *collection of poems* |
|---|---|---|
| | | 詩的 **shiteki** *poetic* |
| | *poetry, poem* | 漢詩 **kanshi** *Chinese poetry* |
| | | 詩歌 **shi'ika** *song, poetry* |

`、 二 三 言 言 言 言 言 計 計 詰 詩 詩`

The Chinese added the element for **temple** 寺 to the element for **say** or **speak** 言 to form the new composite kanji 詩 signifying temple speaking, meaning **poetry** or **poem**. It is pronounced **SHI**, whether it is a word by itself or used in compound words. A 詩人 **SHIJIN**, poem-person, is a **poet**.

| 143 時 10 strokes | ON READING: **JI** KUN READING: **toki** | 時間 **jikan** *hour, time* |
|---|---|---|
| | | 当時 **tōji** *at that time* |
| | *time, hour* | 時々 **tokidoki** *sometimes* |
| | | 砂時計 **sunadokei** *hourglass* |

`丨 冂 冃 日 日 日 時 時 時 時`

They put the element for **temple** 寺 together with the element for **sun** 日 to form the new kanji 時 meaning **time** or **hour**. It was the temple in the early days that measured the movement of the sun and kept the time and calendar. Used as a word by itself it is pronounced **TOKI**. In compound words it is pronounced **JI**. 十時 **JŪJI**, ten-hour, is **ten o'clock**. 三時 **SANJI**, three-hour, is **three o'clock**. 時 has the special pronunciation **TO** when used in the compound word 時計 **TOKEI**, time-measure, which means **clock** or **wristwatch**.

| 144 持 9 strokes | ON READING: **JI** KUN READING: **mo(tsu)** | 持参 **jisan** *bringing* |
|---|---|---|
| | | 支持 **shiji** *support, advocate* |
| | *to have, to hold, to possess* | 持ち物 **mochimono** *belongings* |
| | | 持ち帰る **mochikaeru** *to bring back* |

`一 十 扌 扩 扩 扶 拝 持 持`

The kanji for **hand** 手 is used as an element in many other kanji. It changes shape to fit into the square of the new kanji, depending on where in the square the Chinese decided to finally place it. A common selection was the left-hand side of the square. To fit neatly into this location, the shape of **hand** 手 was changed from 丰 to 扌 and finally to 扌.

The Chinese combined this element for **hand** 扌 with the element for **temple** 寺 and wrote the new kanji 持 to symbolize the meaning of **to have** or **to hold** or **to possess**, since at the time only the temple was allowed to own anything. Used as a word by itself it is pronounced **MO-TSU**. Used in compound words it is pronounced **JI**.

| 145 | ON READING: **SHU** | 主人公 **shujinkō** *main character, protagonist* |
|---|---|---|
| 主 | KUN READINGS: **nushi, omo** | 坊主頭 **bōzuatama** *shaven head* |
| | *master, owner, chief; main, major* | 地主 **jinushi** *land owner*<br>主な **omona** *main, major* |
| 5 strokes | ` 丶 二 亠 主 主 ` | |

The pictograph of an ornate lamp with burning flame 主 became the symbol the Chinese used for lord and master. They simplified it first to 坐 and squared it off to 主, the kanji meaning **master**, **owner**, or **chief**. Used as an adjective it is pronounced 主な **OMO-NA** (the kanji 主 is pronounced **OMO** and the **NA** is an adjectival ending written in kana) and means **main** or **major**. Used as a word by itself it is pronounced **NUSHI**. In compound words it is pronounced **SHU**. 主人 **SHUJIN**, master-person, means **master** or **employer** or **husband**. 持ち主 **MOCHINUSHI**, possess-person, means **owner**.

| 146 | ON READING: **JŪ** | 住所 **jūsho** *address* |
|---|---|---|
| 住 | KUN READING: **su(mu)** | 衣食住 **ishokujū** *food, clothing and housing* |
| | *to reside, to live* | 住み心地 **sumigokochi** *livability*<br>住居 **jūkyo** *living place* |
| 7 strokes | ノ 亻 亻 仁 住 住 住 | |

The Chinese added the element for **person** 人 to the character of the oil lamp with burning flame 主 to make a new kanji 住 symbolizing the placement of a person's master lamp in his or her residence. The kanji 住 means **to reside** or **live**. Used as a word by itself it is pronounced **SU-MU**. In compound words it is pronounced **JŪ**.

| 147 | ON READING: **FU** <br><br> KUN READINGS: **tsu(keru), tsu(ku)** | 付与する **fuyo suru** *to give* <br> 給付金 **kyūfukin** *benefit* <br> 名付け親 **nadukeoya** *godparent* <br> 気付く **kizuku** *to get wise, to find* <br> 付け足し **tsuketashi** *afterthought* |
|---|---|---|
| 付 | *to attach, to stick to, be attached to, to come with; with* | |
| 5 strokes | ノ　イ　仁　付　付 | |

The Chinese put together the element for **person** 人, modified to イ to fit into the left side of a kanji square, with the element for **regulating rules and laws** 寸 (a pictograph of a hand and a pulse) to form a new kanji 付 symbolizing the act of sticking rules and laws onto a person. The kanji 付 means **to attach** or **stick it to** (transitive verb), or **to be attached to** or **stick to** (intransitive verb). Used as a word by itself it is pronounced **TSU-KERU** (transitive), or **TSU-KU** (intransitive). It is sometimes changed to **ZU-KERU** or **ZU-KU** for euphony. 付 is used frequently in menus and ads as a preposition meaning **with**, in the sense of is **attached to** or **comes with**. It is pronounced **TSUKI** to indicate, for example, that the product comes **with** rice or **with** bath. In compound words it is pronounced **FU**.

| 148 | ON READING: **FU** | 政府 **seifu** *government* <br> 京都府 **Kyōtofu** *Kyoto Prefecture* <br> 幕府 **bakufu** *feudal government* <br> 甲府 **Kōfu** *Kofu City* |
|---|---|---|
| 府 | *seat of government; prefecture (Kyoto and Osaka)* | |
| 8 strokes | 丶　亠　广　产　疒　庁　府　府 | |

Inside a pictograph that symbolizes a structure or a building, first drawn as 冂, then modified to 广, and finally to 广, the Chinese put the element for **stick it to** 付 to make the kanji 府, symbolizing the building where they stick it to the people. This means the **seat of government**. It is not used as a word by itself. In compound words it is pronounced **FU**. 府立 **FURITSU**, government-stands-it-up, means **government-operated** or **prefectural (Kyoto and Osaka)**, a library or a hospital, for example.

| 149 | ON READING: **JU** <br><br> KUN READINGS: **u(keru), u(karu)** <br><br><br>*to receive, to pass (an exam)* | 受験 **juken** *(to take) an exam* <br> 受信 **jushin** *(to) receive (a mail, etc.)* <br> 受け取る **uketoru** *to receive, to collect* <br> 受け皿 **ukezara** *saucer* |
|---|---|---|
| 受 <br><br> 8 strokes | ノ　く　く　⺥　⺤　⺤　受　受 | |

As described earlier, two hands reaching for each other 🤝 formed the kanji 友 **friend**. To form the kanji meaning **receive**, the Chinese drew a pictograph of the same two hands, now passing something, in the shape of a bar or a baton ⌒, from one to the other. They needed to change the shape of the upper hand so the kanji for **friend** and the kanji for **receive** would not look alike. In the kanji for **receive**, they modified the upper hand to 𠂆, then to ⺤, and wrote the final kanji for **receive** 受. Used as a word by itself it is pronounced **U-KERU** (transitive), or **U-KARU** (intransitive). In compound words it is pronounced **JU**. 受付 **UKETSUKE**, receive-attach, means **reception** or **receptionist**, and is usually posted on reception desk signs in any kind of building. A sign reading 受付中, **UKETSUKECHŪ**, reception-middle-of, means **now accepting applications**, as for example, rental apartments or school matriculation.

| 150 | ON READING: **SŌ** <br><br> KUN READING: **araso(u)** <br><br><br>*to quarrel, to dispute, to conflict, to struggle* | 競争 **kyōsō** *competition, race* <br> 戦争 **sensō** *war, battle* <br> 争い事 **arasoigoto** *conflict, battle* <br> 論争 **ronsō** *debate, argument* |
|---|---|---|
| 争 <br><br> 6 strokes | ノ　⺈　⺈　争　争　争 | |

The same two hands fighting over the bar or the baton 争, instead of passing it from one to the other, formed the kanji meaning **quarrel**, **dispute**, **conflict**, or **struggle**. The Chinese first drew the pictograph 爭, with the lower hand capturing the bar, then wrote it in the form 爭. Recently the upper hand was further simplified to ⺈. The kanji is now generally written 争 but it is still seen as 爭. Used as a word by itself it is pronounced **ARASO-U**. Used in compound words 争 is pronounced **SŌ**.

| 151 | ON READINGS: **KŌ, KAN** | 甲虫 **kōchū** *beetle* |
| | | 甲板 **kanpan, kōhan** *deck* |
| 甲 | *armor* | 甲高い **kandakai** *high-pitched* |
| | | 手の甲 **te-no-kō** *back of the hand* |
| 5 strokes | 丨　冂　冂　日　甲 |

The Chinese drew a picture of a warrior's shield 㽗 to symbolize the meaning **armor**. They simplified it to 㽗 and finally to 甲. It is rarely used as a word by itself. In compound words it is pronounced **KŌ** or **KAN**.

| 152 | ON READING: **Ō** | 押印 **ōin** *imprint* |
| | KUN READING: **o(su)** | 押し花 **oshibana** *flower pressing* |
| 押 | *to push* | 差し押さえ **sashiosae** *foreclosure* |
| | | 押す **osu** *to push, to press* |
| 8 strokes | 一　才　扌　扌　扣　扣　押　押 |

The Chinese put together the element for **hand** 手, modified to fit the left-hand side of a kanji square 扌, with the element for **armor** 甲 to symbolize a force pushing against the armor, and made the new kanji 押, meaning **push**. Used as a word by itself it is pronounced **O-SU**. Used in compound words it is pronounced **Ō**. It appears on almost all the doors in public places where you are asked to **push** the door, not pull.

| 153 | ON READING: **TAN** | 単独 **tandoku** *independent* |
| | | 単位 **tan-i** *unit, credit* |
| 単 | *sole, simple, single; basic unit* | 簡単な **kantan na** *easy* |
| | | 単純な **tanjun na** *plain, simple* |
| 9 strokes | 丶　丷　丷　丷　兴　兴　甾　単　単 |

The Chinese drew a pictograph of an ancient warrior's weapon, part axe and part broad-blade sword with two thrusting points 單, which was the basic unit in their armory, to signify the concept of **sole** or **simple** or **single** or **basic unit**. They simplified it to 單, then to 單, and then to 單. Recently, they simplified it even further, to 単. The version 単 is now much more common, but 單 is still used. 単 is pronounced **TAN**, used either as a word by itself or in compound words. 単語 **TAN-GO**, basic-unit-language, means a **word** or **vocabulary**. 単一 **TAN-ITSU** (with a special pronunciation for 一, usually pronounced **ICHI** or **HITOTSU**), sole-one, means **single** or **singleness**.

| 154 | ON READING: **SEN** | 戦車 **sensha** *tank* |
|---|---|---|
| | KUN READINGS: **tataka(u), ikusa** | 戦場 **senjō** *battlefield* |
| | | 勝ち戦 **kachi'ikusa** *victory,* |
| 戦 | *to fight, to make war; battle, war* | *triumphant battle* |
| | | 戦う **tatakau** *to fight, to make war* |

| ` | `` | ``` | ⼾ | ⺍ | ⺍ | 当 | 当 | 単 | 単 |
|---|---|---|---|---|---|---|---|---|---|
| 13 strokes 戦 | 戦 | 戦 | | | | | | | |

Another weapon the Chinese used as a model for a kanji was a lance, first drawn 弐. They simplified it to 弋 and the final form became 戈. It is not now used as a kanji by itself but it appears as an element in many other kanji dealing with war or fighting or cutting.

For example, to the element for **lance** 戈 the Chinese added the pictograph of the other ancient weapon, the part axe, part broad-blade sword 単, to make a new kanji 戦 meaning **to fight** or **make war**. Used as a word by itself it is pronounced **TATAKA-U** or **IKUSA**. In compound words it is pronounced **SEN**. 戦争 **SENSŌ**, fight-conflict, means **war**. 大戦 **TAISEN**, big-fight, means **world war**.

| 155 | ON READING: **KYŌ** | 共同体 **kōdōtai** *community* |
|---|---|---|
| | KUN READING: **tomo** | 共通 **kyōtsū** *common* |
| 共 | | 公共 **kōkyō** *public* |
| | *together* | 共働き **tomobataraki** *two incomes* |

| 一 | 十 | 世 | 世 | 共 | 共 |
|---|---|---|---|---|---|
| 6 strokes | | | | | |

Two hands joined in holding up a box together 爲 symbolized togetherness. The Chinese first squared it off to 具 and finally to 共, meaning **together**. Used as a word by itself it is pronounced **TOMO**. Used in compound words it is pronounced **KYŌ**. 共有 **KYŌYŪ**, together-have, means **joint ownership**. 共有者, **KYŌYŪSHA**, joint-ownership-person means **joint owner**.

| 156 | ON READING: **KŌ** | 交通 **kōtsū** *traffic* |
| | KUN READINGS: **ma(jiru),** **ma(zeru), maji(waru),** **ka(wasu)** | 交番 **kōban** *police box, Koban* |
| 交 | | 外交官 **gaikōkan** *diplomat* |
| | *intersection, exchange, mixing; to mix, to blend, to intersect, to exchange* | 交わす **kawasu** *to sign, to exchange* |
| | | 交わる **majiwaru** *to cross, to meet* |
| 6 strokes | ヽ 亠 亣 六 亣 交 | |

To symbolize the concept of intersecting or exchanging, the Chinese drew a pictograph of an X intersection, ✕, topped by 六, the **number 6**, to signify a lot of people involved in the intersecting. They wrote the kanji 交, meaning **intersection**, **exchange**, or **mixing**. Used as a word by itself, generally a verb, its pronunciation is one of many variations of **MA-JIRU**, **MA-ZERU**, **MAJI-WARU** or **KA-WASU**. In compound words 交 is pronounced **KŌ**. 外交 **GAIKŌ**, outside-exchange, means **diplomacy**.

| 157 | ON READING: **KŌ** | 校正 **kōsei** *proofreading* |
| | | 校長 **kōchō** *school principal, president* |
| 校 | *school* | 校庭 **kōtei** *campus, school ground* |
| | | 高校 **kōkō** *high school* |
| 10 strokes | 一 十 才 木 木' 杧 杧 杧 杫 校 | |

The Chinese put together the kanji for **exchange** 交 with the kanji for **tree** 木 to symbolize the early outdoor schoolhouse, where knowledge was exchanged. The final form was written 校, and means **school**. It is not used as a word by itself. In compound words it is pronounced **KŌ**. 母校 **BOKŌ**, mother-school, means **alma mater**.

| 158 | ON READING: **GAKU** | 学習 **gakushū** *learning* |
| | KUN READING: **mana(bu)** | 科学 **kagaku** *science* |
| 学 | | 大学 **daigaku** *university* |
| | *to learn, to study* | 数学 **sūgaku** *mathematics* |
| | | 学ぶ **manabu** *to learn, to study* |
| 8 strokes | 丶 ヽヽ ヽヽヽ 冖 学 学 学 | |

To symbolize the concept **learn**, the Chinese drew a pictograph of two hands ⿰ pouring knowledge, represented by a pair of Xs, ⿳ into the head of a **child** 子 seated under a **roof** 宀. They squared the hands ⺦ ⺕ and wrote the kanji as 學. Recently, this has been simplified by combining the hands and knowledge ⺼ into the symbol for quotation marks, ⿱, and the final form is now written 学. The simplified character is more common but the older character is still used. Either character is pronounced **MANA-BU** when used as a word by itself, and **GAKU** when used in compound words. Some examples:

| | |
|---|---|
| 学生 | **GAKUSEI**, learning-life, is a **student** |
| 学校 | **GAKKŌ** (**GAKUKŌ** pronounced euphonically), learn-school, means **school** |
| 小学校 | **SHŌGAKKŌ**, small-school, is an **elementary school** |
| 中学校 | **CHŪGAKKŌ**, middle-school, is a **junior high school** |
| 大学 | **DAIGAKU**, great-learning, is a **university** |
| 大学生 | **DAIGAKUSEI**, great-learning-life, is a **university student** |
| 学者 | **GAKUSHA**, learn-person, is a **scholar** |
| 科学 | **KAGAKU**, category-learn, means **science** |
| 科学者 | **KAGAKUSHA**, category-learn-person, is a **scientist** |
| 光学 | **KŌGAKU**, light-ray-learning, means **optics** |

| 159 | ON READINGS: **BUN, MON** | 文化 **bunka** *culture* |
|---|---|---|
| | KUN READING: **fumi** | 作文 **sakubun** *composition* |
| 文 | | 文字 **moji** *letter, character* |
| | *writing, text, culture* | 恋文 **koibumi** *love letter* |
| 4 strokes | ヽ 一 ナ 文 | |

The Chinese drew a pictograph of a writing brush 𦥑 to symbolize the idea of writing or text or culture. They simplified the form to 𠂇, then wrote the kanji 文. It means **writing**, **text**, or **culture**. Used as a word by itself it is pronounced **FUMI**. In compound words it is pronounced **BUN** or **MON**. 文学 **BUNGAKU**, text-learn, is **literature**. 文科 **BUNKA**, culture-category, means **liberal arts**. A 文科大学 **BUNKADAIGAKU**, culture-category-big-learning, is a **liberal arts university**.

# SECTION FIVE

## Kanji List

| | | | | | |
|---|---|---|---|---|---|
| 160 支 | 161 枝 | 162 書 | 163 筆 | 164 事 | 165 史 |
| 166 吏 | 167 使 | 168 士 | 169 仕 | 170 化 | 171 花 |
| 172 粧 | 173 比 | 174 皆 | 175 階 | 176 官 | 177 館 |
| 178 反 | 179 坂 | 180 止 | 181 先 | 182 洗 | 183 足 |
| 184 禁 | 185 祭 | 186 際 | 187 各 | 188 路 | 189 客 |
| 190 正 | 191 証 | 192 政 | 193 行 | 194 歩 | 195 渉 |
| 196 渋 | 197 街 | 198 待 | 199 心 | | |

| 160 支<br><br>4 strokes | ON READING: **SHI**<br>KUN READING: **sasa(eru)**<br><br>*branch; to hold up,*<br>*to support* | 支店 **shiten** *branch*<br>支配 **shihai** *control, domination*<br>支払う **shiharau** *to pay*<br>支える **sasaeru** *to hold, to support* |
|---|---|---|
| | 一　十　ｽ　支 | |

A pictograph of a hand ☝ holding up a branch Ψ symbolized both a branch and holding up. The pictograph was first drawn ☝, then simplified to 支. The final form was written 支. It means a **branch** of an organization like a business, trade union, association, or government. It also means **hold up** or **support**. Used as a word by itself it is pronounced **SASA-ERU**, and usually means **support**. In compound words it is pronounced **SHI**. 支持 **SHIJI**, support-hold, means **support**.

| 161 枝<br><br>8 strokes | ON READING: **SHI**<br>KUN READING: **eda**<br><br>*branch of a tree* | 楊枝 **tsumayōji** *toothpick*<br>枝垂れ桜 **shidare-zakura**<br>　　　*overhanging cherry blossom*<br>枝豆 **edamame** *green soybean*<br>小枝 **koeda** *twig, stick* |
|---|---|---|
| | 一　十　オ　木　杧　杧　枝　枝 | |

To denote a branch of a tree, the Chinese added the element for **tree** 木 to the element for **branch** 支 to form the new kanji 枝 meaning **branch of a tree**. Used as a word by itself it is pronounced **EDA**. In compound words it is pronounced **SHI**.

| 162 書<br><br>10 strokes | ON READING: **SHO**<br>KUN READING: **ka(ku)**<br><br>*to write, to compose; writing, book* | 書籍 **shoseki** *book*<br>読書 **dokusho** *reading*<br>書く **kaku** *to write, to compose*<br>書道 **shodō** *calligraphy* |
|---|---|---|
| | ﾌ　ﾌ　ﾖ　ヨ　彐　聿　聿　書　書　書 | |

A pictograph of a hand holding a brush ✍ writing on a piece of paper 📄 formed the character for **write**. The Chinese first drew the pictograph 書, then simplified it to 書, and drew the final kanji 書. Used as a word by itself it is pronounced **KA-KU**. In compound words 書 is pronounced **SHO**. A 書記, **SHOKI**, write-chronicle, is a **secretary**. 文書 **BUNSHO**, text-write, is a **document**.

| 163 | ON READING: **HITSU** | 筆記 **hikki** *note; to write down* |
| | KUN READING: **fude** | 毛筆 **mōhitsu** *writing brush* |
| 筆 | *writing brush* | 絵筆 **enpitsu** *painting brush* |
| | | 筆先 **fudesaki** *brush tip* |

| ノ | ⺊ | ⺇ | ⺊ | ⺮ | 竹 | 笁 | 笁 | 筀 | 筀 |
| 笙 | 筆 | | | | | | | | |

12 strokes

Early writing brushes were made from bamboo, so the Chinese added the element for bamboo ⺮ atop the element for the hand holding a brush 聿 to form the kanji for a **writing brush** 筆. It is pronounced **FUDE** when used as a word by itself, and **HITSU** in compound words.

| 164 | ON READING: **JI** | 無事 **buji** *no damage* |
| | KUN READING: **koto** | 事件 **jiken** *affair, case, matter* |
| 事 | *thing, affair, happening,* | 仕事 **shigoto** *work, job, business* |
| | *matter, event* | 出来事 **dekigoto** *event, happening* |

| 一 | 一 | 一 | 一 | 写 | 写 | 写 | 事 |
| --- | --- | --- | --- | --- | --- | --- | --- |

8 strokes

In the pictograph for **write** 書, the brush is pointed downward, writing on the paper. The Chinese used a pictograph of the brush held in hand, pointed upward, poised and ready to record things as they happen 事 to symbolize the unfolding of events. They simplified the form to 事, then 事, and wrote the final kanji 事. It means **thing**, **affair**, **happening**, **matter**, or **event**. Used as a word by itself it is pronounced **KOTO**. Used in compound words it is pronounced **JI**. 事 is frequently used both in writing and in speech. Some examples are:

大事 　　**DAIJI**, big-matter, means **important**

工事 　　**KŌJI**, tool-things, means **construction**

工事中 　**KŌJICHŪ**, construction-middle, means **under construction**, a sign seen at most construction sites

人事 　　**JINJI**, human-affairs, means **personnel affairs**

| 165 | ON READING: **SHI** | 歴史 **rekishi** *history* |
|---|---|---|
| 史 | *history* | 日本史 **nihonshi** *Japanese history*<br>世界史 **sekaishi** *the history of the world*<br>史跡 **shiseki** *historic sites, lamdmark* |
| 5 strokes | ヽ 冂 口 史 史 | |

To symbolize the passage of history, the Chinese drew a pictograph of a hand holding a counting stick 叏 to mark the passing of events and added a **mouth** 口 to call out each event. They drew the new kanji 史, meaning **history**. It is not used as a word by itself. In compound words it is pronounced **SHI**. 史書 **SHISHO**, history-write, means **history book**. 史学 **SHIGAKU**, history-learning, means the **study of history**.

| 166 | ON READING: **RI** | 官吏 **kanri** *a government official* |
|---|---|---|
| 吏 | *government official* | |
| 6 strokes | 一 厂 冂 口 吏 吏 | |

To the element for **history** 史, the Chinese added a Mandarin's hat ⼀, to illustrate that all history revolves around the officials of the government that has the Mandate of Heaven. They drew the final character 吏, meaning a **government official**. It is not used as a word by itself. In compound words 吏 is pronounced **RI**.

| 167 使 8 strokes | ON READING: **SHI** KUN READING: **tsuka(u)** *servant, messenger, use; to use* | 使命 **shimei** *mission*<br>使用人 **shiyōnin** *servant, employee*<br>大使 **taishi** *ambassador*<br>使い古し **tsukaifurushi** *worn-out* |
|---|---|---|
| | ノ 亻 仁 仁 佇 佇 佳 使 | |

The Chinese combined the element for a **government official** 吏 and the element for **person** 人 and formed a new kanji, 使, symbolizing a person you use to carry out your work and get things done. The modern meaning of 使 is **servant, messenger**, or **use**. Used by itself, as the verb **to use**, it is pronounced **TSUKA-U**. In compound words it is pronounced **SHI**. A 使者 **SHISHA**, messenger-person, is a **messenger**. A 大使 **TAISHI**, big-messenger, is a **government ambassador**. A 小使 **KOZUKAI**, small-servant, is a **person employed to do odd-jobs**. A 天 使 **TENSHI**, heaven-messenger, is an **angel**.

| 168 士 3 strokes | ON READING: **SHI** *warrior, scholar* | 武士 **bushi** *samurai, warrior*<br>紳士 **shinshi** *gentleman*<br>博士 **hakushi, hakase** *doctorate, Ph.D*<br>会計士 **kaikeishi** *accountant* |
|---|---|---|
| | 一 十 士 | |

A pictograph of a man standing erect on the ground with arms outstretched and at the ready 士 symbolized a man prepared to carry out his duty. The Chinese squared off this pictograph to the final kanji form 士. It means **a warrior, a scholar**, or **a man whose job bears responsibilities**, like a Senator or a sumo wrestler. It is not used as a word by itself, and needs another kanji to show what the man's responsibility is. In compound words 士 is pronounced **SHI**. A 学 士 **GAKUSHI**, learned-man, is a **bachelor degree**. A 力士 **RIKISHI**, strength-man, is a **sumo wrestler**.

| 169<br><br>仕<br><br>5 strokes | ON READING: **SHI**<br>KUN READING: **tsuka(eru)**<br><br>*servant; to work, to serve* | 仕返し **shikaeshi** *revenge*<br>仕草 **shigusa** *motion, sign*<br>給仕 **kyūji** *waiter, waitress, server*<br>仕える **tsukaeru** *to serve* |
|---|---|---|
| | ノ イ 仁 什 仕 | |

The Chinese put together the element for a **man who carries out responsibilities** 士 and the element for **person** 人 to symbolize one who carries out tasks for another person, a servant. The final form of the kanji is 仕, and it means **servant** or **carrying out work for others**. When it is used as a word by itself it is pronounced **TSUKA-ERU**. In compound words it is pronounced **SHI**. 仕事 **SHIGOTO**, work-affairs, is the common word meaning **to work at a job or task**.

| 170<br><br>化<br><br>4 strokes | ON READINGS: **KA, KE**<br>KUN READING: **ba(keru)**<br><br>*to change, to transform;*<br>*~-ization* | 化石 **kaseki** *fossil*<br>化粧 **keshō** *makeup*<br>お化け **obake** *ghost*<br>文字化け **mojibake** *to garble* |
|---|---|---|
| | ノ イ 仁 化 | |

A **person** standing up 人 beside a person fallen down, seated on the ground 匕, symbolized a change in state. The Chinese wrote the final form 化, meaning **change** or **transform**. Used as a word by itself it is pronounced **BA-KERU**. In compound words it is pronounced **KA** or **KE**. 文化 **BUNKA**, writing-change, means **culture**. 化学 **KAGAKU**, change-learning, means **chemistry**.

| 171<br><br>花<br><br>7 strokes | ON READING: **KA**<br>KUN READING: **hana**<br><br>*flower* | 花びん **kabin** *vase*<br>花粉症 **kafunshō** *hay fever*<br>花びら **hanabira** *petal*<br>花束 **hanataba** *bouquet* |
|---|---|---|
| | 一 十 サ サ 井 花 花 | |

The element for **change** 化 was added to the pictograph for plants ⁺⁺ to symbolize plants changing into flowers. The Chinese wrote the new composite kanji 花, meaning **flower**. Used as a word by itself it is pronounced **HANA**. In compound words it is pronounced **KA**. 花火 **HANABI**, flower-fire, means **fireworks**. 生花 **IKEBANA**, living-flowers, is the **art of flower arrangement**.

| 172 | ON READING: **SHŌ** | 化粧水 **keshō** *toner, lotion* |
| | | 化粧室 **keshōshitsu** *powder room* |
| 粧 | *makeup* | 雪化粧 **yukigeshō** *layer of snow* |
| | | 厚化粧 **atsugeshō** *heavy makeup* |

| 、 | ゛ | ゛ | 半 | 米 | 米 | 米' | 米' | 籵 | 粁 |
|---|---|---|---|---|---|---|---|---|---|
| 粧 | 粧 | | | | | | | | |

12 strokes

The Chinese combined the element for **rice** 米 with the element for **earth** or **clay** 土 under a shed 广, to signify the place where it was processed into ladies makeup or face powder. They wrote the composite kanji 粧, meaning **makeup**. It is not used as a word by itself. In compound words it is pronounced **SHŌ**. The formal word for **makeup** or **face powder** is 化粧 **KESHŌ**, change-makeup. 化粧品 **KESHŌHIN**, makeup-goods, are **cosmetics**.

| 173 | ON READING: **HI** | 比較 **hikaku** *comparison* |
| | KUN READING: **kura(beru)** | 比例 **hirei** *proportion* |
| 比 | *comparison; to compare* | 比べる **kuraberu** *to compare* |

| 一 | 上 | 比 | 比 | | | | | | |
|---|---|---|---|---|---|---|---|---|---|

4 strokes

A pictograph of two people seated in the same posture facing in the same direction 𣥂 symbolized comparing one to the other. The Chinese squared off the figures and wrote the final form 比, meaning **to compare**. Used as a word by itself, generally as a verb, it is pronounced **KURA-BERU**. In compound words it is pronounced **HI**.

| 174 | ON READING: **KAI** | 皆勤賞 **kaikinshō** *reward for perfect attendance* |
|---|---|---|
| 皆 | KUN READINGS: **mina, minna** | |
| | *all, everyone* | 皆さん **minasan** *everyone*<br>皆目 **kaimoku** *not even* |
| 9 strokes | 一　ヒ　ヒ'　比　比　比　皆　皆　皆 | |

The Chinese drew a pictograph of these same two people, this man and that man 比, and me 自, to symbolize the concept "everyone." They first wrote the kanji 皆, but it looked too tall so they removed one line from the pictograph of "me" (which was drawn of me pointing to my nose) and the final form became 皆, meaning **all, everyone**. Used as a word by itself it is pronounced **MINA**, sometimes **MINNA** with a long **N**. In compound words it is pronounced **KAI**. 皆無 **KAIMU**, all-none, means **none at all**.

| 175 | ON READING: **KAI** | 階段 **kaidan** *stairs, staircase*<br>階級 **kaikyū** *class, rank* |
|---|---|---|
| 階 | *step, floor, rank* | 地階 **chikai** *basement floor*<br>音階 **onkai** *musical scale* |
| | フ　3　阝　阝-　阝　阝'　阝比　阝比　阝比　階 | |
| 12 strokes | 階　階 | |

They took a pictograph of a terraced and graded hillside 畾, simplified to 阝, then to 阝, and finally to 阝, and added it to the element for everyone 皆 to symbolize the moving up of everyone in steps or grades. The Chinese wrote the final form of the composite kanji 階, meaning **steps** or **floors** or **rank**. Used either as a word by itself or in compound words it is pronounced **KAI**. 三階 **SAN-GAI** (**SANKAI** pronounced euphonically), three-floor, means **third-floor**. 二階 **NIKAI**, two-floor, means **second floor** or **upstairs**. 階上 **KAIJŌ**, floor-above, means **rooftop**.

| 176 | ON READING: **KAN** | 官庁 **kanchō** *government office*<br>教官 **kyōkan** *instructor* |
|---|---|---|
| 官 | *government bureaucrat* | 警察官 **keisatsukan** *police officer*<br>司令官 **shireikan** *commander* |
| 8 strokes | ヽ   ʼ   宀   宀   宀   宀   官   官 | |

A man with a full stomach sitting down resting against a wall 𠮟 under a roof ⼍ signified to the Chinese a bureaucrat or government employee. They wrote the kanji first as 𠮟, then simplified it to 官, meaning **government bureaucrat**. It is not used as a word by itself. In compound words it is pronounced **KAN**. 官費 **KANPI** (**KANHI** pronounced euphonically), government-expenses, means **expenses paid by the government**. 士官 **SHIKAN**, man-with-responsibilities-government-bureaucrat, means a **military officer**. 仕官 **SHIKAN**, working-for-others-government-bureaucracy, means **government service**.

| 177 | ON READING: **KAN**<br>KUN READING: **yakata** | 館長 **kan-chō** *director, curator*<br>旅館 **ryokan** *Japanese inn* |
|---|---|---|
| 館 | *official building* | 図書館 **toshokan** *library*<br>水族館 **suizokukan** *aquarium* |
| | ノ   人   𠆢   今   今   今   食   食   食ʼ   食ʼ | |
| 16 strokes | 飠   飠   節   館   館   館 | |

Adding the element for **eat** 食 to the element for **government bureaucrat** 官 symbolizes the quarters set up for bureaucrats to eat when they were on the road on government business. The Chinese wrote the new kanji 館, meaning **an official building**. The meaning was later extended to mean any large building, but predominantly government buildings. Used as a word by itself it is pronounced **YAKATA**. In compound words it is pronounced **KAN**. A 大使館 **TAISHIKAN**, big-messenger-building, is an **Embassy**. 本館 **HONKAN**, origin-building, is **the main building**.

| 178 | ON READING: **HAN, TAN** KUN READINGS: **so(ru), so(rasu)** | 反対 **hantai** *opposite, reverse*<br>違反 **ihan** *infraction, outrage*<br>反り返る **soru** *to roll back*<br>反らす **sorasu** *to arch*<br>反物 **tanmono** *(dry) goods, fabric* |
|---|---|---|
| 反 | *to oppose; reverse, anti-; to be against* | |
| 4 strokes | 一 厂 反 反 | |

To form the character for anti- or oppose, the Chinese combined the element for **hand** Ψ with the element for a **hill** ∫ to symbolize a hand piling up a man-made hill to oppose the progress of an enemy 反. They drew the final kanji 反. It means **oppose, reverse, anti-,** or **be against**. It is pronounced **SO-RU** or **SO-RASU** when used as a word by itself. In compound words it is pronounced **HAN** or **TAN**. 反語 **HANGO**, reverse-talk, means **irony**. 反映 **HAN-EI**, reverse-reflect, is a **reflection of an image**, as from a mirror.

| 179 | ON READING: **HAN** KUN READING: **saka** | 急坂 **kyūhan, kyūzaka** *steep slope*<br>坂道 **sakamichi** *slope*<br>赤坂 **Akasaka** *Akasaka district (in Tokyo)*<br>上り坂 **boborizaka** *uphill* |
|---|---|---|
| 坂 | *slope, hill* | |
| 7 strokes | 一 十 土 扌 圹 坂 坂 | |

To draw the kanji for an actual hill, the Chinese added the element for **earth** 土 to the element for the man-made hill built to thwart the progress of an enemy 反. They wrote the new kanji 坂. It means **slope** or **hill**. It is pronounced **SAKA** when used as a word by itself or in geographical names. In compound words it is pronounced **HAN**. 下り坂 **KUDARIZAKA** (**KUDARISAKA** pronounced euphonically), means **downhill**.

| 180 | ON READING: **SHI**<br><br>KUN READINGS: **to(maru), to(meru)** | 静止 **seishi** *calm, stillness*<br>行き止まり **ikidomari** *dead end*<br>歯止め **hadome** *brake*<br>波止場 **hatoba** *wharf* |
|---|---|---|
| 止<br><br>4 strokes | *to stop* | |

**止 stroke order:** 丨 卜 ⺊ 止

The Chinese drew a pictograph of a stationary footprint to symbolize the act of stopping. They simplified the pictograph to 止, then to 止, and drew the final form 止. It means **stop**. When it is used as a word by itself, it is pronounced **TO-MARU** (intransitive verb) or **TO-MERU** (transitive verb). In compound words it is pronounced **SHI**. 中止 **CHŪSHI**, middle-stop, means **cancel** or **suspend**. 休止 **KYŪSHI**, resting-stop, means **discontinue** or **halt**.

| 181 | ON READING: **SEN**<br>KUN READING: **saki** | 先方 **senpō** *the other end*<br>先頭 **sentō** *head, front*<br>先取り **sakidori** *look-ahead, prefetch*<br>*(computer)*<br>爪先 **tsumasaki** *tiptoe, toe* |
|---|---|---|
| 先<br><br>6 strokes | *already been there; precedent, leading edge; previous* | |

**先 stroke order:** 丿 ⼂ 牛 生 牛 先

They combined the element for **footprint** 止 with the element for **person** 人 to symbolize a person who has already been there and walked the walk. Both elements were modified to fit the square and meet artistic balance: the person was placed in the bottom half of the square and changed its shape to ⼉. The footprint was placed in the top half of the square and changed its shape, first to 生, and then to 土. The final character was written 先. It means **already been there**, **precedent**, **leading edge**, or **previous**. Used as a word by itself it is pronounced **SAKI**. In compound words it is pronounced **SEN**. 舌先 **SHITA-SAKI**, tongue-tip, means **tip of the tongue**. 先生 **SENSEI**, prior-living, is **a teacher**. 先月 **SENGETSU**, previous-month, is **last month**. 先日 **SENJITSU**, previous-day, is **yesterday**.

| 182 | ON READING: **SEN** KUN READING: **ara(u)** | 洗面所 **senmenjo** *restroom* 洗剤 **senzai** *detergent, cleanser* |
|---|---|---|
| 洗 | *washing; to wash* | 洗礼 **senrei** *baptism* 洗う **arau** *to clean, to wash* |
| 9 strokes | ` 丶 冫 氵 氵 氵 泮 泮 泮 洗 | |

To symbolize the act of washing, the Chinese added the element for **water** 水, modified to 氵 to fit into the square, to the element 先 which means **already walked there** (but which itself is composed of the elements for **person** 人 and **foot** 止). The new kanji is written 洗 and means pouring water over one's foot or **washing**. Used as a word by itself it is pronounced **ARA-U**. Used in compound words it is pronounced **SEN**. 手洗い **TE-ARAI**, hand-washing, is a polite name for **restroom**. 手洗い, with the addition of one or two kana for grammar, is the sign directing you to the restroom.

| 183 | ON READING: **SOKU** KUN READINGS: **ashi, ta(riru), ta(su)** | 足跡 **ashiato** *footprint* 遠足 **ensoku** *field trip, picnic* 足音 **ashioto** *footsteps* |
|---|---|---|
| 足 | *leg, foot; to be satisfied, to add to; enough* | 素足 **suashi** *barefoot* 足りる **tariru** *enough* |
| 7 strokes | 丶 冂 口 卩 卩 尸 足 | |

To the pictograph for footprint 凵, which became the kanji 止 meaning **stop**, the Chinese added a picture of a knee ㄱ and drew the kanji meaning **leg** 足. The final form of the kanji was 足, and it means either **leg** or **foot**. Used as word by itself it is pronounced **ASHI**, **TA-RIRU** or **TA-SU**. Used in compound words it is pronounced **SOKU**. One of the Wards in Tokyo is named 足立区 **ADACHI-KU** (**ASHI-DASHI-KU** pronounced euphonically).

| 184 | ON READING: **KIN** | | | | 禁煙 **kin'en** *No smoking* |
|---|---|---|---|---|---|
| 禁 | | | | | 禁酒 **kinshu** *abstinence* |
| | *to forbid; ban, prohibition* | | | | 解禁 **kaikin** *lifting of the ban* |
| | | | | | 禁句 **kinku** *forbidden word* |

| 禁 | 一 | 十 | 才 | 木 | 朮 | 村 | 材 | 林 | 梺 | 埜 |
|---|---|---|---|---|---|---|---|---|---|---|
| 13 strokes | 埜 | 禁 | 禁 | | | | | | | |

The Chinese put two sticks of **wood** 木木 atop an altar 示 to warn that transgressions against the will of the gods bring crucifixion. The final form of the kanji is 禁, meaning **forbid** or **ban**. (The pictograph for altar is not used as a kanji by itself, but often forms part of pictographs for words related to religion.) Used either as a word by itself or in compound words 禁 is pronounced **KIN**. 禁止 **KINSHI**, forbid-stop, means **prohibited**. 立入禁止 **TACHI'IRI-KINSHI**, stand-enter-forbid-stop, means **keep out, entry prohibited**. 禁足 **KINSOKU**, forbid-foot, means **grounded, confined to the house, can't go out**.

| 185 | ON READING: **SAI** KUN READINGS: **matsu(ri), matsu(ru)** | | | | 祭礼 **sairei** *festival* |
|---|---|---|---|---|---|
| 祭 | | | | | 文化祭 **bunkasai** *cultural festival* |
| | *to deify, to worship; festival* | | | | 祭る **matsuru** *to enshrine* |
| | | | | | 秋祭り **akimatsuri** *autumn festival* |

| 祭 | ノ | ク | タ | 夕 | 夗 | 奴 | 奴 | 怒 | 祭 | 祭 |
|---|---|---|---|---|---|---|---|---|---|---|
| 11 strokes | 祭 | | | | | | | | | |

A pictograph of a hand Ψ placing a piece of sacrificial meat (modified to 月) on an altar 示 was simplified and drawn in the final form 祭, symbolizing a sacrificial ceremony. Used as a word by itself it is pronounced **MATSU-RU** as a verb, meaning **to deify** or **to worship**, or **MATSU-RI** (or **MATSURI**) as a noun, meaning **festival**. In compound words it is pronounced **SAI**. A 祭日 **SAIJITSU**, festival-day, is a **holiday**.

| 186 | ON READING: **SAI** | 交際 **kōsai** *contact, association* |
|---|---|---|
| | KUN READING: **kiwa** | この際 **konosai** *in this case* |
| 際 | *to interact, to come into contact* | 窓際 **madogiwa** *window (side)* |
| | | 際どい **kiwadoi** *suggestive, risky* |

| ⁊ | ³ | ⻖ | ⻖' | ⻖⁷ | ⻖⁷ | ⻖⁷ | ⻖⁷⁷ | ⻖⁷⁷ | ⻖⁷⁷ |
|---|---|---|---|---|---|---|---|---|---|
| 14 strokes | 際 | 際 | 際 | 際 | | | | | |

The Chinese added the element for a terraced hillside ⻖ to the element for **festival** 祭 to signify the place where the festival was held and all the people came to meet and interact. The final form of the kanji was written 際, meaning **to interact** or **come into contact**. In compound words it is pronounced **SAI**. Used as a word by itself it is pronounced as **KIWA**. 国際 **KOKUSAI**, country-interact, means **international**.

| 187 | ON READING: **KAKU** | 各自 **kakuji** *each one* |
|---|---|---|
| | KUN READING: **ono-ono** | 各種 **kakushu** *various* |
| 各 | *each and every* | 各位 **kakui** *participant, related persons* |
| | | 各 (各々) **ono-ono** *each* |

| ノ | ク | 夂 | 夂 | 各 | 各 | | | |
|---|---|---|---|---|---|---|---|---|
| 6 strokes | | | | | | | | |

The Chinese drew a pictograph of a person sitting cross-legged 夂 in front of a box 口 taking inventory, checking each and every box. They drew it first 各, then simplified it to 各, and wrote it in its final form 各. It means **each and every**. It is not used as a word by itself. Used as a word by itself it is pronounced **ONO-ONO**. In compound words it is pronounced **KAKU**. 各人 **KAKUJIN**, each-person, means **each and every person**.

| 188 | ON READING: **RO** | 路上 **rojō** *on a street* |
| | KUN READING: **ji** | 道路 **dōro** *road, lane* |
| 路 | *road* | 家路 **eiji** *homeward* |
| | | 旅路 **tabiji** *journey, on a trip* |

| | | | | | | | | | | |
|---|---|---|---|---|---|---|---|---|---|---|
| 13 strokes | ヽ | 口 | 口 | 尸 | 足 | 足 | 足 | 足 | 足 | 跮 |
| | 跮 | 路 | 路 | | | | | | | |

They combined the element for **foot** 足 with the element for **each and every** 各, symbolizing the foot trudging each and every step in forward movement, to form the new kanji 路, meaning **road**. Used as a word by itself it is pronounced **JI**. In compound words 路 is pronounced **RO**.

| 189 | ON READINGS: **KYAKU, KAKU** | 客間 **kyakuma** *guest room* |
| | | 乗客 **jōkyaku** *passenger* |
| 客 | *guest, customer* | お客様 **okyaku-sama** *guest, customer* |
| | | 旅客 **ryokaku** *traveler* |

| | | | | | | | | | |
|---|---|---|---|---|---|---|---|---|---|
| 9 strokes | ヽ | ハ | 宀 | 宀 | 宀 | 安 | 安 | 客 | 客 |

The Chinese put the element for **each and every** 各 under the pictograph for **roof** 宀, symbolizing that each and every person under my roof is my guest, and formed the new kanji 客 meaning **guest** or **customer**. It is not used as a word by itself. In compound words it is pronounced **KYAKU** or **KAKU**. With kana before and after to denote respect, 客 is commonly seen written in and around commercial establishments, referring to their **customers**.

| 190 | ON READINGS: **SEI, SHŌ** <br> KUN READINGS: **masa,** <br> **tada(su), tada(shi'i)** | 正義 **seigi** *justice* <br> 正直 **shōjiki** *honesty* <br> 正しい **tadashi'i** *right* <br> 正す **tadasu** *to correct* <br> 正夢 **masayume** *prophetic dream* <br> 正当な **seitō na** *legitimate* |
|---|---|---|
| 正 <br> 5 strokes | *to correct; proper, right,* <br> *righteous, reasonable,* <br> *legitimate* | |
| | 一　丁　下　正　正 | |

A straight line 一 was added above the element for **footprint** 止 (which had become the kanji meaning **stop**) to symbolize keeping the footprint on the straight and narrow. The new kanji was written 正 and means **correct**, **proper**, **right**, or **righteous**. Used as a word by itself it is pronounced **MASA** or **TADA-SU**. A common adjectival form is **TADA-SHI'I** (written with two kana for the syllables **SHI** and **I**) meaning **righteous** or **reasonable** or **legitimate**. Used in compound words it is pronounced **SEI** or **SHŌ**. It is used in first and last names, usually pronounced **MASA** or **TADA**, but sometimes **SHŌ**. 正力 **SHŌRIKI**, Righteous-Power, is the name of the founder of an important Japanese business empire. 正月 **SHŌGATSU**, proper-month, is **New Year's**.

| 191 | ON READING: **SHŌ** | 証拠 **shōko** *evidence* <br> 証明 **shōmei** *proof* <br> 免許証 **menkyoshō** *certificate* <br> 保険証 **hokenshō** *insurance card* |
|---|---|---|
| 証 <br> 12 strokes | *proof* | |
| | 丶　亠　二　言　言　言　訂　訂　訂 <br> 訂　証 | |

The Chinese put together the element for **say** 言 with the element for **correct** 正 and formed the new kanji 証, meaning **proof**. It is not used as a word by itself. In compound words it is pronounced **SHŌ**. A 証人 **SHŌNIN**, proof-person, is a **witness**. A 学生証, **GAKUSEISHŌ**, student-proof, is a **student ID card**. 証明 **SHŌMEI**, proof-bright, means **proof**. A 証明書 **SHŌMEISHO**, proof-write, is a **certificate** of graduation or other accomplishment.

| 192 | ON READINGS: **SEI, SHŌ**<br>KUN READING: **matsurigoto** | 政治 **seiji** *politics*<br>行政 **gyōsei** *government, public*<br> *administration*<br>摂政 **sesshō** *regent*<br>政治家 **seijika** *politician* |
|---|---|---|
| 政<br>9 strokes | *government* | |

一　丁　下　正　正　正　正　政　政

To symbolize the concept of "coerce" or "force," the Chinese drew a pictograph of a hand holding a stick ready to strike 攴. They first simplified it to 攵, and then its final form it became 攵. This pictograph is no longer used as a kanji alone, but it appears in many kanji as an element that brings the meaning of **to cause** or **pressure to happen**.

The Chinese combined this element for coerce or force 攴 with the element for **correct** or **proper** 正 (modified slightly to 㐬 to better fit the square) and formed a new kanji 政 meaning **government**. Used as a word by itself it is pronounced **MATSURIGOTO**. It is not used as a word by itself. In compound words it is pronounced **SEI** or **SHŌ**. 政府 SEIFU, government-government, means **government**. The 中央政府 CHŪ-ŌSEIFU, central-government is the **central government**.

| 193 | ON READINGS: **KŌ, GYŌ**<br>KUN READINGS: **i(ku),<br>yu(ku), okona(u)** | 旅行 **ryokō** *journey, trip*<br>行列 **gyōretsu** *line*<br>行く **iku, yuku** *to go (to)*<br>行う **okonau** *to do, to act, to hold*<br>行儀 **gyōgi** *manner* |
|---|---|---|
| 行<br>6 strokes | *line, row; to go, to do, to<br>act, to hold* | |

丿　彳　彳　行　行

The pictograph for crossroads was drawn 行. It was simplified to 彳亍 and then the final form was written 行, meaning **go**. Used as a word by itself it is pronounced **I-KU**, **YU-KU** or **OKONA-U**. In compound words 行 is pronounced **KŌ** or **GYŌ**. 行事 GYŌJI, go-thing, means **event** or **function** or **program**.

Another of the very few instances where two or more different Chinese pictographs were simplified and stylized to a point where they became identical is the character for walk. (An earlier example was the modified version of **meat** and the kanji for **moon**, both written 月).

| 194 | ON READINGS: **HO, BU** | 歩道 | **hodō** *sidewalk* |
|---|---|---|---|
| 歩 | KUN READINGS: **aru(ku), ayu(mu)** | 進歩 | **shinpo** *advance, progress* |
| | | 歩合 | **buai** *commission* |
| | *to walk* | 歩く | **aruku** *to walk, to step* |
| | | 歩む | **ayumu** *to follow, to walk* |

| 8 strokes | ー | ├ | ﻠﻟ | 止 | 止 | 步 | 步 | 歩 | |
|---|---|---|---|---|---|---|---|---|---|

The Chinese pictograph for **walk** was drawn as a left foot being put in front of a right foot 步. The left foot was simplified first to 止, and finally to 凹, which, as described earlier, became the kanji 止 meaning **stop**.

The right foot was the flip side of the left, and was simplified first to 𠂆, and then to 丄丄, and finally squared off into an aesthetic form 少 so the bottom half of the kanji would not be just the mirror image of the top. This right-foot element is written exactly as is the kanji for **a few** 少.

The kanji for walk was drawn 歩 in final form. Used as a word by itself, it is pronounced **ARU-KU** or **AYU-MU**. In compound words it is pronounced **HO** or **BU**. 歩行 **HOKŌ**, walk-go, is **walking**. A 歩行者 **HOKŌSHA** is a **pedestrian**, and pedestrian walkways are so marked.

| 195 | ON READING: **SHŌ** | 干渉 | **kanshō** *interference* |
|---|---|---|---|
| 渉 | | 渉外 | **shōgai** *external affairs* |
| | *to cross over carefully, to cross, to liaison with* | | |

| | ` | ﾉ | 氵 | 氵 | 氵 | 氵 | 涉 | 涉 | 涉 | 涉 |
|---|---|---|---|---|---|---|---|---|---|---|
| 11 strokes | 渉 | | | | | | | | | |

The Chinese drew a pictograph for walk on water by combining the element for **walk** 歩 with the element for **water** 氵. They drew the final kanji 渉, meaning **cross over carefully from one side to the other** or **be in liaison with**. It is not used by itself as a word. In compound words it is pronounced **SHŌ**. 交渉 **KŌSHŌ**, exchange-liaison, means **negotiate**. 渉外 **SHŌGAI**, liaison-outside, means **public relations**.

| 196 | ON READING: **JŪ** | 渋滞 **jūtai** *traffic jam* |
| | KUN READINGS: **shibu,** | 苦渋 **kujū** *anguished* |
| | **shibu(i), shibu(ru)** | 渋柿 **shigaki** *sour persimmon* |
| 渋 | *to hesitate, to be reluctant;* | 渋い **shibui** *cool, bitter* |
| | *quiet, sober, tasteful* | 渋る **shiburu** *to hold back; to be reluctant* |

| ` | ; | シ | シ | シ | シ | 泮 | 渋 | 渋 | 渋 |
|---|---|---|---|---|---|---|---|---|---|
| 渋 | | | | | | | | | |

11 strokes

They combined three footprint elements 歮 with the element for **flowing water** シ to symbolize the disruption of the free flow of water when roiled by footprints. They first drew the kanji as 澁, which indicates disruption. The Chinese further abbreviated the kanji to 渋, and the old way of writing is rarely seen now.

渋 means **to hesitate**, **to be reluctant**, or **to be a fly in the ointment**. It also means **quiet**, **sober**, or **tasteful**, and in this definition has become a favorite description in Western culture of Japanese refined and laid-back taste. Used as a word by itself it is pronounced **SHIBU**, **SHIBU-I** or **SHIBU-RU**. In compound words it is pronounced **JŪ**.

| 197 | ON READINGS: **GAI, KAI** | 街頭 **gaitō** *in the street* |
| | KUN READING: **machi** | 商店街 **shōtengai** *shopping district* |
| 街 | *street, avenue* | 街道 **kaidō** *way* |
| | | 街角 **machikado** *street corner* |

| ' | ' | 彳 | 彳 | 彳 | 往 | 往 | 往 | 往 | 往 |
|---|---|---|---|---|---|---|---|---|---|
| 街 | 街 | | | | | | | | |

12 strokes

The Chinese took the pictograph for crossroads, meaning **go** 行, then widened the roads 彳 丁 and dropped in a double-fill of **earth** 圭 to make a new kanji 街, meaning **street** or **avenue**. Used by itself it is pronounced **MACHI**. In compound words it is pronounced **GAI** or **KAI**.

| 198 待 9 strokes | ON READING: **TAI**<br>KUN READING: **ma(tsu)**<br><br>*to wait* | 待機 **taiki** *waiting*<br>期待 **kitai** *expectation, hope*<br>待つ **matsu** *to wait*<br>待ち遠しい **machidōshi'i** *can hardly wait* |
| --- | --- | --- |

ノ　ノ　イ　彳　彳　行　待　待　待

When the crossroads 行 meaning **go** is used as an element in other kanji, just one side of the street is used. For example, the Chinese put the abbreviated element for **go** 彳 on the left-hand side of a new composite kanji, and put the kanji for **temple** 寺 on the right-hand side. The new kanji 待 symbolizes going to the temple, and was used to mean "go and wait for me at the temple." It now means simply **wait**. Used as a word by itself it is pronounced **MA-TSU**. In compound words it is pronounced **TAI**.

| 199 心 4 strokes | ON READING: **SHIN**<br>KUN READING: **kokoro**<br><br>*heart* | 心身 **shinshin** *mind and body*<br>感心 **kanshin** *admiration*<br>心待ちにする **kokoromachi ni suru** *to wait in anticipation*<br>親心 **oyagokoro** *parental feeling* |
| --- | --- | --- |

ヽ　心　心　心

A picture of a heart meant **heart**. The Chinese first drew it, then simplified it to. They wrote the final kanji as 心. Used as a word by itself it is pronounced **KOKORO**. In compound words it is pronounced **SHIN**. In Japanese, 心 means about the same as **heart** in English. It is not only a vital organ but the center of the spirit and emotions as well. 心理学 **SHINRIGAKU**, heart-manage-study, means **psychology**. 中心 **CHŪSHIN**, center-heart, means **center** in the broad sense, where things revolve around the center, as for example the center of a town, a central principle, or the sun as center of the solar system. 心中 **SHINJŪ** (**SHINCHŪ** pronounced euphonically) means a **double suicide**. 小心 **SHŌSHIN**, small-heart, means **cowardly**, and a 小心者 **SHŌSHINMONO**, small-heart-person, is a coward.

# SECTION SIX

## Kanji List

| | | | | | |
|---|---|---|---|---|---|
| 200 羽 | 201 非 | 202 不 | 203 悲 | 204 愛 | 205 急 |
| 206 音 | 207 意 | 208 味 | 209 目 | 210 注 | 211 相 |
| 212 省 | 213 直 | 214 亡 | 215 盲 | 216 忘 | 217 帽 |
| 218 市 | 219 見 | 220 自 | 221 習 | 222 具 | 223 貝 |
| 224 費 | 225 算 | 226 首 | 227 県 | 228 耳 | 229 聖 |
| 230 取 | 231 最 | 232 歯 | 233 鼻 | 234 公 | 235 松 |
| 236 私 | 237 和 | 238 秋 | | | |

| 200 | ON READING: U | 羽毛 **umō** *feather, down* |
| | KUN READINGS: **ha, hane, wa (ba, pa)** | 羽根 **hane** *wing, feather, blade* |
| 羽 | *wing* | 羽布団 **hanebuton** *down quilt*<br>一羽 **ichi-wa** *one (bird)* |
| 6 strokes | フ ヲ ヲ 羽 羽 羽 | |

The Chinese drew a pictograph of a bird's wings as 翔, two wings flying in the same direction. They simplified it to 羽 and wrote the final kanji 羽. It means the **wing** of anything that flies, bird, butterfly, angel, or airplane. Used as a word by itself it is pronounced **HANE, HA** or **WA (BA, PA)**. In compound words it is pronounced **U**. 羽田 **HANEDA** is the name of an airport near Tokyo.

| 201 | ON READING: **HI** | 非難 **hinan** *criticism, responsibility* |
| 非 | *not, non-, un-* | 非常口 **hijōguchi** *emergency exit*<br>非公式 **hikōshiki** *unofficial* |
| 8 strokes | ノ ナ ヲ ヺ 刋 非 非 非 | |

Then they drew a pictograph of two wings flying in opposite directions 刋片 to symbolize things flying off in opposite directions. They simplified it first to 刋片, and wrote the final kanji 非. It means **not, non-**, or **un-**. It is not used as a word by itself. In compound words it is pronounced **HI**. 非行 **HIKŌ**, un-going, means **misconduct** or **mischief**.

| 202 | ON READINGS: **FU, BU** | 不当な **futō na** *unfair* |
| 不 | *negative, wrong, false, unjust; dis-, in-, mis-* | 不利な **furi na** *adverse, inconvenient*<br>不用心 **buyōjin** *careless* |
| 4 strokes | 一 フ 不 不 | |

Another prefix, meaning **negative** or **dis-** or **in-** or **mis-**, was represented by a pictograph of a bird trying to fly straight up toward heaven but being blocked from ever reaching there 丕. The pictograph was squared and simplified and the final form became 不. It is not used as a word by itself. In compound words it is pronounced **FU** or **BU**. 不明 **FUMEI**, un-clear, means **unclear**. 不正 **FUSEI**, in-correct, means **wrong, false**, or **unjust**. 不十分 **FUJŪBUN**, not-enough, means **not enough**.

| 203 | ON READING: **HI** | 悲痛 **hitsū** *heartbreaking* |
| | KUN READINGS: **kana(shi'i),** | 悲運 **hiun** *unhappiness, fate* |
| | **kana(shimu)** | 悲しい **kanashi'i** *sad, unhappy* |
| 悲 | *sad* | 悲しみ **kanashimi** *sadness* |

| ) | ) | ) | ヲ | ヨ | 扌 | 扌 | 非 | 非 | 非 | 悲 |
| 悲 | 悲 | | | | | | | | | |

12 strokes

The Chinese added the element for **not** or **un-**, 非, to the element for **heart** 心 to form a new composite kanji 悲, meaning **sad**. It is pronounced **KANA-SHI'I** or **KANA-SHIMU** when used as a word by itself. In compound words it is pronounced **HI**.

| 204 | ON READING: **AI** | 愛情 **aijō** *love* |
| | | 愛読書 **aidokusho** *favorite book* |
| | *love* | 恋愛 **renai** *love affair* |
| 愛 | | 愛犬家 **aikenka** *dog-lover* |

| 一 | ハ | ハ | 丷 | 爫 | 爫 | 爫 | 愛 | 愛 | 愛 |
| 愛 | 愛 | 愛 | | | | | | | |

13 strokes

To form the character for **love**, the Chinese drew a pictograph of someone sitting down, cross-legged 夊, with a hand ⺈ holding a support ⌐ to control a fluttering **heart** 心. The finished kanji was written 愛, and means **love**. Used either as a word by itself or in compound words it is pronounced **AI**. 愛好 **AIKŌ**, love-like, means **to love**, **to be fond of**. An 愛好者 **AIKŌSHA**, fond-of-person, is a **fan**. An 愛国者 **AIKOKUSHA**, love-country-person, is a **patriot**.

| 205 | ON READING: **KYŪ** | 救急車 **kyūkyūsha** *ambulance* |
| | KUN READING: **iso(gu)** | 急に **kyū ni** *suddenly* |
| 急 | *sudden, urgent; in a hurry* | 特急 **tokkyū** *limited express (train)* |
| | | 急ぐ **isogu** *hurry up* |
| 9 strokes | ノ ｱ ⺈ 刍 刍 刍 急 急 急 | |

For the kanji symbolizing "to be in a hurry" or "be involved in urgent matters," the Chinese drew a pictograph combining a **heart** 心 with a hand outstretched ⺕ to grab a running man ⺈ from behind. They simplified the pictograph to 急 and wrote the final kanji 急. It means **sudden** or **urgent** or **to be in a hurry.** Used as a word by itself 急 is pronounced **ISO-GU**. In compound words it is pronounced **KYŪ**. 急行 **KYŪKŌ**, fast-go, means **express**, as in trains or buses.

| 206 | ON READINGS: **ON, IN** | 音楽 **ongaku** *music* |
| | KUN READING: **oto, ne** | 福音 **fukuin** *good news, gospel* |
| 音 | *sound* | 物音 **mono-oto** *sound* |
| | | 音色 **neiro** *tone* |
| 9 strokes | ﹑ 亠 䒑 立 立 立 音 音 音 | |

The Chinese combined the element for **sun** 日 with the element for **stand** or **rise up** 立 to symbolize the sounds of life awakening that accompany the sun's rising at dawn. They wrote the composite kanji 音, meaning **sound**. It is pronounced **OTO** or **NE** when used as a word by itself, and **ON** or **IN** when used in compound words. 足音 **ASHI-OTO**, foot-sound, is the **sound of footsteps.** 母音 **BO-IN**, mother-sound, is a **vowel**, and a 子音 **SHI'IN**, child-sound, is a **consonant**.

| 207 | ON READING: **I** | 意見 **iken** *opinion, voice, mind* |
| | | 意味 **imi** *meaning* |
| 意 | *thoughts, intentions, the mind* | 決意 **ketsui** *resolve, determination* |
| | | 意思 **ishi** *resolve, will* |
| | ､    一    十    立    立    产    音    音    音 | |
| 13 strokes | 意 意 意 | |

The Chinese combined the element for **sound** 音 with the element for **heart** 心 to symbolize the sounds of the heart, and wrote the new kanji 意, meaning **thoughts** or **intentions** or **the mind**. It is not used as a word by itself. 意 is pronounced **I** in compound words. 意外 **IGAI**, thoughts-outside, means **unexpected**.

| 208 | ON READING: **MI** | 味覚 **mikaku** *sense of taste* |
| | KUN READINGS: **aji,** | 味見 **ajimi** *tasting* |
| 味 | **aji(wau)** | 塩味 **sio-aji** *salty taste* |
| | *to taste* | 味わい **ajiwai** *flavor* |
| 8 strokes | ) 𠃌 口 口⁻ 叮 吐 味 味 | |

The Chinese combined the element for **not yet there**, **unfinished** 未 with the element for **mouth** 口 to symbolize the idea of tasting something cooking, to see how it is coming along. The new kanji was written 味, and means **to taste**. Used as a word by itself it is pronounced **AJI** or **AJI-WAU**. Used in compound words it is pronounced **MI**. 意味 **IMI**, thoughts-taste, means **mean**, as in "What does that word mean?" 中味 **NAKAMI**, inside-taste, means **contents**, of a box, for example.

| 209 | ON READINGS: **MOKU, BOKU** | 目的 **mokuteki** *purpose, object* |
|---|---|---|
| | KUN READINGS: **me, ma** | 面目 **menmoku** *one's honor* |
| 目 | | 目立つ **medatsu** *to stand out* |
| | *eye* | 目の当たり **ma-no-atari** *with one's own eyes* |
| 5 strokes | 丨 冂 刀 月 目 | |

The Chinese drew the pictograph for eye as it looked ◁▷. Then they stood the pictograph on end ⊖ to make the kanji tall and narrow instead of wide and squat so it would fit properly into a kanji square, and drew the final form 目. It means **eye**. It is also used to express the ordinal suffix in counting order (watching the numbers march by), as in first, second, third. Used as a word itself, and also as the counting suffix, it is pronounced **ME** or **MA**. In compound words it is pronounced **MOKU** or **BOKU**. 目上 **ME-UE**, eyes-above, means **those superior to you in age or station**. 目下 **MESHITA**, eyes-below, means the opposite, namely those inferior to you in age or station. 一日目 **ICHINICHIME** means **the first day**. 三丁目 **SANCHŌME** means **Block Number 3**, as used in street addresses.

| 210 | ON READING: **CHŪ** | 発注する **hatchū suru** *to order* |
|---|---|---|
| | KUN READING: **soso(gu)** | 注文 **chūmon** *order* |
| 注 | | 注ぐ **sosogu** *to pour* |
| | *to pour, to be careful; to pay attention* | 注ぎ口 **sosogiguchi** *spout, lip* |
| 8 strokes | 丶 冫 氵 汈 氿 汁 注 注 | |

The element for **master**, which is a pictograph of a dwelling's oil lamp that is always lit 主, was added to the element for water, modified to fit the square 氵, to form a new kanji 注 symbolizing the pouring of the oil, without fail, into the lamp so it never goes out. 注 means **to pour** and also **to pour your attention on so you don't make mistakes**, that is, **to be careful**. Used as a word by itself, generally as a verb meaning **to pour**, it is pronounced **SOSO-GU**. In compound words it is pronounced **CHŪ**. 注目 **CHŪMOKU**, attention-eyes, means **pay attention**. 注意 **CHŪ-I**, attention-thoughts, means **pay attention** or **take care**.

| 211 | ON READINGS: **SŌ, SHŌ**<br>KUN READING: **ai**<br><br>*to observe closely; mutual* | 相談 **sōdan** *conference*<br>首相 **shushō** *prime minister*<br>相棒 **aibō** *buddy, pal* |
| :-- | :-- | :-- |
| 相<br><br>9 strokes | 一　十　才　木　札　札　相　相　相 | |

The Chinese drew a pictograph of an **eye** 目 peering from behind a **tree** 木 to check things out. The kanji's form was 相, meaning **to observe closely to determine worth**. It also means **a person with whom you do a mutual activity after checking them out**. Used as a word by itself, it is pronounced **AI**. In compound words it is pronounced **SŌ** or **SHŌ**. 相手 **AITE**, observe-hand, means **the other party in an activity**. 手相 **TESŌ** (the same two kanji in reverse order), hand-observe, means **palm-reading**. 相愛 **SŌAI**, mutual-love, means **a couple mutually in love**.

| 212 | ON READINGS: **SHŌ, SEI**<br>KUN READING: **habu(ku),**<br>**kaeri(miru)**<br><br>*government ministry;*<br>*to omit, to save* | 外務省 **gaimushō** *Ministry of*<br>　　　　　　　　　　 *Foreign Affairs*<br>財務省 **zaimushō** *Ministry of Finance*<br>省略 **shōryaku** *abbreviation*<br>省く **habuku** *to omit, to save* |
| :-- | :-- | :-- |
| 省<br><br>9 strokes | ノ　丿丶　小　少　少　劣　省　省　省 | |

The element for **a few** 少 was combined with the element for **eyes** 目 to form a new kanji 省, symbolizing a few eyes inspecting closely. It means either a **government ministry,** or **to scrutinize** as a government ministry is wont to do. Used as a word by itself it is pronounced **KAERI-MIRU** or **HABU-KU**. In compound words it is pronounced **SHŌ** or **SEI**.

| 213 | ON READINGS: **CHOKU, JIKI** <br><br> KUN READINGS: **nao(ru), nao(su), su(gu), tada(chi-ni)** | 直接 **chokusetsu** *direct* <br> 直筆 **jikihitsu** *autograph* <br> 仲直りする **nakanaori suru** *to make peace* <br> 直す **naosu** *to fix, to repair* |
|---|---|---|
| 直 <br><br> 8 strokes | *honest, straight; immediately, at once; proper; to make straight, to fix* | 直ちに **tadachi ni** *immediately* <br> 真っ直ぐ **massugu** *straight* |

一　十　广　市　市　肻　直　直

They drew a pictograph of **ten** 十 **eyes** 目 staring into a corner ∟ to see what's going on, and formed the kanji 直 to symbolize the idea that "we're watching you, don't hide anything, bring it all out in the open, keep it straight, do it right, fix it up." 直 means **straight** or **straight and narrow** or **honest** or **proper** as a noun or adjective, and means **make straight** or **fix** or **correct** as a verb, and **straight away** (as the British say) or **at once** as an adverb. When used as a word by itself, it is pronounced **NAO-RU** or **NAO-SU** as a verb, and **SU-GU** or **TADA-CHINI** as an adverb. In compound words it is pronounced **CHOKU** or **JIKI**. 正 直 **SHŌJIKI**, both kanji being separate pictographs of the concept straight-and-narrow, means **honest**. 直立 **CHOKURITSU**, straight-stand, means **stand erect, at attention**.

| 214 | ON READINGS: **BŌ, MŌ** <br> KUN READING: **na(ki)** | 亡命 **bōmei** *exile* <br> 死亡 **shibō** *death* |
|---|---|---|
| 亡 <br><br> 3 strokes | *to die, to escape, to lose* | 亡くなる **nakunaru** *to pass away* <br> 亡きがら **nakigara** *dead body* |

丶　亠　亡

The Chinese drew a pictograph of a **person** 人 departing from a hiding place in a corner of a house ∟ to symbolize the ultimate departure. They modified the shape of person to fit the square aesthetically ⼇, and wrote the kanji 亡, meaning **to die**, **to escape**, or **to lose**. When used as a word by itself, it is pronounced **NA-KI**. It is rarely used as a word by itself. In compound words it is pronounced **BŌ** or **MŌ**. A 亡者 **MŌJA** (**MŌSHA** pronounced euphonically), dead-person, is **the deceased**.

亡 is used as an element in other kanji, where it brings the meaning of **the ultimate departure**, **die**, **escape**, or **lose**.

| 215 盲 8 strokes | ON READING: **MŌ** KUN READING: **mekura** *blind* | 盲点 **mōten** *blind spot* 盲目 **mōmoku** *blind* 盲腸 **mōchō** *appendicitis* 盲判 **mekuraban** *unread* |
|---|---|---|

| ` | 亠 | 亡 | 亡 | 盲 | 盲 | 盲 | 盲 |

The element for the ultimate departure 亡, in its meaning **to lose**, was put together with the element for **eye** 目 to form a new kanji 盲 meaning **blind**. Used as a word by itself it is pronounced **MEKURA**, which is the common word for a **blind person**. In compound words it is pronounced **MŌ**. 盲人 **MŌJIN**, blind-person, is a more formal word for a **blind person**. 文盲 **MONMŌ**, writing-blindness, means **illiteracy**.

| 216 忘 7 strokes | ON READING: **BŌ** KUN READING: **wasu(reru)** *to forget* | 忘年会 **bōnenkai** *year-end party* 健忘症 **kenbōshō** *amnesia* 物忘れ **monowasure** *forgetfulness* 忘れ物 **wasuremono** *lost property* |
|---|---|---|

| ` | 亠 | 亡 | 亡 | 忘 | 忘 | 忘 |

The element for the ultimate departure 亡, in its meaning **to escape**, was put together with the element for **heart** 心 to form a new kanji 忘 meaning **forget**. Used as a word by itself it is pronounced **WASU-RERU**. In compound words 忘 is pronounced **BŌ**.

| 217 | ON READING: **BŌ** | 帽子屋 **bōshi-ya** *hatter* |
|---|---|---|
| | | 綿帽子 **watabōshi** *Japanese wedding veil* |
| **帽** | *hat* | 脱帽する **datsubō suru** *to take one's hat off to someone* |
| | | 赤帽 **akabō** *porter, redcap* |

| | | | | | | | | | |
|---|---|---|---|---|---|---|---|---|---|
| 丨 | 冂 | 巾 | 巾丶 | 巾冖 | 帆 | 帊 | 帊 | 帽 | 帽 |

**12 strokes** 帽 帽

To symbolize the meaning **cloth**, the Chinese drew a pictograph of a salesman using his hands to measure a length of cloth 帠. The pictograph in final form was drawn 巾. It is seldom used as a kanji by itself but often appears as an element in other kanji, where it brings the meaning **cloth**.

The element for **cloth** 巾 was added to the elements for **sun** 日 and **eye** 目 to form the pictograph of a piece of cloth used to keep the sun out of your eyes 帽. This is how they wrote the kanji meaning **hat**. In this kanji, the element for **sun** 日 is written slightly wider than the element for **eye** 目 (although the two elements when written alone have the same width) to make it easier to distinguish the seven horizontal lines in the right side of the square. 帽 is not used as a word itself. In compound words it is pronounced **BŌ**. Hats in general are called 帽子 **BŌSHI**, hat-little. A 学帽 **GAKUBŌ**, study-hat, is the **student's cap** worn with school uniforms.

| 218 | ON READING: **SHI** | 市民 **shimin** *citizen* |
|---|---|---|
| | KUN READING: **ichi** | 都市 **toshi** *city* |
| **市** | *city, central marketplace* | 市場 **ichiba** *market* |
| | | 朝市 **asaichi** *morning market* |

| | | | | | |
|---|---|---|---|---|---|
| 丶 | 亠 | 广 | 产 | 市 | |

**5 strokes**

The Chinese placed atop the salesman as he measured a length of **cloth** 巾 a cap bearing the badge of authority 一 to form the kanji 市, meaning either a **central marketplace** or a **full-blown city**, which in ancient days was about the same thing. When used as a word by itself, 市 is pronounced **ICHI** in its meaning **marketplace** and **SHI** in its meaning **city**. In either meaning, it is pronounced **SHI** in compound words. 立川市 **TACHIKAWA-SHI** is the **City of Tachikawa**.

| 219 見 7 strokes | ON READING: **KEN** KUN READINGS: **mi(ru), mi(eru), mi(seru)** *to see* | 見学 **kengaku** *observation* 下見 **shitami** *preview* 見える **mieru** *visible, to see, to appear* 見世物 **misemono** *show* |
| --- | --- | --- |
| | 丨 冂 冃 目 目 貝 見 | |

The element for **person** 人, modified to fit the bottom of the square 儿, was placed below the element for **eye** 目 to form the kanji meaning **see** 見. Used as a word by itself it is pronounced **MI-RU**, **MI-ERU** or **MI-SERU**. In compound words it is pronounced **KEN**. A 見本 **MIHON**, see-original, is **a sample**. 意見 **IKEN**, thought-see, means **opinion**.

Another of the very few instances where an element in one kanji looks exactly like another element in different kanji (previous examples were: 月 for **meat** and **moon**; 少 for **a few** and **the left foot**; and 田 for **rice-paddy** and a **piece of fruit**) is the simplified pictograph for eye 目. It is used both as a kanji by itself and as an element in other kanji. The form of this pictograph 目 is a very generic one, with two vertical lines connected by four horizontal lines. It looks like it could represent almost anything. It is the pictograph the Chinese drew for eye, and is also the simplified pictograph they arrived at for **a nose, a neck, a cabinet, a shell**, and other symbols.

| 220 自 6 strokes | ON READING: **JI, SHI** KUN READING: **mizuka(ra)** *self* | 自由 **jiyū** *freedom* 各自 **kakuji** *each one* 自然 **sizen** *nature* 自ら **mizukara** *oneself* |
| --- | --- | --- |
| | ⼃ 丿 冂 自 自 自 | |

One example is the kanji meaning **self**. The Chinese formed it from a pictograph for nose 𦣹 with a person's finger pointing at the nose ⼃ to indicate that "this is me, myself." They simplified the pictograph first to 𦣹, and drew it in final form 自. The final pictograph of nose looks very much like the pictograph for eye 目, except for the finger pointing to it, and in fact it is written exactly the same as is the pictograph of **eye**, with the same number of strokes, the same stroke order, and the same spacing. The Chinese drew it as a finger pointing to a nose but, if it is easier to remember as a finger pointed to an eye, there is no reason not to do so. In either case, 自 means **self**.

自 is rarely used as a word by itself. When used as a word by itself, it is pronounced **MIZUKA-RA**. In compound words it is pronounced **JI** or **SHI**. The common word for self is 自分 **JIBUN**, self-part. 自信 **JISHIN**, self-trust, means **self-confidence**.

| 221 | ON READING: **SHŪ** | 練習 **renshū** *exercise* |
| | KUN READING: **nara(u)** | 習字 **shūji** *calligraphy* |
| 習 | *to learn* | 習い事 **naraigoto** *culture lesson* |
| | | 習性 **shūsei** *behavior, habit* |
| | ㇆ ㇆ ㋻ ㋻㇀ ㋻㇀ ㋻㇀ ㋻㇀ ㋻㇀ 習 習 | |
| 11 strokes | 習 | |

The Chinese combined the element for **self** 自 with the element for **wings** 羽, symbolizing fly-on-your-own-wings, and formed the character 習, meaning **learn**. They first wrote the kanji with the element for **self** 自 complete, but the two middle lines of 自 too often blurred together because the final kanji was so tall and narrow. They dropped one of the interior lines in self 自 and wrote the final kanji 習. It is pronounced **NARA-U** when used as a word by itself, and pronounced **SHŪ** when used in compound words. A 見習い **MI-NARAI**, see-learn, is an **apprentice**. 学習 **GAKUSHŪ**, study-learn, means **learning**.

| 222 | ON READING: **GU** | 具体的な **gutaiteki na** *specific* |
| | | 道具 **dōgu** *tool* |
| 具 | *utensil, tool* | 具合 **guai** *condition* |
| | | 具材 **guzai** *ingredient, filling* |
| 8 strokes | ｜ 冂 月 月 目 且 具 具 | |

Another example of a kanji containing the simplified pictograph 目 with a meaning other than eye is the kanji meaning **utensil** or **tool**. The Chinese drew a pictograph of a storage cabinet with drawers to hold the utensils or the tools 圓, then simplified it to 目, which looks exactly like an **eye**. They placed the storage cabinet atop a pictograph of a work bench 𠀎, which they later simplified to 𠂉, to make the final form of the kanji 具, meaning **utensil** or **tool**. It is rarely used as a word by itself. In compound words it is pronounced **GU**. A 工具 **KŌGU**, tool-tool, is the generic word for **tool**.

| 223 | KUN READING: **kai** | 貝がら **kaigara** *seashell* |
| | | 貝塚 **kaiduka** *shell heap* |
| 貝 | *shell, shellfish* | 平貝 **tairagai** *fan-mussel* |
| | | ほら貝 **horagai** *trumpet shell* |
| 7 strokes | 丨 冂 冃 月 目 貝 貝 | |

The pictograph for **seashell** or **shellfish** is another example of a kanji using an element that looks just like **eye** 目. It was first drawn by the Chinese 𓆉. They simplified it to 𣎴, and then drew the final form 貝, meaning **shell** or **shellfish**. It is written exactly the same as the kanji for eye, with two shellfish fins added at the bottom. 貝 means **shell** or **shellfish**. In the early days, shells were used for money, so 貝 was extended to mean **money**. When 貝 is used as an element in other kanji, it almost always means **money**. When 貝 is used as a separate kanji, whether as a word by itself or in compound words, it almost always means **shell** or **shellfish**. In all cases, it is pronounced **KAI**.

| 224 | ON READING: **HI** | 費用 **hiyō** *cost, expense* |
| | KUN READING: **tsui(yasu)** | 消費税 **shōhizei** *consumption tax* |
| 費 | *expense, expenditure;* *to spend* | 交通費 **kōtsūhi** *transportation fee* |
| | | 費やす **tsuiyasu** *to spend, to consume* |
| | 一 二 弓 弔 弗 弗 弗 弗 費 費 | |
| 12 strokes | 費 費 | |

The Chinese put a Chinese dollar sign 弗 atop the element for **shell** 貝 to symbolize the idea of expense or expenditure. They squared off the Chinese dollar sign to 弗, and wrote the final kanji 費, meaning **expense** or **expenditure**. Used as a word by itself, usually as a verb, it is pronounced **TSUI-YASU**. Used in compound words it is pronounced **HI**. 学費 GAKUHI, study-expense, are **school fees**. 自費 JIHI, self-expenditure, means **at your own expense**.

| 225 | ON READING: **SAN** | 予算 **yosan** *budget* |
|---|---|---|
| 算 | *to calculate* | 暗算 **anzan** *mental calculation*<br>掛け算 **kakezan** *multiplication*<br>足し算 **tashizan** *addition* |

| ノ | � | ⺅ | ⺭ | 竹 | 竹 | 竹 | 竹 | 笞 | 笞 |
|---|---|---|---|---|---|---|---|---|---|

| 笪 | 笪 | 算 | 算 |
|---|---|---|---|

**14 strokes**

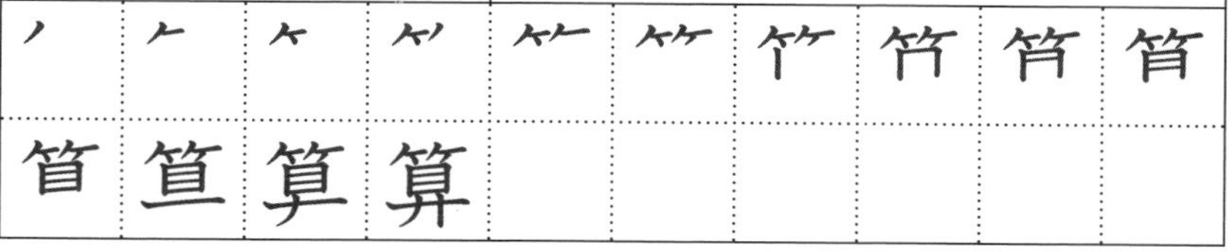

Still another example of a pictograph the Chinese drew which, after being simplified and stylized, looked exactly like their element for **eye** 目, was the pictograph of an abacus ▦. They simplified it first to ▦, then to ▦, and its final form was 目. They put the element for **bamboo** 竹 above the element for abacus 目, since that is what an early abacus was made of, and then at the bottom placed two hands ㄚㄜ, stylized first to ㄚ ㄜ then to ⺽, to operate it. They wrote the final form of the kanji as 算, meaning **to calculate**. It is not used as a word by itself. In compound words it is pronounced **SAN**. 算数 **SANSŪ**, calculate-numbers, means **mathematics**. 計算 **KEISAN**, measure-calculate, means **to calculate**.

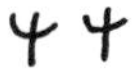

| 226 | ON READING: **SHU**<br>KUN READING: **kubi** | 船首 **senshu** *bow, prow* |
|---|---|---|
| 首 | *neck, head* | 自首 **jishu** *surrender*<br>首飾り **kubikazari** *necklace*<br>足首 **ashikubi** *ankle* |

| ` | ⺀ | ⺷ | 丷 | 产 | 产 | 首 | 首 | 首 |
|---|---|---|---|---|---|---|---|---|

**9 strokes**

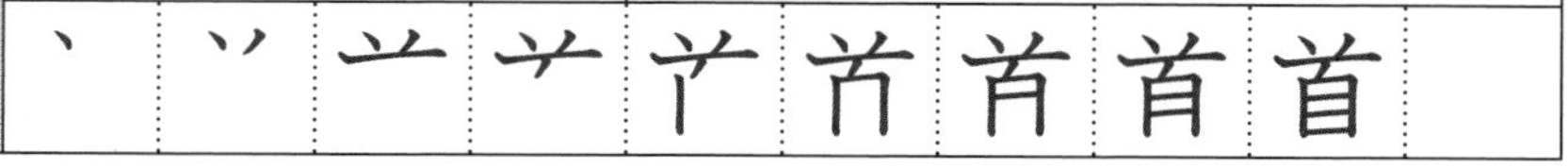

A pictograph of a human head 😊 with hair on top ㄚㄜ was first drawn 😊 to represent a human **head** or **neck**. The Chinese simplified it to 首, and then wrote it in final form 首. It means **head** or **neck**, and was extended to mean **the head of a group or organization**. The part below the hair looks very much like an eye, and is drawn exactly the same as eye, but the Chinese meant it as the picture of a human **head** without the hair. Used as a word by itself, it is pronounced **KUBI**, which is the generic word for **neck**. In compound words it is pronounced **SHU**. 首切り **KUBIKIRI** (written with a kana at the end to represent the grammatical ending of the verb **cut**), head-cut, means **decapitation**. **KUBIKIRI** is also a popular way to say fired from employment. 首府 **SHUFU**, head-government, means **nation's capital**. 首相 **SHUSHŌ**, head-collaborator, means **Prime Minister**.

| 227 | ON READING: **KEN** | 県庁 **kenchō** *prefectural government* |
| --- | --- | --- |
| 県 | *prefecture, state* | 県営 **ken-ei** *prefecture-run*<br>県民 **kenmin** *citizen in a prefecture* |
| 9 strokes | | １　冂　冃　月　目　目　睍　県　県 |

The Chinese drew a pictograph of a head turned upside down hanging from a **tree** 木 to symbolize a severed head hung upside down from a tree as punishment for transgression against authority. They simplified the pictograph to 県, and then drew the final form 県, meaning **Prefecture** or **State**, the seat of political authority. In compound words it is pronounced KEN. 県立 **KENRITSU**, Prefecture-stand, means **Prefecture-operated**, for example, a school or hospital.

| 228 | ON READING: **JI**<br>KUN READING: **mimi** | 中耳炎 **chūjien** *infection of the middle ear* |
| --- | --- | --- |
| 耳 | *ear* | 耳たぶ **mimitabu** *earlobe*<br>耳鳴り **miminari** *buzzing, tinnitus*<br>耳飾り **mimikazari** *earring* |
| 6 strokes | | 一　丆　下　下　耳　耳 |

The Chinese saw a human ear as. They drew the pictograph, then simplified it to, and drew the final form 耳, meaning **ear**. Used as a word by itself it is pronounced **MIMI**. In compound words it is pronounced **JI**. 早耳 **HAYAMIMI**, fast-ears, means **to be in the know**.

| 229 | ON READING: **SEI** | 神聖な **shinsei na** *holy* |
|---|---|---|
| | | 聖火 **seika** *torch* |
| 聖 | *holy, sacred* | 大聖堂 **daiseidō** *cathedral* |
| | | 聖歌 **seika** *carol* |

一　丆　丆　丆　丐　耳　耵　耶　耵　取

13 strokes 耵　聖　聖

They combined the elements for **ear** 耳, **mouth** 口, and **Ruler** 王 to symbolize "from the Ruler's lips to my ears." They wrote the new kanji 聖, meaning **holy** or **sacred**. In compound words it is pronounced **SEI**. 聖書 **SEISHO**, holy-book, is **the bible**. A 聖人 **SEIJIN**, holy-man, is **a saint**.

| 230 | ON READING: **SHU** | 取材 **shuzai** *coverage* |
|---|---|---|
| | KUN READING: **to(ru)** | 取得する **shutoku suru** *to take out* |
| 取 | *to take* | 切り取る **kiritoru** *to crop* |
| | | 頭取 **tōdori** *president* |

一　丆　丆　丆　丐　耳　取　取

8 strokes

To symbolize the meaning **take**, the Chinese drew a pictograph of a hand taking an ear right off an enemy's head ⬚, which was how a battlefield body count was done in the early days. They combined the element for **hand** ψ and the element for **ear** 耳 into a new kanji 取, meaning **take**. Used as a word by itself, it is pronounced **TO-RU**. In compound words it is pronounced **SHU**. 受取る **UKETO-RU**, receive-take, means **to receive**, usually an object as opposed to receiving something like a visit from someone or a knock on the head. 受取り **UKETO-RI** (the noun form of **UKETO-RU**), receive-take, means **a receipt**, as you would get from a restaurant or store.

| 231 | ON READING: **SAI**<br>KUN READING: **motto(mo)**<br><br>*the most, the highest degree* | 最小 **saishō** *minimum*<br>最近 **saikin** *recently, late*<br>最先端 **saisentan** *cutting edge*<br>最も **mottomo** *most* |
|---|---|---|
| 最<br><br>12 strokes | ノ 冂 冂 日 旦 早 早 早 早 冔<br>最 最 | |

The Chinese added the element for **sun** 日 above the element for **take** 取 to symbolize a grasping for the sun, the highest taking of all. They wrote the kanji 最, meaning **the most, the highest degree**. It also translates as **–est**, the grammatical ending indicating superlative. When used by itself as a word, it is pronounced **MOTTO-MO**. In compound words it is pronounced **SAI**. 最大 **SAIDAI**, most-big, means **biggest**. 最古 **SAIKO**, most-old, means **oldest**. 最愛 **SAI-AI**, most-love, means **dearly beloved**.

| 232 | ON READING: **SHI**<br>KUN READING: **ha**<br><br>*tooth, teeth* | 歯医者 **haisha** *dentist*<br>歯ブラシ **haburashi** *toothbrush*<br>歯みがき **hamigaki** *toothpaste;*<br>*brush one's teeth*<br>出っ歯 **deppa** *buckteeth* |
|---|---|---|
| 歯<br><br>12 strokes | ノ 卜 止 止 歩 歩 歩 歩 歩 歩<br>歯 歯 | |

To write the kanji meaning **teeth**, the Chinese drew a picture of a set of teeth inside a mouth beneath a nose 𘉽. They simplified it to 𦥑, and then to 𡲕, meaning **tooth** or **teeth**. Finally, it was simplified to 歯. Used as a word by itself it is pronounced **HA**. In compound words it is pronounced **SHI**. 入歯 **IREBA**, insert-teeth (written with a kana to provide the grammatical ending of "**insert**"), are **dentures**. A 歯科 **SHIKA**, tooth-department, is the **dental wing of a hospital**.

| 233 | ON READING: **BI** <br> KUN READING: **hana** | 耳鼻科 **jibika** *otological* <br> 鼻血 **hanaji** *nose bleeding* <br> 鼻水 **hanamizu** *snivel* <br> 鼻声 **hanagoe** *nasal* |
|---|---|---|
| 鼻 <br><br> 14 strokes | *nose* | |

| ′ | ⺊ | ⼞ | ⼢ | 白 | 自 | 自 | 鳥 | 鳥 | 鳥 |
|---|---|---|---|---|---|---|---|---|---|
| 畠 | 畠 | 鼻 | 鼻 | | | | | | |

The Chinese drew a picture of the full-front view of the nose 𦣻 to mean the
**nose**. They simplified it to 畠, then in final form they drew the kanji 鼻, meaning **nose**. Used as a word by itself it is pronounced **HANA**. In compound words
it is pronounced **BI**. A 鼻音 **BI-ON**, nose-sound, is **a nasal sound**.

| 234 | ON READING: **KŌ** <br> KUN READING: **ōyake** | 公平な **kōhei na** *fair, impartial* <br> 不公平な **fukōhei na** *unfair, unjust* <br> 公園 **kōen** *park* <br> 公開 **kōkai** *publicity* |
|---|---|---|
| 公 <br><br> 4 strokes | *public* | |

| ノ | 八 | 公 | 公 | | | | |
|---|---|---|---|---|---|---|---|

They drew a picture of the side view of a nose 厶 to symbolize the idea of
**private** (not public), **me myself alone**, or **the private self**. They simplified the
pictograph to 厶. It cannot form a kanji alone, however, and must be combined
with other elements to become a character.

The Chinese added the element for **eight** 八 (a pictograph of a vertical line
| divided), which also carries the meaning **split** or **divide**, to the element for
**private** 厶, and formed the kanji 公. This character symbolizes something
split from private, and means **public**. Used as a word by itself it is pronounced
**ŌYAKE**. In compound words it is pronounced **KŌ**. 公立 **KŌRITSU**, public-
standing, means **public-operated**, as in libraries or hospitals. A 公人 **KŌJIN**,
public-person, is a **government-employee** or a **politician**. 公休 **KŌKYŪ**, public-
vacation, means **government non-work days**. 公費 **KŌHI**, public-expense,
means **at public expense**.

| 235 | ON READING: **SHŌ**<br>KUN READING: **matsu** | 青松 **seishō** *pine tree*<br>松本市 **Matsumoto-shi** *Matsumoto City*<br>門松 **kadomatsu** *New Year's ornament*<br>松茸 **matsutake** *pine mushroom* |
|---|---|---|
| 松<br><br>8 strokes | *pine tree* | |
| | 一　十　才　木　杉　松　松　松 | |

The element for **public** 公 was added to the element for **tree** 木 to form the kanji 松, meaning a **public tree**, the tree that is everywhere, the pine tree. Used as a word by itself it is pronounced **MATSU**. Used in compound words, it is pronounced **SHŌ**. 松 is very popular in proper names, where it is almost always pronounced **MATSU**. 小松 **KOMATSU**, small-pine, is the name of a leading Japanese machinery manufacturer. 松下 **MATSUSHITA**, pine-below, is the name of a well-known electrical equipment manufacturer.

| 236 | ON READING: **SHI**<br>KUN READINGS: **watakushi, watashi** | 私語 **shigo** *talking*<br>私生活 **shiseikatsu** *private life*<br>私用 **shiyō** *private business*<br>私事 **watakushigoto** *personal matter* |
|---|---|---|
| 私<br><br>7 strokes | *I, my, me, mine* | |
| | 一　二　千　升　禾　私　私 | |

The pictograph of the side-view of a nose ム, symbolizing the self or private, was combined with the element for **a stalk of grain growing in the field** 禾 to form the kanji 私 meaning "me and my possessions," **private**, in the sense of not public, or **I**, **my**, **me**, or **mine**. Used as a word by itself 私 is pronounced **WATAKUSHI** or **WATASHI**, the most common Japanese word for **I**, **my**, **me**, or **mine**. In compound words it is pronounced **SHI**. 私立 **SHIRITSU**, private-standing, means **private**, as in "private school." 私費 **SHIHI**, private-expenses, means **at your own expense**.

| 237 | ON READING: **WA** | 和服 **wafuku** *Japanese-style clothing, kimono* |
|---|---|---|
| 和 | KUN READINGS: **nago(mu), yawa(ragu)** | 和風 **wafū** *Japanese style* |
| | *peace, harmony; to moderate, to ameliorate, to abate, to lessen; Japanese style* | 平和 **heiwa** *peace* |
| | | 和らぐ **yawaragu** *to ease off, to dull, to moderate* |
| | | 和む **nagomu** *calm* |
| 8 strokes | ノ 二 千 千 禾 禾 和 和 | |

The element for **a stalk of grain** 禾 was combined with the element for **mouth** 口 to symbolize the peace and harmony people feel when they have enough to eat. The Chinese drew the final form 和. Used as a noun, it means **peace** or **harmony**. Used as a verb, it means **to moderate**, **to ameliorate**, **to abate**, or **to lessen**, in other words to make a situation more peaceful and harmonious. When used as a word by itself, generally as a verb, it is pronounced **YAWA-RAGU** or **NAGO-MU**. In compound words it is pronounced **WA**. 和 often means, in compound words, **JAPAN** or **JAPANESE**. 大和 **YAMATO** (a very special pronunciation of both kanji) is an older word for **Japan**. The same two kanji, 大和, pronounced the regular way, **DAIWA**, great-peace, is the name of a well-known Japanese bank. Another well-known bank is 協和 **KYŌWA**, cooperate-in-harmony.

| 238 | ON READING: **SHŪ** | 秋分の日 **shūbun-no-hi** *Autumnal Equinox Day* |
|---|---|---|
| 秋 | KUN READING: **aki** | 晩秋 **banshū** *late autumn* |
| | *autumn* | 秋風 **akikaze** *autumn breeze* |
| | | 秋田県 **Akita-ken** *Akita Prefecture* |
| 9 strokes | ノ 二 千 千 禾 禾 禾ノ 秒 秋 | |

After the harvest, **fire** 火 was added to the remaining stalks of grain 禾 to burn and clear the fields. The Chinese combined these elements into a new composite kanji 秋, meaning **autumn**, which was harvest season. Used as a word by itself it is pronounced **AKI**. In compound words 秋 is pronounced **SHŪ**.

# SECTION SEVEN

## Kanji List

| | | | | | |
|---|---|---|---|---|---|
| 239 兄 | 240 税 | 241 説 | 242 競 | 243 険 | 244 保 |
| 245 厄 | 246 危 | 247 回 | 248 同 | 249 尚 | 250 常 |
| 251 堂 | 252 高 | 253 宮 | 254 党 | 255 車 | 256 庫 |
| 257 転 | 258 軍 | 259 運 | 260 送 | 261 用 | 262 通 |
| 263 道 | 264 雨 | 265 傘 | 266 雪 | 267 申 | 268 神 |
| 269 電 | 270 汽 | 271 気 | 272 周 | 273 週 | 274 干 |
| 275 刊 | 276 舟 | 277 船 | 278 机 | 279 航 | |

| 239 | ON READINGS: **KEI, KYŌ** | 父兄 **fukei** *guardian* |
| | KUN READING: **ani** | 義兄 **gikei** *brother-in-law* |
| 兄 | *elder brother* | 兄弟 **kyōdai** *brother* |
| | | 兄さん **ni'isan** *one's elder brother* |
| 5 strokes | ㇓ 丆 口 尸 兄 | |

The Chinese drew a pictograph of a man with a big mouth 兄 to symbolize the meaning "elder brother." They simplified the pictograph and drew the final form 兄, meaning **elder brother**. Used as a word by itself it is pronounced **ANI**. Used in compound words it is pronounced **KEI** or **KYŌ**.

| 240 | ON READING: **ZEI** | 税金 **zeikin** *tax* |
| | | 免税 **menzei** *duty free* |
| 税 | *taxes* | 印税 **inzei** *royalty* |
| | | 節税 **setsuzei** *tax saving* |
| | 一 二 千 千 禾 禾 禾' 禾' 秒 秒 | |
| 12 strokes | 秒 税 | |

The Chinese added horns ゛to the element for **elder brother** 兄 to make him a real "big brother" 兑. Then they combined this element 兑 with the element for a **stalk of grain** 禾 to symbolize the grain you pay to big brother in taxes. They wrote the final kanji form as 税, meaning **taxes**. Used either as a word by itself or in compound words it is pronounced **ZEI**. 税関 **ZEIKAN**, tax-barrier, means **a customs house**. 国税 **KOKUZEI**, country-tax, means **national taxes**.

| 241 | ON READINGS: **SETSU, ZEI**<br>KUN READING: **to(ku)** | 演説 **enzetsu** *speech*<br>遊説 **yūzei** *campaign*<br>説得 **settoku** *persuasion* |
|---|---|---|
| 説 | *opinion, theory; to preach, to explain* | 説く **toku** *to preach, to teach*<br>説教 **sekkyō** *preach* |

| ` | 二 | 三 | 言 | 言 | 言 | 言 | 言 | 言′ | 訂′ |
|---|---|---|---|---|---|---|---|---|---|
| **14 strokes** 訳 | 詋 | 訝 | 説 | | | | | | |

The same **big brother with horns** 兄 was combined with the element for **say** 言 to form a composite kanji 説 meaning **an opinion** or **a theory** as a noun, and meaning **to preach** or **to explain** as a verb. 説 is pronounced **TO-KU** by itself and **SETSU** or **ZEI** in compound words. 説明 **SETSUMEI**, explain-clear, means **explanation**. A 説明書 **SETSUMEISHO**, explain-clear-writing, is **an instruction manual**. A 小説 **SHŌSETSU**, small-explain, is a **novel**. A 学説 **GAKUSETSU**, learn-theory, is a **theory**.

| 242 | ON READINGS: **KYŌ, KEI**<br>KUN READINGS: **se(ru), kiso(u)** | 競馬 **keiba** *horse racing*<br>徒競走 **tokyōsō** *foot race* |
|---|---|---|
| 競 | *to compete* | 競る **seru** *to bid*<br>競う **kisou** *to compete* |

| ヽ | 亠 | 宁 | 立 | 立 | 产 | 音 | 音 | 产 | 竞 |
|---|---|---|---|---|---|---|---|---|---|
| **20 strokes** 竞′ | 竟 | 竞 | 竞 | 競 | 競 | 競 | 競 | 競 | 競 |

The Chinese took the element for **elder brother** 兄 and doubled it to make two **elder brothers** 兄兄. Then added **stand** 立立 to each to pit them one against the other to form the composite kanji 競 meaning **to compete**. Used as a word by itself 競 is pronounced **SE-RU** or **KISO-U**. In compound words it is pronounced **KYŌ** or **KEI**. 競争 **KYŌSO**, compete-struggle, means **competition**.

| 243 | ON READING: **KEN** KUN READING: **kewa(shi'i)** | 危険 **kiken** *dangerous* 健康保険 **kenkō hoken** *health insurance* 生命保険 **seimei hoken** *life insurance* 険しい **kewashi'i** *hard, steep, rough* |
|---|---|---|
| 険 | *risky, steep, dangerous* | |
| 11 strokes | ⁷ ³ ß ß' ß˄ ß˄ ß⋏ ß⋏ ß⋏ 険 険 | |

They added the pictograph of a terraced hillside to the elements of two **elder brothers** 兄兄 talking together under a canopy appraising the condition of the hillside they fear may be sliding down. They first drew the pictograph. They wrote the kanji, and there it stayed for several thousand years until they simplified it again, to 険. The old form is still occasionally seen. Either form means **risky**, **steep**, or **dangerous**. Used as a word by itself, 険 is pronounced **KEWA-SHI'I**. In compound words it is pronounced **KEN**.

| 244 | ON READING: **HO** KUN READING: **tamo(tsu)** | 保存 **hozon** *keeping, save* 保安 **hoan** *security* 保留 **horyū** *suspension, deferment* 保つ **tamotsu** *to keep* |
|---|---|---|
| 保 | *to preserve, to maintain, to protect, to keep* | |
| 9 strokes | ノ イ イ' 伊 伊 但 保 保 保 | |

To symbolize the idea of maintaining something in its original condition and protecting it to let it grow and prosper, the Chinese drew a pictograph of a baby, still in swaddling clothes, strapped to a wooden board carried on the back of a **person** 人 who protects the baby. The pictograph was first drawn, then simplified to, and finally to 保. It means **preserve**, **maintain**, or **protect**. Used as a word by itself, it is pronounced **TAMO-TSU**. Used in compound words it is pronounced **HO**. 保険 **HOKEN**, protect-risk, means **insurance**. 保険証 **HOKENSHŌ**, protect-risk-proof, means **insurance card**. 保証人 **HOSHŌNIN**, protect-proof-person, means a **guarantor**. 保証書 **HOSHŌSHO**, protect-proof-writing, means a **product-warranty card**.

| 245 厄 4 strokes | ON READING: **YAKU** / bad luck, misfortune, disaster | 厄年 **yakudoshi** *unlucky/critical year* <br> 災厄 **saiyaku** *disaster* <br> 厄除け **yakuyoke** *against evils* |
|---|---|---|

一 厂 厂 厄

The Chinese drew a pictograph of a cliff ∫ with a person who had fallen off it lying twisted on the ground below ⺆. They simplified it to ⺆, then drew the final character 厄. It means **bad luck**, **misfortune**, or **disaster**. Used either by itself or in compound words it is pronounced **YAKU**. A 厄日 **YAKUBI**, misfortune-day, is an **unlucky day**.

| 246 危 6 strokes | ON READING: **KI** <br> KUN READINGS: **abu(nai)**, **aya(ui)** / dangerous | 危害 **kigai** *harm* <br> 危機 **kiki** *pinch, crisis* <br> 危ない **abunai** *dangerous* <br> 危うい **ayaui** *fragile, risky* |
|---|---|---|

ノ ク ⺈ 产 产 危

Atop the element for **misfortune** 厄 the Chinese added a man peering over the edge of the cliff looking for his friend who had fallen off and is lying twisted on the ground below. They drew the final form 危, meaning **dangerous**. Used as a word by itself it is pronounced **ABU-NAI** or **AYA-UI**. In compound words it is pronounced **KI**. This kanji appears on all trucks carrying dangerous cargo, sometimes alone and sometimes in a compound word that shows what type of dangerous cargo it is. It also appears on signs marking danger zones you should avoid. 危険 **KIKEN**, dangerous-risky, means **danger**.

| 247 回 6 strokes | ON READING: **KAI** <br> KUN READINGS: **mawa(su)**, **mawa(ru)** / to rotate, to revolve, to go around, to circulate | 回転 **kaiten** *rotation, spinning* <br> 次回 **jikai** *next time* <br> 回り道 **mawarimichi** *roundabout* <br> 手回し式 **temawashi shiki** *wind-up type* |
|---|---|---|

丨 冂 冂 冋 冋 回

A pictograph of swirling water in a whirlpool (ⓔ) was drawn to symbolize the idea of going round and round. The Chinese first simplified it to ⓞ, then squared it off to fit the square and wrote the final kanji 回. It means **to rotate** or **revolve**, **to go around**, or **circulate**. It is used by itself mainly as a verb, pronounced **MAWARU** (intransitive) or **MAWA-SU** (transitive). In compound words it is pronounced **KAI**. 二回 **NIKAI**, two-rotations, means **two times**, or **second inning**, or **second round**, depending on the context. 回路 **KAIRO**, circulate-road, means **electric circuit**. 三回目 **SANKAIME**, three-times-ordinal, means the **third time**.

| 248 | ON READING: **DŌ** | 同情する **dōjō suru** *to feel sympathy, to pity* |
|---|---|---|
| 同 | *same* | 混同 **kondō** *confusion*<br>同じ **onaji** *same*<br>同い年 **onaidoshi** *same age* |
| 6 strokes | 丨 冂 冃 冋 同 同 | |

The Chinese put the elements for **one** 一 and **mouth** 口 inside a house 冂 to symbolize the idea that all inside the house have one voice and all speak the same. They wrote the final kanji 同, meaning **same**. Used as a word by itself, 同 is pronounced **ONA-JI**. In compound words it is pronounced **DŌ**. 同時 **DŌJI**, same-time, means **the same time**, as in "they both arrived at the same time."

| 249 | ON READING: **SHŌ**<br>KUN READING: **NAO** | 尚早 **shōsō** *early stage*<br>和尚 **oshō, wajō** *Buddhist saint*<br>高尚な **kōshō na** *lofty, magnificent* |
|---|---|---|
| 尚 | *further, furthermore, still more* | |
| 8 strokes | 丿 丶丿 丷 丷 尚 尚 尚 尚 | |

A pictograph of a tall building 冏 with smoke rising higher and higher from the roof 丷 symbolized the idea of further and further. The Chinese wrote the final kanji 尚, meaning **further**, **furthermore**, **still more** (or **still less**). It is used mainly as a word by itself, pronounced **NAO**. In compound words it is pronounced **SHŌ.** It is also used as an element in other kanji.

| 250 | ON READING: **JŌ**<br>KUN READINGS: **tsune, toko** | 常備 **jōbi** *regular stock*<br>通常 **tsūjō** *commonly, usually* |
|---|---|---|
| 常<br><br>11 strokes | *always, usual* | 常に **toko ni** *always, every time*<br>常夏 **tokonatsu** *everlasting summer* |

| 丶 | 丷 | 丷 | 丷 | 丷 | 丷 | 尚 | 尚 | 常 | 常 |
|---|---|---|---|---|---|---|---|---|---|
| 常 | | | | | | | | | |

The Chinese added the element for **further** 尚 to the element for **cloth** 巾 to symbolize a thread forever unraveling from the cloth and going further and further, ad infinitum. They wrote the new kanji 常, meaning **always** or **usual**. Used by itself, it is pronounced **TSUNE** or **TOKO**. In compound words it is pronounced **JŌ**. 日常 **NICHIJŌ**, day-always, means **daily**. 非常 **HIJŌ**, non-usual, means **emergency**.

| 251 | ON READING: **DŌ** | 堂々と **dōdō to** *nobly, sonorously*<br>礼拝堂 **reihaidō, raihaidō** *chapel* |
|---|---|---|
| 堂<br><br>11 strokes | *hall, building (temple, chapel, etc.)* | 講堂 **kōdō** *hall*<br>議事堂 **gijidō** *congress hall* |

| 丶 | 丷 | 丷 | 丷 | 丷 | 丷 | 尚 | 尚 | 堂 | 堂 |
|---|---|---|---|---|---|---|---|---|---|
| 堂 | | | | | | | | | |

They put the pictograph of a tall building with smoke rising higher and higher 尚 atop the element for a mound of **ground** 土 to make the building look even higher and wrote a new kanji 堂, meaning **a high and stately building**. It usually refers to an important building or a temple or a great hall. It is not used as a word by itself. In compound words it is pronounced **DŌ**. A 食堂 **SHOKUDŌ**, eat-building, is **a dining hall**. A 聖堂 **SEIDŌ**, holy-building, is a **temple**, **church**, or **holy sanctuary**.

| 252 高 10 strokes | ON READING: **KŌ** KUN READINGS: **taka(i), taka, taka(maru), taka(meru)** *tall, high, expensive* | 高級 **kōkyū** *luxury, premium* 売上高 **uriagedaka** *sales, proceeds* 高まる **takamaru** *to increase* 高める **takameru** *to be increased* |
|---|---|---|

` 　一　广　宀　古　户　高　高　高　高

A pictograph of a tall building with a royal roof 髙 symbolized tall or high. The Chinese simplified the pictograph to 髙, then drew the final form 高, meaning **tall** or **high**. Used as a word by itself, generally as an adjective, it is pronounced **TAKA-I, TAKA, TAKA-MARU** or **TAKA-MERU**. Used in compound words it is pronounced **KŌ**. 最高 **SAIKŌ**, most-tall, means **the tallest** or **the highest**. A 高校生 **KŌKŌSEI**, high-school-student, is **a high-school student**. 高知県 **KŌCHIKEN**, lofty-wisdom-prefecture, is the name of Kōchi Prefecture on the island of Shikoku.

| 253 宮 10 strokes | ON READING: **KYŪ, GŪ** KUN READING: **miya** *palace, temple, shrine* | 宮殿 **kyūden** *palace* 宮廷 **kyūtei** *court* 神宮 **jingū** *shrine* 宮城県 **miyagi-ken** *Miyagi Prefecture* |
|---|---|---|

` 　丶　宀　宀　宀　宀　宀　宀　宮　宮

The Chinese drew a pictograph of a palace or a temple 宮 showing several buildings in a courtyard. They simplified it to 宮, then wrote the final form 宮, meaning **a palace**, **temple**, or **shrine**. Used as a word by itself it is pronounced **MIYA**. Used in compound words it is pronounced **KYŪ** or **GŪ**. 宮中 **KYŪCHŪ**, palace-inside, is **the Court**. 大宮 **ŌMIYA**, great-shrine, is the name of a district in Saitama Prefecture.

| 254 党 10 strokes | ON READING: **TŌ** | 悪党 **akutō** *bad guys* |
| | *faction, party (political), bloc, caucus* | 甘党 **amatō** *a sweet tooth* |
| | | 保守党 **hoshutō** *conservative party* |

| ` | ` | ` | ` | ` | ` | ` | ` | ` | ` |
|---|---|---|---|---|---|---|---|---|---|
| ⼀ | ⼁ | ⼂ | ⼃ | ⼄ | ⼅ | ⼆ | ⼇ | ⼈ | 党 |

Inside the element for **tall building** 尚 the Chinese put a **person** 人, modified to 儿 to fit the bottom of the square, to symbolize a like-minded group of people assembling to collaborate with each other toward an end. They wrote the new kanji 党, meaning **faction** or **bloc** or **caucus** or **cabal**. Used by itself or in compound words it is pronounced **TŌ**. A 政党 **SEITŌ**, government-faction, means **political party**. The 党首 **TŌSHU**, faction-head, is the **party or faction chief**.

| 255 車 7 strokes | ON READING: **SHA** KUN READING: **kuruma** | 車輪 **sharin** *wheel* |
| | | 車庫 **shako** *garage* |
| | *car, cart* | 電車 **densha** *train* |
| | | 歯車 **haguruma** *gear wheel* |

| 一 | 厂 | 冂 | 戸 | 百 | 亘 | 車 |
|---|---|---|---|---|---|---|

The pictograph for car or cart was simplified to 車 and then squared off to the final form 車, meaning **car** or **cart**. It is used also as an element in other kanji, where it brings the meaning of a wheeled-vehicle of any type. Used as a word by itself it is pronounced **KURUMA**. In compound words it is pronounced **SHA**. A 人力車 **JINRIKISHA**, man-powered-vehicle, is a **rickshaw**. A 車体 **SHATAI**, car-body, is **a car body** or **chassis**. 自動車税 **JIDŌSHAZEI**, car-tax, means **vehicle tax**.

| 256 庫 10 strokes | ON READING: **KO** | 倉庫 **sōko** *warehouse, storehouse* |
| | | 文庫本 **bunkobon** *paperback edition* |
| | *storage shed, storehouse* | 金庫 **kinko** *cashbox, safe* |

| ` | 亠 | 广 | 广 | 庐 | 庐 | 庐 | 盲 | 庫 |
|---|---|---|---|---|---|---|---|---|

The Chinese drew a pictograph of a shed or lean-to 厂 and put the element for **car** or **cart** 車 inside for storage. They drew the final kanji 庫, meaning **storage**

**shed** or **storehouse**. It is not used as a word by itself. In compound words it is pronounced **KO**. A 車庫 **SHAKO**, car-shed, is **a garage**.

| 257 | ON READING: **TEN** | 回転 **kaiten** *turning, spin* |
|---|---|---|
| | KUN READINGS: **koro(bu), koro(garu)** | 運転 **unten** *driving* |
| 転 | | 転ぶ **korobu** *to fall down* |
| | *to tumble, to turn, to roll* | 転がる **korogaru** *to roll over* |
| | 一 | 厂 | 亇 | 亘 | 自 | 亘 | 車 | 車 | 軡 | 転 |
| 11 strokes | 転 | | | | | | | | | |

The element for a **cart** 車 was added to a pictograph containing the element for **two** 二 above the side-view of a nose ム that means **me**, **myself** to symbolize me-myself doing cartwheels, going around twice. The final form of the composite kanji was written 転, meaning **to tumble**, **turn**, or **roll**. Used as a word by itself, generally a verb, it is pronounced **KORO-BU** or **KORO-GARU**. In compound words it is pronounced **TEN**. A 自転車 **JITENSHA**, self-roll-vehicle, is **a bicycle**. 転校 **TENKŌ**, turn-school, means **transfer to a different school**.

| 258 | ON READING: **GUN** | 軍隊 **guntai** *forces, military* |
|---|---|---|
| | | 従軍 **jūgun** *to join an army* |
| 軍 | *armed forces, military* | 将軍 **shōgun** *general, Shogun* |
| | | 軍手 **gunte** *cotton work gloves* |
| | ノ | 冖 | 宀 | 肎 | 肎 | 肎 | 旨 | 亘 | 軍 | |
| 9 strokes | | | | | | | | | | |

An iron bumper 冖 mounted on the element for **cart** 車 symbolized a military armored cart used when circling the wagons for protection. The Chinese drew the final form of the kanji 軍, which at first meant **a military armored vehicle**. It was extended to mean an armored regiment and then to mean the army as a whole. 軍 now means **the armed forces** or **military**. Used either as a word by itself or in compound words it is pronounced **GUN**. A 軍人 **GUNJIN**, military-person, is a **soldier**, **sailor**, **airman**, or **marine**. 空軍 **KŪGUN**, sky-military, means **air force**. Used as an element in other kanji, 軍 brings the original meaning of an armored cart, as used for circling the wagons.

| 259 | ON READING: **UN** | 運動 **undō** *exercise, movement* |
|---|---|---|
| | KUN READING: **hako(bu)** | 幸運 **kōun** *good fortune, good luck* |
| 運 | *to transport, to carry* | 運命 **unmei** *fate, fortune* |
| | | 運ぶ **hakobu** *to transport, to carry* |

| | ' | 一 | 一 | 尸 | 肙 | 肙 | 冒 | 宣 | 軍 | 軍 |
|---|---|---|---|---|---|---|---|---|---|---|
| 12 strokes | 運 | 運 | | | | | | | | |

To symbolize the meaning of movement, generally movement from one location to another, the Chinese combined the element for **go** 行, modified to fit into the left-hand side of the square 彳, with the element for **stop** 止 (which itself is the pictograph of a footprint) into a new pictograph 辵. They simplified this pictograph first to 辵 then to 辶, and drew the final pictograph 辶. This is not used as a kanji by itself but it appears as an element in many other kanji, where it brings the meaning of movement.

For example, the Chinese added the element for **armored cart** 軍 to the element for **movement** 辶 and made the new kanji 運, meaning **transport** or **carry**. Used as a word by itself, usually as a verb, it is pronounced **HAKO-BU**. In compound words it is pronounced **UN**. 運転 **UNTEN**, transport-turn, means **drive**, as in a car. An 運転手 **UNTENSHU**, transport-turn-hand, is a **driver** or **chauffeur**.

| 260 | ON READING: **SŌ** | 送別会 **sōbetsukai** *farewell party* |
|---|---|---|
| | KUN READING: **oku(ru)** | 放送 **hōsō** *broadcasting* |
| 送 | *to send* | 送金 **sōkin** *(cash) transfer, remittance* |
| | | 送る **okuru** *to send, to drive* |

| | ` | ⺍ | ⺍ | 兰 | 关 | 关 | 关 | 送 | 送 |
|---|---|---|---|---|---|---|---|---|---|
| 9 strokes | | | | | | | | | |

To symbolize the idea of shipping something from one place to another, the Chinese drew a pictograph of a road 二 with a barrier across it to control the flow of goods and collect the tolls 关, then added the element that means **movement from one location to another** 辶. The final character became 送, meaning **to send**. Used as a word by itself it is pronounced **OKU-RU**. In compound words it is pronounced **SŌ**. 運送 **UNSŌ**, carry-send, means **transport** or **ship freight** or **move goods**. 送料 **SŌRYŌ**, send-fee, means **shipping charge**. 見送り **MI-OKU-RI** (with the addition of a kana for the grammatical ending of the verb send), see-send, means **to see someone off**.

| 261 | ON READING: **YŌ** | 用意 **yōi** *preparation* |
|---|---|---|
| | KUN READING: **mochi(iru)** | 使用法 **shiyōhō** *usage method,* |
| 用 | | *directions* |
| | *to use, to put to use* | 費用 **hiyō** *cost, expense* |
| | | 用いる **mochi'iru** *to use* |
| 5 strokes | ) 几 月 月 用 | |

To symbolize the meaning **use** or **put to use** or the **use of a thing** for a specific pur-pose, the Chinese drew a pictograph of the fence they used to enclose their land or livestock 冊. They simplified it to ㄁ㄅ, then wrote the final kanji 用. Used as a word by itself, generally a verb, it is pronounced **MOCHI-IRU**. In compound words it is pronounced **YŌ**. 用心 **YŌJIN**, use-heart, means **be careful**, **use cau-tion**, or **watch out for**. 用事 **YŌJI**, use-affair, means **errand** or **business** or **thing to take care of**. 学生用 **GAKUSEIYŌ**, student-use, means **a thing specifically for students to use**, like a special type of student's briefcase. 用品 **YŌHIN**, use-goods, means **articles** or **equipment** or **supplies**, **used for a specific purpose**.

| 262 | ON READING: **TSŪ** | 普通 **futū** *usually, generally* |
|---|---|---|
| | KUN READINGS: **tō(ru)**, | 通り **tōri** *street, lane* |
| 通 | **tō(su), kayo(u)** | 通す **tōsu** *to go through, to run through* |
| | *to go through, to commute* | 通う **kayou** *to commute, to attend* |
| 10 strokes | ㄱ マ 尸 甬 甬 甬 甬 `甬 通 通 | |

The Chinese combined the element for **use** 用, itself a pictograph of a fence, with the element for **sun** 日 into a pictograph showing the sun emerging from below the fence and breaking into the clear 甬. They simplified it first to 甬, and then to 甬. They then wrote the final form 甬, meaning **emerge** or **break clear**. It is not used as a kanji by itself but appears in other kanji, where it brings the meaning of **break clear** or **pass through**.

They put together the element meaning **movement** ⻌ with the element mean-ing **pass through** 甬 to make a new kanji 通 meaning **go through** or **commute**. Used as a word by itself, generally a verb, it is pronounced **TŌ-RU**, **TŌ-SU**, or **KAYO-U**. In compound words it is pronounced **TSŪ**. 通行 **TSŪKŌ**, pass-go, means **go through** or **traffic**. 通行止 **TSŪKŌDOME** (with the addition of a kana for the grammatical ending of the verb "stop"), traffic-stop, means **closed to traffic** or **no thoroughfare**. 大通 **ŌDORI** (with the addition of a kana for the grammatical ending of the verb **go through**), big-go-through, means **main road**.

| 263 | ON READINGS: **DŌ, TŌ**<br>KUN READING: **michi** | 道路 **dōro** *road, way, lane*<br>報道 **hōdō** *news, report*<br>神道 **shintō** *Shinto (religion)*<br>近道 **chikamichi** *shortcut* |
|---|---|---|
| 道 | *way, road* | |
| | 丶 ` 丷 ` 丷 ` ` 产 丷 首 首 首 `道 | |
| 12 strokes | 道 道 | |

They added the element for movement 辶 to the element for **head** or **chief** 首 to symbolize an even bigger main road for traveling on, or a main road or way to advance a philosophy. They wrote the new kanji 道, meaning **an important way**, as in philosophy, or **an important road**, as in a thoroughfare. Used as a word by itself it is pronounced **MICHI**. In compound words it is pronounced **DŌ** or **TŌ**. The 東海道 **TŌKAIDŌ**, east-sea-road, historically the main road between Tokyo and Kyoto, is the subject of many well-known wood-block prints drawn by Japanese artists. 車道 **SHADŌ**, car-road, means **roadway**. 水道 **SUIDŌ**, water-road, means **city waterworks**. 道 is the kanji used for the Chinese philosophy of Taoism, and generally translates as **the Way**.

| 264 | ON READING: **U**<br>KUN READINGS: **ame, ama** | 雨季 **uki** *rainy season*<br>雨降り **amefuri** *rainy weather*<br>雨雲 **amagumo** *rain cloud*<br>雨戸 **amado** *shutter* |
|---|---|---|
| 雨 | *rain* | |
| 8 strokes | 一 厂 厂 币 币 雨 雨 雨 | |

The Chinese pictured rain as raindrops falling from a cloud ☁. They first drew the kanji as 雨, then simplified it to 雨. They wrote the final form as 雨, meaning **rain**. Used as a word by itself it is pronounced **AME**, and occasionally **AMA**. In compound words it is pronounced **U**. 大雨 **ŌAME** means **heavy rain**. 雨天 **UTEN**, rain-sky, means a **rainy day**. 雨具 **AMAGU**, rain-utensils, means **rain gear**.

| 265 | ON READING: **SAN**<br>KUN READING: **kasa** | 傘下 **sanka** *affiliated*<br>落下傘 **rakkasan** *parachute*<br>傘立て **kasatate** *umbrella stand*<br>長傘 **nagakasa** *stick umbrella* |
|---|---|---|
| 傘<br><br>12 strokes | *umbrella* | |

| ノ | 入 | 仌 | 仌 | 仌 | 仌 | 仌 | 仌 | 仌 | 仌 |
|---|---|---|---|---|---|---|---|---|---|
| 傘 | 傘 | | | | | | | | |

They first drew a pictograph of an umbrella 宀 as 个, then added people 仌仌 underneath it. They wrote the final form of the kanji 傘, meaning **umbrella**. Used as a word by itself it is pronounced **KASA**. In compound words it is pronounced **SAN**. 雨傘 **AMAGASA**, rain-umbrella, is an **umbrella for rain**. 日傘 **HIGASA**, sun-umbrella, is an **umbrella for sun** or a **parasol**.

| 266 | ON READING: **SETSU**<br>KUN READING: **yuki** | 降雪 **kōsetsu** *snowfall, downfall*<br>積雪 **sekisetsu** *snow cover*<br>初雪 **hatsuyuki** *first snowfall*<br>雪だるま **yukidaruma** *snowman* |
|---|---|---|
| 雪<br><br>11 strokes | *snow* | |

| 一 | 厂 | 后 | 帀 | 帀 | 帀 | 帀 | 雨 | 雪 | 雪 |
|---|---|---|---|---|---|---|---|---|---|
| 雪 | | | | | | | | | |

The Chinese added a broom ⇒ to the element for rain 雨 to symbolize the **snow**, which can be swept away. They simplified the broom first to ⇒, then to ⇒, and wrote the final kanji 雪. It is now often written with the broom-handle cut off even more 雪. Used as a word by itself it is pronounced **YUKI**. In compound words it is pronounced **SETSU**. 雪国 **YUKIGUNI**, snow-country, means the **north country** where snow piles up for months. 雪見 **YUKIMI**, snow-see, means **a trip to see the snow scenery**.

| 267 | ON READING: **SHIN** | 申告 **shinkoku** *declaration* |
|---|---|---|
| | KUN READING: **mō(su)** | 申請 **shinsei** *application* |
| 申 | *to expound* | 内申書 **naishinsho** *school recommendation* |
| | | 申し出 **mōshide** *offer* |
| 5 strokes | 丨 冂 冃 日 申 | |

A pictograph of a jagged bolt of lightning ⚡ was first drawn ⚡. It was simplified to ⚡, and then to a line hurled toward the earth by the hands of the gods ⚡. The Chinese drew the final kanji, 申, meaning **lightning**, with the extended meaning of **speak like lightning** or **expound**. Used as a word by itself it is pronounced **MŌ-SU**. In compound words 申 is pronounced **SHIN**.

The opening greeting of every Japanese telephone caller, meaning roughly "I have something important to say," is derived from 申す **MŌ-SU**. It is generally written completely in kana, but can also be written 申し申し **MOSHI-MOSHI**.

| 268 | ON READINGS: **SHIN, JIN** | 精神 **seishin** *mind, spirit* |
|---|---|---|
| | KUN READING: **kami** | 神社 **jinja** *shrine* |
| 神 | *God* | 神様 **kamisama** *God* |
| | | 女神 **megami** *Goddess* |
| 9 strokes | ㇒ ㇆ ㇅ ネ ネ 初 初 袙 神 | |

The Chinese drew a pictograph of a sacrificial altar with the sacrifice atop it 示 then simplified it to 示 and squared it off to 示. They placed this pictograph, modified to ネ to fit the kanji square, with the element for the jagged bolt of **lightning** 申 hurled toward the earth by the gods to form a new composite kanji 神 meaning **God**. Used as a word by itself 神 is pronounced **KAMI**. In compound words it is pronounced **SHIN** or **JIN**. A 神宮 **JINGU**, god-shrine, is a **shrine**.

| 269 | ON READING: **DEN** | 電気 **denki** *electricity* |
|---|---|---|
| | | 電報 **denpō** *telegram* |
| | *electricity* | 発電所 **hatsudensho** *power plant* |
| | | 電話番号 **denwabangō** *phone number* |

一 厂 戸 雨 雨 雨 雨 雨 雷 雷

雷 雷 電

13 strokes

The Chinese added the element for **lightning** 申, modified slightly so it would fit the kanji square 电, to the element for **rain** 雨 to symbolize the lightning bolt that comes from clouds and brings electric charges. They wrote the new kanji 電, meaning **electricity**. Used either as a word by itself or in compound words, it is pronounced **DEN**. A 電車 **DENSHA**, electric-car, is a **streetcar** or **trolley**. A 電圧 **DEN-ATSU**, electricity-pressure, is a **volt**. A 電力 **DENRYOKU**, electricity-power, is a **watt**. A 電話 **DENWA**, electricity-talk, is a **telephone**.

| 270 | ON READING: **KI** | 汽船 **kisen** *steamboat, steamship* |
|---|---|---|
| | *steam* | 汽笛 **kiteki** *(air) whistle* |
| | | 汽水 **kisui** *brackish water* |

丶 冫 氵 氵 汸 汽 汽

7 strokes

Their pictograph for vapor was a few ephemeral lines 〰. They simplified the lines to 气, then drew the final form 气. This is not used as a kanji by itself but appears in other kanji with other elements that show what kind of vapor it is. For example, the Chinese added the element for water 氵 and made the new composite kanji 汽, meaning **steam**. Used as either a word by itself or in compound words it is pronounced **KI**. A 汽車 **KISHA**, steam-car, is a **steam train**.

| 271 | ON READINGS: **KI, KE** | 気体 **kehai** *gas* |
| | | 元気 **genki** *cheer, energy* |
| 気 | *spirit, unseen force* | 気配 **kehai** *hint, sign of presence* |
| | | 火の気 **hi-no-ke** *heat of fire* |
| 6 strokes | ノ　ー　ケ　气　気　気 | |

Adding the element for **rice** 米 to the element for **vapor** 气 symbolizes the vapor that rises from cooking rice, the staff of life. The Chinese wrote kanji 氣, meaning **unseen force** or **spirit**. It was recently simplified to 気 by replacing rice with an ✕. Used either as a word by itself or in compound words, it is pronounced either **KI** or **KE**. 気分 **KIBUN**, spirit-part, means **frame of mind**, **feeling**, **mood**. 気持 **KIMOCHI** (written with a kana to show the grammatical ending of **MOTSU**) spirit-have, means **feeling** or **mood**. 天気 **TENKI**, sky-mood, means the **weather**. 電気 **DENKI**, electricity-spirit, means **electric**.

| 272 | ON READING: **SHŪ** | 周囲 **shūi** *circuit, round; to surround* |
| | KUN READING: **mawa(ri)** | 円周 **enshū** *circle, circumference* |
| 周 | *circumference; around* | 周る **mawaru** *to surround* |
| | | 周期 **shūki** *cycle, period* |
| 8 strokes | ノ　几　月　円　用　周　周 | |

The Chinese put the element for **land** 土 with the element for **mouth** 口 (signifying the head of household), and then drew a line around it ⌷ to indicate the perimeter of the land that a head of household needs to feed his family. They wrote the new kanji 周, meaning **circumference** or **around**, as in "gather around me." Used as a word by itself it is pronounced **MAWA-RI**. In compound words it is pronounced **SHŪ**. 一周 **ISSHŪ** (**ICHISHŪ** pronounced euphonically), one-circumference, means **one lap**.

| 273 | ON READING: **SHŪ** | 週刊 **shūkan** *weekly* |
| | | 今週 **konshū** *this week* |
| | *week* | 週休二日 **shūkyū futsuka** *five-day week* |

週

) 丁 几 几 用 用 周 周 `周 调

週

11 strokes

Then they put the element for **movement** 辶 with the element for **around** 周 to symbolize movement around a time cycle, and wrote the new composite kanji 週 meaning **a week**. Used either as a word by itself or in compound words it is pronounced **SHŪ**. 毎週 **MAISHŪ**, every-week, means **every week**. 先週 **SENSHŪ**, precede-week, means **last week**. 週末 **SHŪMATSU**, week-extremity, means **week-end**.

| 274 | ON READING: **KAN** | 若干 **jakkan** *a little bit, a few* |
| | KUN READINGS: **ho(su)**, | 物干し **monohoshi** *drying area* |
| | **hi(ru)** | 干物 **himono** *dried fish (or food)* |
| | *dry* | 潮干狩り **shiohigari** *clam digging* |

干

一 二 干

3 strokes

The Chinese drew a pictograph of a clothesline-pole 干 (which they copied from the pictograph of an ancient weapon 干 used in peacetime as a clothesline-pole) to symbolize drying. They wrote the final form of the kanji as 干, meaning **dry**, referring to drying out anything, food, laundry, or bodies of water. Used as a word by itself, generally as a verb, it is pronounced **HO-SU** or **HI-RU**. In compound words it is pronounced **KAN**. 干菓子 **HIGASHI** (**HI** is the noun form of the verb **to dry**; **GASHI** is **KASHI** pronounced euphonically), dry-cake, means Japanese pastries, sembei, for example, that have been dried to last longer. 干し 肉 **HOSHINIKU** (the syllable **SHI** in the word **HOSHI** is the grammatical part of the verb and is written with a kana), dry-meat, means **dried meat**.

| 275 | ON READING: **KAN** | 朝刊 **chōkan** *morning paper*<br>夕刊 **yūkan** *evening paper* |
| 刊 | *to publish* | 刊行する **kankō suru** *to publish*<br>月刊 **gekkan** *monthly* |
| 5 strokes | 一　二　干　刊　刊 | |

The element for dry 干 was added to the element for sword 刀, modified to 刂 to fit the right side of the square, to symbolize "dry cutting" or engraving a block of wood into a printer's plate. They wrote the final form of the kanji 刊, meaning **to publish**. It is pronounced **KAN**, either as a word by itself or in compound words. 週刊 SHUKAN, week-publish, means **weekly edition**. 日刊 NIKKAN, day-publish, means **daily edition**.

| 276 | ON READING: **SHŪ**<br>KUN READINGS: **fune, funa** | 舟運 **shū-un** *water transport*<br>小舟 **kobune** *boat, small boat* |
| 舟 | *small ship, boat* | 舟遊び **funa-ashobi** *boating*<br>箱舟 **hakobune** *(Noah's) ark* |
| 6 strokes | ′　丿　几　丹　舟　舟 | |

The Chinese drew a pictograph of a boat 𦩘 to write the word boat. They first simplified the pictograph to 𦨉, then to 𠂤, and wrote the final kanji 舟, meaning a **small ship** or **boat**. Used as a word by itself it is pronounced **FUNE** or **FUNA**. In compound words it is pronounced **SHŪ**.

| 277 | ON READING: **SEN**<br>KUN READINGS: **fune, funa** | 乗船 **jōsen** *boarding*<br>大船 **Ōfuna** *Ofuna district (in Kanagawa Prefecture)* |
| 船 | *boat, ship* | 船旅 **funatabi** *trip by boat*<br>船賃 **funachin** *boat fare* |
| 11 strokes | ′　丿　几　丹　舟　舟　舟ノ　舟ハ　舟ハ　船<br>船 | |

The Chinese added a crew of eight, in the shape of the element for **eight** 八 and the element for **mouth** 口, to the element for **boat** 舟 and made a composite kanji 船 meaning **boat** or **ship**, this one referring to a large boat. Used as a word by itself it is also pronounced **FUNE** or **FUNA**, so in spoken language you can call any size boat **FUNE** and you won't be wrong. In compound words 船 is pronounced **SEN**. 船客 **SENKYAKU**, ship-guest, is a **ship's passenger**. A 汽船 **KISEN**, steam-ship, is a **steamship**.

| 278 机 6 strokes | ON READING: **KI** KUN READING: **tsukue** *desk* | 机上の **kijō no** *academic, bookish* 机上論 **kijōron** *desk plan* 文机 **fumizukue** *writing desk* 勉強机 **benkyōzukue** *student desk* |
|---|---|---|
| | 一　十　才　木　机　机 | |

The pictograph for desk was first drawn ⎕, then simplified to ⎕, and drawn in final form 几. It is not a kanji by itself but is used as an element in other kanji, to which it brings the meaning **desk**. For example, the Chinese drew the kanji for the formal word for **desk** by adding the element for **wood** 木 to the element for desk 几 and made the composite kanji 机. Used as a word by itself it is pronounced **TSUKUE**. In compound words 机 is pronounced **KI**.

| 279 航 10 strokes | ON READING: **KŌ** *voyage* | 航空便 **kōkūbin** *airmail* 航路 **kōro** *channel, (sea) course* 欠航 **kekkō** *flight cancellation* |
|---|---|---|
| | ′　丿　丿　丿　舟　舟′　舟′　舟　航 | |

The element for **person** 人, modified to ⼇ to fit the square, was put behind the element for **desk** 几. Then this was added to the element for **ship** 舟 to symbolize the captain of a ship, seated behind his desk in his cabin, setting out on a voyage. The composite kanji was written 航, meaning **voyage**. Used either as a word by itself or in compound words it is pronounced **KŌ**. 航空 **KŌKŪ**, voyage-sky, means **aviation**. 日本航空 **NIHONKŌKŪ**, Nihon-aviation, is Japan Airlines, sometimes abbreviated 日航 **NIKKŌ** (**NICHIKŌ** pronounced euphonically). 航海 **KŌKAI**, voyage-sea, means a **cruise** or **sea voyage**.

# SECTION EIGHT

## Kanji List

| | | | | | |
|---|---|---|---|---|---|
| 280 重 | 281 動 | 282 働 | 283 罪 | 284 買 | 285 売 |
| 286 商 | 287 読 | 288 員 | 289 円 | 290 門 | 291 聞 |
| 292 問 | 293 間 | 294 関 | 295 開 | 296 閉 | 297 戸 |
| 298 是 | 299 頁 | 300 題 | 301 豆 | 302 腐 | 303 頭 |
| 304 馬 | 305 尺 | 306 駅 | 307 駐 | 308 長 | 309 帳 |
| 310 鳥 | 311 島 | 312 西 | 313 煙 | 314 集 | 315 曜 |
| 316 至 | 317 室 | 318 屋 | 319 店 | 320 局 | 321 部 |
| 322 産 | 323 業 | | | | |

| 280 | ON READINGS: **JŪ, CHŌ** | 貴重 **kichō** *valuable, precious* |
| | KUN READINGS: **omo(i), e, kasa(neru)** | 二重 **nijū, futae** *twofold, double; duplex* |
| 重 | *heavy, grave, layered* | 重たい **omotai** *heavy* |
| | | 重ね着 **kasanegi** *layered look* |
| 9 strokes | 一　二　仁　一　一　一　一　一　重 | |

The pictograph the Chinese drew for **heavy** was a man weighed down by a heavy pack on his back 𠂤. They first simplified it to 重 and then to 重, then wrote the final kanji 重. It means **heavy** in weight, and also means **heavy** in burden, **grave**. As a word by itself it is pronounced **OMO-I, E,** or **KASA-NERU**. In compound words it is pronounced **JŪ** or **CHŌ**. 体重 **TAIJŪ**, body-heavy, means **body weight**, as in "how much do you weigh?" 重大 **JŪDAI**, heavy-big, means **serious**. 重力 **JŪRYOKU**, heavy-power, means **gravity**, as in the law of gravity.

| 281 | ON READING: **DŌ** | 動物 **dōbutsu** *animal* |
| | KUN READING: **ugo(ku)** | 活動 **katsudō** *activity, movement* |
| 動 | *to move* | 身動き **miugoki** *motion* |
| | | ゆれ動く **yureugoku** *to sway, to waver* |
| 11 strokes | 一　二　仁　一　一　一　一　重　重　動　動 | |

They placed the element for **heavy** 重 beside the element for **power** or **strength** 力 to form the new kanji 動 symbolizing the application of power to a heavy object, and meaning **to move**. Used as a word by itself it is pronounced **UGO-KU**. In compound words it is pronounced **DŌ**. 自動 **JIDŌ**, self-move, means **automatic**. 自動車 **JIDŌSHA**, automatic-car, means **automobile**. 手動 **SHUDŌ**, hand-move, means **manually operated**. 運動 **UNDŌ**, carry-move, means **movement**, either physical movement, as in exercise, or political and social movements, as in a traffic safety campaign or an anti-nuclear protest.

| 282 | ON READING: **DŌ** <br> KUN READING: **hatara(ku)** | 重労働 **jūrodō** *hard work* <br> 実働時間 **jitsudō jikan** *actual working hours* |
|---|---|---|
| 働 | *work; to work* | 働き者 **hatarakimono** *hard worker* <br> ただ働き **tadabataraki** *to work with no pay* |

| ノ | イ | イ | 仁 | 仁 | 仵 | 佫 | 佫 | 俥 | 俥 |
|---|---|---|---|---|---|---|---|---|---|
| 俥 | 働 | 働 | | | | | | | |

13 strokes

They added the element for **man** 人 to the kanji for **movement** 動 and formed the new composite kanji 働 meaning **work**. Used as a word by itself, generally as a verb, it is pronounced **HATARA-KU**. Used in compound words 働 is pronounced **DŌ**.

| 283 | ON READING: **ZAI** <br> KUN READING: **tsumi** | 犯罪 **hanzai** *crime* <br> 罪悪感 **zaiakukan** *guilt* |
|---|---|---|
| 罪 | *crime, sin* | 罪深い **tsumibukai** *sinful* <br> 罪状 **zaijō** *guilty* |

| 丶 | 冂 | 罒 | 罒 | 罒 | 罪 | 罪 | 罪 | 罪 | 罪 |
|---|---|---|---|---|---|---|---|---|---|
| 罪 | 罪 | 罪 | | | | | | | |

13 strokes

The Chinese drew a pictograph of the net they used to catch things 网, then simplified it first to 网 and then to 罒. They added this to the element for **non-** 非 (which was the pictograph for two wings of the same bird flying off in opposite directions) to symbolize the act of catching in the net the one who does the opposite of what society asks. They wrote the final kanji 罪, meaning **crime** or **sin**. Used as a word by itself it is pronounced **TSUMI**. In compound words it is pronounced **ZAI**. A 罪人 **ZAININ**, crime-person, is a **criminal**. A 重罪 **JŪZAI**, heavy-crime, is a **felony**. 有罪 **YŪZAI**, have-crime, means **guilty**, as found in a court of law. 無罪 **MUZAI**, no-crime, means **not guilty**.

| 284 | ON READING: **BAI** | 買収 **baishū** *buyout, corruption* |
| | KUN READING: **ka(u)** | 売買 **baibai** *marketing, trade* |
| **買** | *to buy* | 買い物 **kaimono** *shopping* |
| | | 買いだめ **kaidame** *hoarding* |

| ヽ | 冖 | 冖 | 冊 | 皿 | 罒 | 罒 | 罒 | 買 | 買 |
|---|---|---|---|---|---|---|---|---|---|
| 買 | 買 | | | | | | | | |

12 strokes

They put the element for **net** ⌐ over the element that signifies **money** 貝 (which is the kanji meaning **seashell**), to symbolize the casting of a net to gather shells and build a stock of money, and made the new kanji 買, meaning **to buy**, which is what you do with money. Used as a word by itself 買 is pronounced **KA-U**. In compound words it is pronounced **BAI**.

| 285 | ON READING: **BAI** | 商売 **shōbai** *business* |
| | KUN READING: **u(ru)** | 売り出し **uridashi** *sale* |
| **売** | *to sell* | 売れ行き **ureyuki** *sales, demand* |
| | | 売り物 **urimono** *articles for sale* |

| 一 | 十 | 士 | 声 | 声 | 声 | 売 |
|---|---|---|---|---|---|---|

7 strokes

To write the kanji meaning **sell**, the Chinese put the element for **to put out** 出 atop the kanji for **buy** 買 to symbolize putting out on display what people want to buy. Without modifying the element **to put out** 出, the new kanji meaning **sell** would be much too tall to fit into a square, however, so the Chinese flattened 出 to 土, then drew the form 賣, meaning sell. This character was simplified further in the last hundred years to 売, but the older form is still seen. Used as a word by itself, it is pronounced **U-RU**. In compound words it is pronounced **BAI**. 売買 **BAIBAI**, buy-sell, means **trade** or **transactions**.

| 286 | ON READING: **SHŌ**<br>KUN READING: **akina(u)**<br><br>*trading, doing business* | 商業 **shōgyō** *commerce, trade*<br>商社 **shōsha** *trading company*<br>商品 **shōhin** *commercial goods, item*<br>商い **akinai** *business* |
|---|---|---|
| 商<br><br>11 strokes | ` 、　　一　　亠　　六　　产　　向　　向　　商　　商 `<br>` 商 ` | |

A pictograph of a merchant opening a box to display his wares 商 symbolized trading or dealing in business. They simplified it first to 商, and then to 商, and wrote the final form 商, meaning **trading** or **doing business**. Used as a word by itself, usually as a verb, it is pronounced **AKINA-U**. In compound words it is pronounced **SHŌ**. A 商人 **SHŌNIN**, trading-person, is a **merchant**. 商売 **SHŌBAI**, trading-sell, means **business**. A 商店街 **SHOTENGAI**, trading-shops-street, is a **shopping market**.

| 287 | ON READINGS: **DOKU, TŌ**<br>KUN READING: **yo(mu)**<br><br>*to read* | 読書 **dokusho** *reading*<br>句読点 **kutōten** *punctuation*<br>読み物 **yomimono** *reading material*<br>読む **yomu** *to read, to divine* |
|---|---|---|
| 読<br><br>14 strokes | ` 、　　二　　三　　言　　言　　言　　訓　　計　　訓 `<br>` 訐　　読　　読　　読 ` | |

The Chinese combined the element for **sell** 売 with the element for **sayings** 言 and formed the new composite kanji 読, meaning **to read**. Used as a word by itself, usually a verb, it is pronounced **YO-MU**. In compound words it is pronounced **DOKU** or **TŌ**. 読売 **YOMI-URI**, read-sell, is the name of a leading Japanese newspaper. 読者 **DOKUSHA**, read-person, means **readers** or **the reading public**.

| 288 | ON READING: **IN** | 満員 **man-in** *crowded* |
| --- | --- | --- |
| 員 | | 定員 **tei'in** *capacity* |
| | *member, employee, staff* | 社員 **sha-in** *employee, staff* |
| | | 委員会 **i'inkai** *commission* |
| 10 strokes | ヽ　冖　口　戸　貝　貝　目　目　員　員 | |

The element for **shell** 貝, in its meaning **money**, was combined with the element for **mouth** 口, indicating persons, open-mouthed and talking, to symbolize the members of an organization discussing money, which is the core issue of many groups. The new kanji was written in final form 員, and means a **member, employee, staff**, or **executive of an organization**. It is pronounced **IN**, whether it is used as a word by itself or used in compound words. A 党員 **TŌ-IN**, party-member, is a **member of a political party**. A 船員 **SEN-IN**, ship-staff, is a **member of a ship's crew**. A 工員 **KŌ-IN**, build-employee, is a **factory worker**.

| 289 | ON READING: **EN** | 円高 **endaka** *high value of the yen* |
| --- | --- | --- |
| 円 | KUN READING: **maru(i)** | 円形 **enkei** *circle, round shape* |
| | *yen, circle, round* | 円み **marumi** *roundness* |
| | | だ円 **daen** *ellipse* |
| 4 strokes | 丨　冂　冂　円 | |

The Chinese placed the element for the staff member talking money 員 on top of a rounded coin ○ to form a new kanji 圓 meaning **yen**, **circle**, or **round** (as in a yen coin). They squared the circle and made the form 圓. This kanji was later replaced by the simplified element 円, which originally was a pictograph of a bank-teller's window 冊. The old form of yen 圓 is also used, particularly on documents and checks, presumably because it is harder to forge or misread than the simplified version. Either version is pronounced **EN**, both when used as a word by itself or in compound words. 十円 **JŪ-EN** is 10 yen. 円 can also be pronounced **MARU-I**, meaning **round**.

| 290 門 8 strokes | ON READING: **MON** KUN READING: **kado** — *gate* | 専門家 **senmonka** *professional* 門限 **mongen** *curfew* 門出 **kadode** *departure* 肛門 **kōmon** *anus* |
|---|---|---|

| | | | | | | | | |
|---|---|---|---|---|---|---|---|---|
| 丨 | 冂 | 冂 | 冂 | 冂 | 門 | 門 | 門 | |

The Chinese drew a pictograph of a swinging gate 門 and, without much simplification, drew the final kanji 門, meaning **gate**. Used as a word by itself it is pronounced **MON** or **KADO**. In compound words it is pronounced **MON**. A 正門 **SEIMON**, straight-gate, is the **main gate**. A 水門 **SUIMON**, water-gate, is a **sluice gate** or a **floodgate**. A 入門 **NYŪMON**, enter-gate, as a verb means **enter a school**, and as a noun means **a primer** or an **introductory text**.

| 291 聞 14 strokes | ON READINGS: **BUN, MON** KUN READING: **ki(ku)** — *to hear, to ask* | 新聞 **shinbun** *newspaper* 見聞 **kenbun** *knowledge, experience* 前代未聞 **zendaimimon** *unheard of, unprecedented; record-breaking* 聞き違い **kikichigai** *miscommunication* |
|---|---|---|

| | | | | | | | | | |
|---|---|---|---|---|---|---|---|---|---|
| 丨 | 冂 | 冂 | 冂 | 冂 | 門 | 門 | 門 | 門 | 門 |
| 門 | 聞 | 聞 | 聞 | | | | | | |

They put the element for **ear** 耳 at the entry to the **gate** 門, eavesdropping, to form a new kanji 聞 meaning **to hear** or **to ask** (asking so that you may hear the answer). Used as a word by itself, generally as a verb, it is pronounced **KI-KU**. In compound words 聞 is pronounced **BUN** or **MON**.

| 292 | ON READING: **MON** KUN READINGS: **to(u), to(i), ton** | 問題 **mondai** *problem, matter, question* 訪問する **hōmon suru** *to visit* 問い合わせ **toiawase** *inquiry* 問屋 **ton-ya** *wholesaler* |
|---|---|---|
| 問 | *to ask, to inquire* | |
| | 丨 冂 冂 冃 冃 門 門 門 門 問 | |
| 11 strokes | 問 | |

They added the element for **mouth** 口 at the entry to the **gate** 門, speaking, and formed a composite kanji 問 meaning **to ask** or **to inquire**. 問 means **ask** more in the sense of to question or interrogate than in the sense of "please tell me," as the kanji 聞 means. Used as a word by itself, generally as a verb, 問 is pronounced **TO-U**, **TO-I**, or **TON**. In compound words it is pronounced **MON**. 学問 GAKUMON, learn-inquire, means **studies, knowledge, scholarship**.

| 293 | ON READINGS: **KAN, KEN (GEN)** KUN READINGS: **aida, ma** | 中間 **chūkan** *interlevel* 世間 **seken** *public* 間柄 **aidagara** *relation* 間違える **machigaeu** *to mistake; making a mistake* |
|---|---|---|
| 間 | *between (time or space), space* | |
| | 丨 冂 冂 冃 冃 門 門 門 門 間 | |
| 12 strokes | 間 間 | |

The Chinese put the element for **sun** 日 shining through the space between the swinging doors of the **gate** 門 to symbolize the idea of time between or space between. They wrote the new kanji 間, meaning **time or space between**. As a word by itself it is pronounced **AIDA** or **MA**. In compound words it is pronounced **KAN** or **KEN**. 人間 NINGEN (NIN-KEN pronounced euphonically), person-between, means **human being** or **humankind**. 時間 JIKAN, time-between, means **time interval**. 一時間 ICHIJIKAN, one-hour-between, means **one hour**. 中間 CHŪKAN, middle-between, means **midway**.

| 294 | ON READING: **KAN** KUN READING: **seki, kaka(waru)** | 関節 **kansetsu** *joint* 関係 **kankei** *relationship* 関取 **sekitori** *sumo wrestler* |
|---|---|---|
| 関 | *barrier* | 関わる **kakawaru** *to have a relationship* |

| 丨 | 冂 | 冂 | 冃 | 冃' | 門 | 門 | 門 | 門 | 門 |
|---|---|---|---|---|---|---|---|---|---|
| 門 | 門 | 関 | 関 | | | | | | |

14 strokes

They put the element for **barrier** 关 (a pictograph of a road 二 with a barrier 人 across it) in front of the gate 門 to form a new kanji 関 meaning **barrier**. Used as a word by itself it is pronounced **SEKI** or **KAKA-WARU**. In compound words it is pronounced **KAN**. 関東 **KANTŌ**, barrier-east, refers to the **Kanto area**, the Tokyo-Yokohama region, east of the old boundary between Tokyo and Osaka. 税関 **ZEIKAN**, tax-barrier, means a **customs house**. The same two kanji in reverse order, 関税 **KANZEI**, barrier-tax, means the **customs duty you pay**. 大関 **ŌZEKI**, big-barrier, is the **second highest Sumo rank**.

| 295 | ON READING: **KAI** KUN READINGS: **hira(ku), a(ku), a(keru)** | 開始 **kaishi** *to start, to open* 再開 **saikai** *renewal; to restart* 開き戸 **hirakido** *swinging door* |
|---|---|---|
| 開 | *to open* | 開け放し **akehanashi** *opened* |

| 丨 | 冂 | 冂 | 冃 | 冃' | 門 | 門 | 門 | 門 | 門 |
|---|---|---|---|---|---|---|---|---|---|
| 開 | 開 | | | | | | | | |

12 strokes

To the element for **gate** 門, the Chinese added a pictograph of two hands taking down the bar which blocked the gate 𠬞 (simplified first to 廾廾, then to 开) allowing the gate to open. They drew the final kanji 開, meaning **open**. Used as a word by itself, generally a verb, it is pronounced **HIRA-KU**, **A-KU** or **A-KERU**. In compound words it is pronounced **KAI**. 公開 **KŌKAI**, public-open, means **open to the public**. 切開 **SEKKAI** (**SETSU-KAI** pronounced euphonically), cut-open, means **an incision** or **operation**. 開戦 **KAISEN**, open-war, means **to start a war**.

| 296 | ON READING: **HEI** <br> KUN READINGS: **shi(meru),** **to(jiru)** | 閉店 **heiten** *closed* <br> 密閉 **mippei** *seal* <br> 閉じ込める **tojimomeru** *to seal, to keep in, to lock in* <br> 閉め切り **shimekiru** *closing* |
| --- | --- | --- |
| 閉 | *to close* | |

| 丨 | 冂 | 冃 | 冃 | 冃' | 門 | 門 | 門 | 門 | 閉 |
| --- | --- | --- | --- | --- | --- | --- | --- | --- | --- |

11 strokes    閉

To the element for **gate** 門, the Chinese added a pictograph of a bar propped into place and braced 才 to close and block the gate after it was closed. They drew the final form of the kanji 閉, meaning **to close**. Used as a word by itself, generally a verb, it is pronounced **SHI-MERU** or **TO-JIRU**. In compound words it is pronounced **HEI**. 閉口 **HEIKŌ**, close-mouthed, means **speechless, dumbfounded**.

| 297 | ON READING: **KO** <br> KUN READING: **to** | 一戸建 **ikkodate** *single-family house* <br> 戸主 **koshu** *householder* <br> 戸別に **kobetsu ni** *door-to-door* <br> 江戸時代 **Edo jidai** *Edo period* |
| --- | --- | --- |
| 戸 | *door* | |

| 一 | ㄱ | ヨ | 戸 | | | | | | |
| --- | --- | --- | --- | --- | --- | --- | --- | --- | --- |

4 strokes

A pictograph of half a gate 戸 means **door**. There is not much simplification that can be done on this pictograph but the Chinese did make it more aesthetic and wrote the final kanji 戸. Used as a word by itself it is pronounced **TO**. In compound words it is pronounced **KO**. 戸口 **TOGUCHI**, door-opening, is a **doorway**. 戸外 **KOGAI**, door-outside, means **outdoors**.

| 298<br><br>是<br><br>9 strokes | ON READING: **ZE**<br>KUN READING: **kore**<br><br>*right, proper; this* | 是認 **zenin** *approval, endorsement*<br>社是 **shaze** *company creed*<br>国是 **kokuze** *national policy* |
|---|---|---|
| | ㇔ 　 冂 　 冃 　 日 　 旦 　 早 　 昻 　 昻 　 是 | |

The Chinese put the element for the **sun** 日 above the element for **correct and proper** 正, modified slightly to give aesthetic proportion to the square, to form the new kanji 是, symbolizing that the sun is in the heavens and all is right with the world. 是 means **really correct and proper**. It is not often used as a word by itself. When it is, it is pronounced **KORE**. In compound words it is pronounced **ZE**. 是正 **ZESEI**, proper-correct, means **to correct**. 是非 **ZEHI**, proper-opposite, means **at all costs**, or **by any means**.

| 299<br><br>頁<br><br>9 strokes | KUN READING: **pēji**<br><br>*page* | 何頁 **nan pēji** *how many pages* |
|---|---|---|
| | 一 　 ㇐ 　 厂 　 㐅 　 厎 　 百 　 百 　 頁 　 頁 | |

From a pictograph of a head with hair on it ☺, meaning **head** or **neck**, the Chinese drew a kanji 首 meaning **head** or **neck**, as described earlier. They also formed another kanji from the same pictograph of a head, but without the hair this time, and with human legs attached, 頁, to mean just head. It was later extended to mean a **written page**, the head part of a book. 頁 is used rarely as a kanji by itself, and when it is, it only has the extended meaning of a **page**. In this case, it is pronounced **PĒJI**, which is the Japanicized pronunciation of the English word "page." Otherwise, the kanji 頁 is used as an element in other kanji 頭, where it brings the meaning **head**.

| 300 | ON READING: **DAI** | 出題 **shutsudai** *setting a question (for test/exam)* |
| | | 宿題 **shukudai** *homework* |
| 題 | *subject, theme, title* | 課題 **kadai** *challenge, assignment* |
| | | 題材 **daizai** *material, subject* |

| | | | | | | | | | | |
|---|---|---|---|---|---|---|---|---|---|---|
| 丶 | 冂 | 冃 | 日 | 旦 | 早 | 是 | 是 | 是 | 是 | 是 |

| 18 strokes | 是 | 是 | 題 | 題 | 題 | 題 | 題 | 題 | | |

Then the Chinese combined the element for **proper** 是 with the element for **head** (or **page**) 頁 and formed a new kanji 題 meaning **subject** or **theme** or **title**. It is not used as a word by itself. In compound words it is pronounced **DAI**. 話題 **WADAI**, talk-subject, means **the topic of conversation, the talk of the town**. 問題 **MONDAI**, inquire-subject, means **the problem**. A 題名 **DAIMEI**, subject-name, is the **title** of a book or a movie.

| 301 | ON READINGS: **TŌ, ZU** KUN READING: **mame** | 豆腐 **tōfu** *bean curd, tofu* |
| | | 豆苗 **tōmyo** *pea sprouts* |
| 豆 | *beans; very small, miniature* | 枝豆 **edamame** *green soybean* |
| | | 豆本 **mamebon** *miniature book* |

| | | | | | | | |
|---|---|---|---|---|---|---|---|
| 一 | 厂 | 戸 | 豆 | 戸 | 豆 | 豆 | |

| 7 strokes | | | | | | | |

The Chinese drew a pictograph of a covered pot where beans are cooked 豆 to symbolize the beans. They simplified it first to 豆, then wrote the final form 豆, meaning **beans** or **very small** or **miniature**. Used as a word by itself it is pronounced **MAME**. In compound words it is pronounced **TŌ** or **ZU**. 大豆 **DAIZU**, big-beans, are **soybeans**. 小豆 **AZUKI**, small-beans, are **red beans**, the second most popular bean in Japan after soybeans. 豆本 **MAMEHON**, bean-books, are special **miniature books**, less than about 3 inches high and 2 inches wide.

| 302 | ON READING: **FU** KUN READING: **kusa(ru)** *to rot, to decay, to spoil* | 腐心 **fushin** *struggle* 腐敗 **fuhai** *corruption, rot, decay* 腐る **kusaru** *to rot, to decay, to spoil* 腐った **kusatta** *rotten, damaged* |
|---|---|---|
| 腐 14 strokes | `丶 亠 广 广 疒 庐 府 府 府 府 腐 腐 腐 腐` | |

The Chinese combined the element for **government** 府 with the element for **meat** 肉 to symbolize decay or something rotten. They wrote the final form of the kanji 腐 , by extending the walls of the government building 广 down to cover up the rotting meat. As a word by itself, usually a verb, it is pronounced **KUSA-RU**. In compound words it is pronounced **FU**. 腐 means **rot** or **decay** or **spoil**. 豆腐 **TŌFU**, bean-decay, is **tofu, bean curd**.

| 303 | ON READING: **TŌ, ZU** KUN READINGS: **atama, kashira** *head, leader* | 頭部 **tōbu** *head* 頭痛 **zutsū** *headache* 頭金 **atamakin** *deposit, down-payment* 頭文字 **kashiramoji** *capital letter, initials* |
|---|---|---|
| 頭 16 strokes | `一 厂 厅 豆 豆 豆 豆 豆 豆 豆 頭 頭 頭 頭 頭 頭` | |

They combined the element for bean (a slang word for head) 豆, with the element for **head** (without the hair; also used to mean the page of a book) 頁 to form a new kanji 頭 meaning **head**, a human head or a literal head. Used as a word by itself 頭 is pronounced **ATAMA** or **KASHIRA**. In compound words it is pronounced **TŌ** or **ZU**. A 舟頭 **SENTŌ**, ship-head, is a **ship's captain**. A 先頭 **SENTŌ**, precede-head, is the **leader of the pack**.

| 304 | ON READING: **BA** | 乗馬 **jōba** *horse riding* |
| | KUN READINGS: **uma, ma** | 馬小屋 **umagoya** *stable* |
| 馬 | *horse* | 絵馬 **ema** *wooden plaque* |
| | | 河馬 **kaba** *hippopotamus* |
| 10 strokes | | |

| 丨 | 厂 | 𠚤 | 厈 | 軍 | 馬 | 馬 | 馬 | 馬 | 馬 |

The Chinese drew a picture of a horse 🐎 to mean **horse**. They drew the pictograph as mainly mane and legs 🐎, then simplified it to 🐎. They squared it off to make the final form 馬. Used as a word by itself it is pronounced **UMA** or **MA**. In compound words it is pronounced **BA**. A 木馬 **MOKUBA**, wood-horse, is a **wooden horse**. A 回転木馬 **KAITENMOKUBA**, around-revolve-wood-horse, is a **merry-go-round**. 馬力 **BARIKI**, horse-power, is **horsepower**. A 馬車 **BASHA**, horse-car, is a **carriage** or **wagon**. 競馬 **KEIBA**, compete-horse, is a **horse-race**. 竹馬 **TAKE-UMA**, bamboo-horse, are **stilts**.

| 305 | ON READING: **SHAKU** | 尺度 **shakudo** *scale* |
| | | 長尺 **chōjaku** *long (length)* |
| 尺 | *foot (unit of length), scale* | 縮尺 **shukushaku** *reduced scale* |
| 4 strokes | | |

| ⊐ | ⊐ | 尸 | 尺 | |

They drew a pictograph of a man, wearing the headband that workers tie around their heads when they are on the job, leaning on his shovel 🐎, measuring with his foot the width of the path he is clearing. They wrote the final kanji 尺, meaning **foot**, the measurement. It is not used as a word by itself. In compound words it is pronounced **SHAKU**. 一尺 **ISSHAKU** (**ICHI-SHAKU** pronounced euphonically) is **one shaku**, one Japanese foot in length. A Japanese foot is virtually the same as the English foot (six one-thousandths short). A 尺八 **SHAKU-HACHI**, shaku-eight, is a **Japanese flute**. One shaku equals ten sun (the kanji for sun is 寸, indicating the distance between the bottom of a hand and the pulse). The length of the Japanese flute was one shaku, eight sun, hence the name **shakuhachi**.

| 306 | ON READING: **EKI** | 駅長 **ekichō** *station master* |
| | | 駅伝 **ekiden** *long-distance relay* |
| 駅 | *station* | 駅舎 **ekisha** *station building* |
| | | 丨　厂　丌　斤　斤　馬　馬　馬　馬　馬 |
| 14 strokes | | 馬ㄱ　馬ㄱ　馬尸　駅 |

The Chinese put the element for the worker with the headband leaning on the shovel as he cleaned up behind the horses at the stagecoach station 尺, with the element for **horses** 馬 to write the new kanji 駅, meaning the **station**. It now refers to bus or railroad stations. Used either as a word by itself or in compound words it is pronounced **EKI**. An 駅員 **EKI'IN**, station-employee, is an **employee of the station**. 東京駅 **TŌKYŌEKI** is Tokyo Station.

| 307 | ON READING: **CHŪ** | 駐在員 **chūzai'in** *resident officer* |
| | | 駐車場 **chūshajō** *parking lot* |
| 駐 | *to stop, to stay, to reside* | 駐輪場 **chūrinjō** *bicycle-parking lot* |
| | | 丨　厂　丌　斤　斤　馬　馬　馬　馬　馬 |
| 15 strokes | | 馬丶　馬ㄎ　駐丁　駐十　駐 |

They combined the element for **horse** 馬 with the element for **master** 主 (which was the oil lamp, always lit, placed upon the hearth) into a new kanji 駐, meaning **to stop** or **stay** or **reside**. It is not used as a word by itself. In compound words it is pronounced **CHŪ**. 駐車 **CHŪSHA**, stop-car, means **parking**. 駐日 **CHŪNICHI**, reside-Japan, means **resident in Japan**. 駐日大使 **CHUNICHI-TAISHI**, reside-Japan-big-messenger, means **Ambassador to Japan**.

| 308 | ON READING: **CHŌ** | 長所 **chōsho** *good point, advantage* |
|---|---|---|
| 長 | KUN READING: **naga(i)** | 成長 **seichō** *growth, progress* |
| | *long, senior; the boss* | 長さ **nagasa** *length* |
| | | 長崎 **Nagasaki** *Nagasaki (Prefecture)* |
| 8 strokes | 丨 　厂 　F 　F 　⻑ 　長 　長 　長 | |

To symbolize the meaning long, the Chinese drew a pictograph of a long, flowing mane of hair on the head of an old man leaning on a cane 髟. They first simplified the pictograph to cane 髟, and then to 長. The final form of the kanji was 長, meaning **long** or **senior**. By extension, it came to also mean **the boss**. Used as a word by itself, it is pronounced **NAGA-I**. In compound words it is pronounced **CHŌ**. 長女 **CHŌJO**, senior-daughter, is **the eldest daughter**. 校長 **KŌCHŌ**, school-boss, means **principal** or **headmaster**. 学長 **GAKUCHŌ**, education-boss, means **university president** or **chancellor**. 長期 **CHŌKI**, long-term, means **long term** or **a long time**.

| 309 | ON READING: **CHŌ** | 帳面 **chōmen** *notebook* |
|---|---|---|
| 帳 | | 帳消し **chōkeshi** *to cancel; erasing* |
| | *notebook, register* | 台帳 **daichō** *ledger* |
| | 丨　口　巾　忄　忄　忄　忄　帐　帐　帳 | |
| 11 strokes | 帳 | |

They added the element for **long** 長 to the element for **cloth** 巾 to symbolize the long scroll of cloth used by the ancients, since paper hadn't been invented yet, to write down important information. They combined both elements into the new kanji 帳, meaning **notebook** or **register**. Used either as a word by itself or in compound words it is pronounced **CHŌ**. 記帳 **KICHŌ**, write down-register, means **to sign a visitor's register** or **make an entry in a register**. 手帳 **TECHŌ**, hand-notebook, means **small notebook**. 通帳 **TSŪCHŌ**, pass-through-register, means **bankbook**.

| 310 | ON READING: **CHŌ** <br> KUN READING: **tori** | 野鳥 **yachō** *wild bird* <br> 鳥かご **torikago** *bird cage* <br> 鳥居 **tori'i** *tori'i, a Shinto gateway* |
|---|---|---|
| 鳥 | *bird* | |

| ' | イ | 广 | 户 | 户 | 自 | 鳥 | 鳥 | 鳥 | 鳥 |
|---|---|---|---|---|---|---|---|---|---|
| 鳥 | | | | | | | | | |

11 strokes

The Chinese drew a pictograph of a bird 🐦 to mean **a bird**. They simplified it first to 🐦, then to 🐦, and wrote the final kanji 鳥. The four dots at the bottom represent the bird's tail feathers, whereas the four dots at the bottom of the kanji for horse represent the horse's legs, although in both kanji the dots are written the same way. Used as a word by itself, 鳥 is pronounced **TORI**. In compound words it is pronounced **CHŌ**. A 白鳥 **HAKUCHŌ**, white-bird, is **a swan**. A 小鳥 **KOTORI**, small-bird, is a **small bird**. 鳥肉 **TORINIKU**, bird-meat, is **chicken meat**. 一石二鳥 **ISSEKI-NICHŌ**, one-stone-two birds, is the proverb meaning **kill two birds with one stone**.

| 311 | ON READING: **TŌ** <br> KUN READING: **shima** | 半島 **hantō** *peninsula* <br> 列島 **rettō** *archipelago* <br> 島国 **shimaguni** *island country,* <br> *island nation* |
|---|---|---|
| 島 | *island* | |

| ' | イ | 广 | 户 | 户 | 自 | 鳥 | 鳥 | 島 | 島 |
|---|---|---|---|---|---|---|---|---|---|

10 strokes

They put the element for **bird** 鳥 above the element for **mountain** 山 to form a new kanji 嶌, meaning **island**. The Chinese soon decided the character was too tall. They eliminated the bird's tail feathers and re-drew the final kanji as 島. Used as a word by itself or in family names it is pronounced **SHIMA**. In compound words it is pronounced **TŌ**. Some common family names are:

| 中島 | **NAKAJIMA** | Middle-island |
|---|---|---|
| 川島 | **KAWASHIMA** | River-island |
| 松島 | **MATSUSHIMA** | Pine-island |

| 312 | ON READINGS: **SAI, SEI** <br> KUN READING: **nishi** | 東西 **tōzai** *east and west* <br> 西暦 **seireki** *the Christian Era, A.D.,* <br> *Western calendar* <br> 北西 **hokusei** *north and west* <br> 西向き **nishimuki** *westward* |
|---|---|---|
| **西** | *west* | |
| 6 strokes | 一 丆 厂 襾 西 西 | |

A pictograph of a bird returning to its nest ⟨image⟩, as it does at dusk when the sun is setting in the west, meant **west**. The Chinese simplified it first to ⟨image⟩, and then to ⟨image⟩. They wrote the final kanji 西. Used as a word by itself or in family names, it is pronounced **NISHI**. In compound words it is pronounced **SAI** or **SEI**. 関西 **KANSAI**, barrier-west, refers to the **Kansai Area**—the Osaka-Kyoto-Kobe region west of the ancient boundary between Tokyo and Osaka. (Recall that 関東 **KANTŌ**, barrier-east, is the Tokyo-Yokohama area). 西日本 **NISHINIHON**, Japan-west, means **Far-West Japan**. 西口 **NISHIGUCHI**, west-opening, means **west entrance** or **west exit**. Some family names that include the kanji 西 are:

| 西山 | **NISHIYAMA** | West-mountain |
|---|---|---|
| 西林 | **NISHIBAYASHI** | West-woods |
| 中西 | **NAKANISHI** | Mid-west |

| 313 | ON READING: **EN** <br> KUN READINGS: **kemuri,** <br> **kemu(i)** | 煙突 **entosu** *chimney* <br> 喫煙 **kitsuen** *smoking* <br> 煙たい **kemutai** *not feeling* <br> *comfortable* <br> 黒煙 **kokuen** *black smoke* |
|---|---|---|
| **煙** | *smoke* | |
| 13 strokes | 、 ⺍ ⺌ 火 灯 灯 炉 炉 煙 煙 <br> 煙 煙 煙 | |

To symbolize the smoke blown from a fire in the fields by the prevailing winds from the west, the Chinese combined the elements for **fire** 火, **earth** 土, and **west** 西. They wrote the new kanji 煙, meaning **smoke**. Used as a word by itself it is pronounced **KEMURI** or **KEMU-I**. In compound words it is pronounced **EN**. 禁煙 **KIN-EN** means **no smoking**. 煙草 **TABAKO** (a very special pronunciation for both kanji, taken from the English word tobacco; the kanji literally means smoke-grass), means **tobacco**.

| 314 | ON READING: **SHŪ**<br><br>KUN READINGS:<br>**atsu(maru), atsu(meru), tsudo(u)** | 集合 **shūgō** *aggregation, gathering*<br>集まる **atsumaru** *to aggregate, to collect, to get together*<br>人集め **hitoatsume** *to assemble*<br>集い **tsudoi** *meeting, session* |
|---|---|---|
| 集 | *to gather together, to collect* | |
| | ノ　イ　イ'　广　仁　仕　隹　隹　隹　隼 | |
| 12 strokes | 集　集 | |

The Chinese drew another pictograph of bird, this one a short-tailed bird 🐦, to symbolize a bird alighting in a tree. They simplified the bird at ō first to 🐦, and then to 隹, and squared it off to 隹. This bird cannot be used as a character by itself, and has to be combined with other elements to make a kanji.

The Chinese set three of these birds 雥 in a tree 木 to make the kanji 雧, meaning **gather together** or **collect**. After a while, they decided to simplify the character and dropped two of the birds, leaving just one in the tree 集. The meaning and the pronunciation stayed the same. Used as a word by itself, generally as a verb, it is pronounced **ATSU-MARU** (intransitive), **ATSU-MERU** (transitive) or **TSUDO-U**. In compound words 集 is pronounced **SHŪ**. 集中 **SHŪCHŪ**, collect-center, means **concentrate**. 集計 **SHŪKEI**, gather-account, means **make a total of all the costs**.

| 315 | ON READING: **YŌ** | 曜日 **yōbi** *a day of the week*<br>七曜表 **shichiyōhyō** *calendar*<br>日曜大工 **nichiyōdaiku**<br>*do-it-yourself* |
|---|---|---|
| 曜 | *day of the week* | |

| | | | | | | | | | |
|---|---|---|---|---|---|---|---|---|---|
| 丨 | 冂 | 冃 | 日 | 日勹 | 日刁 | 日ヨ | 日彐勹 | 日彐彐 | 日彐彐 |
| 日彐ヨ | 日彐ヨ | 日彐刁 | 日彐刁 | 日彐刄 | 日彐羊 | 日彐隹 | 曜 | | |

18 strokes

The Chinese combined the element for the **short-tailed bird** 隹 with the element for **flying wings** 羽 and the element for **sun** 日, symbolizing the sun flying across the sky, which takes one day, like a bird on the wing. They wrote the new kanji 曜, meaning **day of the week**. It is not used as a word by itself. In compound words it is pronounced **YŌ**. The Japanese names of the days of the week are taken from the names of the seven basic nature symbols: sun, moon, fire, water, wood, gold, and earth. To these symbols are added the kanji 曜, **day of the week**, and then the kanji 日, **day**, to emphasize the day. The days of the week are:

| 日曜日 | **NICHIYŌBI** | Sun-day | Sunday |
|---|---|---|---|
| 月曜日 | **GETSUYŌBI** | Moon-day | Monday |
| 火曜日 | **KAYŌBI** | Fire-day | Tuesday |
| 水曜日 | **SUIYŌBI** | Water-day | Wednesday |
| 木曜日 | **MOKUYŌBI** | Wood-day | Thursday |
| 金曜日 | **KINYŌBI** | Gold-day | Friday |
| 土曜日 | **DOYŌBI** | Earth-day | Saturday |

| 316 | ON READING: **SHI** | 夏至 **geshi** *Summer Solstice* |
| | KUN READING: **ita(ru)** | 冬至 **tōji** *Winter Solstice* |
| 至 | *to reach, to arrive at* | 必至 **hisshi** *unavoidable, inevitable* |
| | | 至る所 **itarutokoro** *everywhere* |
| 6 strokes | 一 乙 云 云 至 至 | |

A pictograph of a bird diving from the sky and reaching the ground, beak first ✸, symbolized the idea of arriving at a goal. The Chinese first simplified the pictograph to ⚉, and then to ⚎. They wrote the final form of the kanji 至. It means **to reach** or **arrive at**, usually referring to a conclusion or opinion. It also means **the way that leads to where you want to go.** It is not a common word but is an element in other useful kanji. Used as a word by itself, usually as a verb, it is pronounced **ITA-RU**. In compound words it is pronounced **SHI**. 至急 **SHIKYŪ**, reach-hurry, means **right away** or **as soon as possible**. 至 will appear on direction signs to indicate where a road leads; 至東京 **ITARU-TŌKYŌ** means **to Tokyo**.

| 317 | ON READING: **SHITSU** | 客室 **kyakushitsu** *guest room* |
| | KUN READING: **muro** | 温室 **onshitsu** *glasshouse* |
| 室 | *room (in a house)* | 教室 **kyōshitsu** *classroom* |
| | | 氷室 **himuro** *ice storage room* |
| 9 strokes | ' 宀 宀 宀 宀 宏 宏 室 室 | |

The element for **arrive** 至 was put under the element for **roof** 宀 to form a new kanji 室, meaning **a room in a house**. It is not used as a word by itself and needs one or two other kanji preceding it to tell what kind of **room** it is. Used as a word by itself it is pronounced **MURO**. In compound words it is pronounced **SHITSU**. A 和室 **WASHITSU**, Japanese-room, is a **Japanese-style room**. A 空室 **KŪSHITSU**, sky-room, is a **vacant room**. 地下室 **CHIKASHITSU**, ground-below-room, means **basement**. 室内 **SHITSUNAI**, means **inside the room**.

| 318 | ON READING: **OKU** | 屋外 **okugai** *outdoors* |
|---|---|---|
| 屋 | KUN READING: **ya** | 家屋 **kaoku** *house* |
| | *shop, building, house* | 屋根 **yane** *roof* |
| 9 strokes | | 花屋 **hana-ya** *flower shop* |

一 コ 尸 尸 尸 居 居 屋 屋

The Chinese combined the element for **arrive** 至 with the element for the worker at the station wearing a headband leaning on his shovel, but this time without the shovel 厂, and formed a new kanji 屋 symbolizing a place where work is done. 屋 means **a shop**, **a building**, or **a house**. Used as a word by itself it is pronounced **YA**. In compound words it is pronounced **OKU**. A tradesman's shop will end with the kanji 屋, preceded by the kanji which show his or her type of trade. A 肉屋 **NIKU-YA**, meat-shop, is a **butcher shop**. A 本屋 **HON-YA**, book-shop, is a **book store**. Many department stores use the kanji 屋 at the end of their name. The 高島屋, **TAKA-SHIMA-YA**, High-island-shop, is a large Department Store in Tokyo. 松阪屋, **MATSU-ZAKA-YA**, Pine-hill-shop, is another. 屋上 **OKUJŌ**, building-above, means **rooftop**.

| 319 | ON READING: **TEN** | 店員 **ten-in** *sales clerk, shop assistant* |
|---|---|---|
| 店 | KUN READING: **mise** | 代理店 **dairiten** *agency* |
| | *shop, store* | 売店 **baiten** *kiosk, newsstand* |
| 8 strokes | | 書店 **shoten** *bookstore* |

丶 亠 广 广 广 店 店 店

Another pictograph the Chinese drew for **shop** or **store** showed a long-nosed clerk standing behind a shop-counter 占 set up under a lean-to 厂. They wrote the final kanji 店. When used as a word by itself it is pronounced **MISE**. In compound words it is pronounced **TEN**. A 書店 **SHOTEN**, writing-shop, is a **book store**. A 本店 **HONTEN**, root-store, is the **main store**, though it looks at first glance as if it should be a book store (by custom a 本屋, **HON-YA**, is a **book store**, and so is a 書店 **SHOTEN**.) A 支店 **SHITEN**, branch-shop, is a **branch store**. 開店時間 **KAITENJIKAN**, open-store-hour, is the **shop opening time**.

| 320 | ON READING: **KYOKU** | 郵便局 **yūbinkyoku** *post office* |
| | | 放送局 **hōsōkyoku** *broadcasting station* |
| 局 | *office, department* | 結局 **kekkyoku** *definitely, in the end* |
| 7 strokes | ｺ ｺ 尸 尽 号 局 局 | |

The Chinese drew a pictograph of a worker wearing a headband, but without his shovel, 尸 standing by the desk in his corner cubicle ｺ in a government building to symbolize a place where official work is done. They wrote the final kanji 局, meaning **an office** or **a department**, usually in a government. It is not used as a word by itself. In compound words 局 is pronounced **KYOKU**.

| 321 | ON READING: **BU** | 全部 **zenbu** *whole, everything* |
| | | 部長 **buchō** *(division) manager* |
| 部 | *part, department, division* | 部門 **bumon** *branch, division* |
| | | 一部 **ichibu** *part* |
| 11 strokes | ' ㆍ ㄎ ㄎ 立 产 音 音 音ㄱ 音彡 部 | |

They put the element meaning **stand** 立 above the element for **a box** or a **circumscribed space** 口 and beside the element for a **terraced hillside village** 阝, and drew a new composite kanji 部, symbolizing a man standing on his part in the hillside village. 部 means **a part,** or **department,** or **devision**. It is not used as a word by itself. In compound words it is pronounced **BU**, with one exception, where it has the special pronunciation **HE**. The exception is the word 部屋 **HEYA**, part-building, which means **a room in a building or a house**. A 本部 **HONBU**, root-part, is **a headquarters**. 部下 **BUKA**, part-below, means **one's subordinates**, who follow orders. 部品 **BUHIN**, part-goods, means **parts**, usually of a machine. 部分 **BUBUN**, part-divide, means **portion**.

| 322 | ON READING: **SAN** | 出産 **shussan** *childbirth, delivery* |
| | KUN READINGS: **u(mu)**, | 産休 **sankyū** *maternity leave* |
| | **u(mareru), ubu** | 産む **umu** *to bear, to deliver* |
| 産 | *to give birth, to produce; naive* | 産な **ubu na** *naive, innocent* |

| | 丶 | 亠 | 产 | 产 | 立 | 产 | 产 | 产 | 产 | 産 |
| 11 strokes | 産 | | | | | | | | | |

The Chinese put the element for giving birth 生 below the element of a cliff 丿 on which a person stands 立 to symbolize a person observing the birth below that produces a new cycle of life. They wrote the new kanji 産, meaning **give birth** or **produce**, of either human beings or products. Used as a word by itself, generally as a verb, it is pronounced **U-MU** (transitive) **U-MARERU** (intransitive) or **UBU**. In compound words it is pronounced **SAN**. 生産 **SEISAN**, birth-produce, means **to produce** or **to manufacture**. A 生産者 **SEISANSHA**, produce-person, is a **manufacturer**. 月産 **GESSAN**, month-produce, is **monthly production**. 名産 **MEISAN**, name-product, is a **famous product**. 不動産 **FUDŌSAN**, un-movable-product, is **real estate**.

| 323 | ON READINGS: **GYŌ, GŌ** | 職業 **shokugyō** *occupation, career* |
| | KUN READING: **waza** | 卒業 **sotsugyō** *graduation* |
| | | 自営業 **jieigyō** *a self-employed* |
| 業 | *profession, occupation* | *business* |
| | | 軽業 **karuwaza** *acrobatics* |

| | 丿 | 丿丿 | 丿丿丿 | 丿丿丿丿 | 业 | 业 | 业 | 业 | 业 | 丵 |
| | 丵 | 丵 | 業 | | | | | | | |
| 13 strokes | | | | | | | | | | |

The Chinese drew a pictograph of a complicated ancient musical instrument made from bells, string, and wooden pegs, difficult to build and play, 丵 to symbolize the work it takes to do something right. They simplified the pictograph to 丵, then added **wood** 木 and wrote the final kanji 業, meaning **a profession** or **an occupation**. Used as a word by itself it is pronounced **WAZA**. In compound words it is pronounced **GYŌ** or **GŌ**. 産業 **SANGYŌ**, produce-occupation, means **an industry**. 開業 **KAIGYŌ**, open-occupation, means **open a business**. A 業者 **GYŌSHA**, profession-person, is a **businessman** or an **industrialist**.

# SECTION NINE

## Kanji List

| | | | | | |
|---|---|---|---|---|---|
| 324 楽 | 325 薬 | 326 牛 | 327 乳 | 328 半 | 329 物 |
| 330 貨 | 331 金 | 332 銀 | 333 座 | 334 園 | 335 特 |
| 336 羊 | 337 洋 | 338 美 | 339 様 | 340 毛 | 341 形 |
| 342 刑 | 343 平 | 344 豚 | 345 家 | 346 安 | 347 案 |
| 348 字 | 349 漢 | 350 魚 | 351 漁 | 352 糸 | 353 係 |
| 354 幾 | 355 機 | 356 戒 | 357 械 | 358 泉 | 359 線 |
| 360 綿 | 361 冬 | 362 終 | 363 氏 | 364 紙 | |

| 324 | ON READINGS: **RAKU, GAKU**<br><br>KUN READINGS: **tano(shi'i), tano(shimu)**<br><br>*music, pleasure* | 楽園 **rakuen** *paradise*<br>楽天家 **rakutenka** *optimist*<br>音楽家 **ongakuka** *musician*<br>楽しみ **tanoshimi** *fun, pleasure*<br>楽勝 **rakusho** *easy victory, runaway* |
|---|---|---|

| 楽 | | ′ | イ | 冂 | 白 | 白 | 白 | 泊 | 泊 | 泊 | 泊 |
|---|---|---|---|---|---|---|---|---|---|---|---|
| | 13 strokes | 楽 | 楽 | 楽 | | | | | | | |

A pictograph of a Chinese drum and cymbal set 🥁, played at all the festivals, symbolized music and pleasure. The Chinese first simplified it to 🥁, then wrote the final form 楽, meaning **music** or **pleasure**. Used as a word by itself, generally meaning **pleasure**, it is pronounced **TANOSHI'I** or **TANO-SHIMU**. In compound words it is pronounced **RAKU** or **GAKU**. 音楽 **ONGAKU**, sound-music, means **music**. 気楽 **KIRAKU**, spirit-pleasure, means **happy-go-lucky** or **carefree**. A 楽器 **GAKKI**, music-utensil, is **a musical instrument**.

| 325 | ON READING: **YAKU**<br><br>KUN READING: **kusuri**<br><br>*medicine, drugs* | 薬剤 **yakuzai** *drug, medicant*<br>薬品 **yakuhin** *drug*<br>飲み薬 **momigusuri** *a medicinal<br>drink, oral medicine*<br>薬指 **kusuriyubi** *ring finger, fourth<br>finger* |
|---|---|---|

| 薬 | | 一 | 十 | 廾 | 艹 | 艹 | 苎 | 苢 | 苢 | 苩 | 苩 |
|---|---|---|---|---|---|---|---|---|---|---|---|
| | 16 strokes | 苩 | 苗 | 薬 | 薬 | 薬 | 薬 | | | | |

The Chinese added the element for plants ⁺⁺ to the element for **pleasure** 楽 to form a new kanji 薬 meaning **medicine** or **drugs**. Used as a word by itself it is pronounced **KUSURI**. Used in compound words it is pronounced **YAKU**. A 薬屋 **KUSURI-YA**, medicine-shop, is **a drugstore**. A 薬局 **YAKKYOKU** (**YAKUKYOKU** pronounced euphonically), medicine-department, is a fancier word for **drugstore**. 火薬 **KAYAKU**, fire-medicine, is **dynamite**.

| 326<br><br>牛<br><br>4 strokes | ON READING: **GYŪ**<br>KUN READING: **ushi**<br><br>*cow, bull* | 牛乳 **gyūnyū** *milk*<br>牛丼 **gyūdon** *a bowl of rice topped with beef*<br>乳牛 **nyūgyū** *dairy cow* |
|---|---|---|
| | ノ  ゝ  ⺧  牛 | |

The kanji for a cow started as a picture of its face 𤘈. The Chinese simplified it first to 𠂒, and then to 牛. The final form was written 牛 and means **cow** or **bull**. As a word by itself it is pronounced **USHI**. In compound words it is pronounced **GYŪ**. A 子牛 **KOUSHI**, child-cow, is **a calf**. 牛肉 **GYŪNIKU**, cow-meat, is **beef**. A 水牛 **SUIGYŪ**, water-cow, is a **water buffalo**.

| 327<br><br>乳<br><br>8 strokes | ON READING: **NYŪ**<br>KUN READINGS: **chichi, chi**<br><br>*milk* | 乳児 **nyūji** *baby, infant*<br>乳液 **nyūeki** *emulsion*<br>乳房 **chibusa** *breasts*<br>母乳 **bonyū** *breast milk* |
|---|---|---|
| | ⺊  ⺅  ⺹  ⺹  孚  孚  孚  乳 | |

The Chinese drew a pictograph of a **hand** 爫 holding a **child** 子 against a **breast** し to form the kanji 乳 meaning **milk**. It is not used as a word by itself. Used as a word by itself it is pronounced **CHICHI** or **CHI**. In compound words it is pronounced **NYŪ**. 牛乳 **GYŪNYŪ**, cow-milk, means **milk**.

| 328<br><br>半<br><br>5 strokes | ON READING: **HAN**<br>KUN READING: **naka(ba)**<br><br>*half* | 半面 **hanmen** *half-faced*<br>大半 **taihan** *large portion, most part*<br>半額 **hangaku** *half price*<br>半ば **nakaba** *half, middle, halfway* |
|---|---|---|
| | 、  ゛  ⺌  半  半 | |

They put the element for **divide** 八 atop the element for **cow** 牛 to symbolize dividing the cow in half. They dropped the horn, leaving 丰, and wrote the final kanji 半, meaning **half**. Used as a word by itself it is pronounced **NAKA-BA**. In compound words it is pronounced **HAN**. 半分 **HANBUN** (usually pronounced **HAMBUN** for euphony), half-part, is the common word for **half**. A 半島 **HANTŌ**, half-island, means a **peninsula**. 十時半 **JŪJIHAN**, ten-hour-half, means **ten-thirty**. 半半 **HANHAN**, half-half, is a colloquialism meaning a **fifty-fifty division**. 半月 **HANGETSU**, half-moon, means a **half-moon**.

| 329 | ON READINGS: **BUTSU, MOTSU**<br><br>KUN READING: **mono** | 人物 **jinbutsu** *character*<br>食物 **shokubutsu** *food*<br>禁物 **kinmotsu** *taboo* |
|---|---|---|
| 物 | *things* | 物足りない **monotarinai**<br>*not enough* |
| 8 strokes | `,  ー  牛  牛  牜  牞  物  物` | |

The element for **cow** 牛 was added to a pictograph of an **elephant** 𓃰 to symbolize the meaning **diverse things**. To make this kanji, they simplified the pictograph for elephant to show just his head with trunk and tusks 勿, and slightly modified the element for cow to 牜. They wrote the final kanji 物, meaning **things**. Used as word by itself, 物 is pronounced **MONO**. In compound words it is pronounced **BUTSU** or **MOTSU**. 品物 **SHINAMONO**, things-things, means **goods** or **articles**, generally those for sale. 物産 **BUSSAN** (**BUTSUSAN** pronounced euphonically), thing-produce, means **products**. 動物 **DŌBUTSU**, move-thing, means **animal**. A 物語 **MONOGATARI**, thing-tell, is **a tale** or **a narrative**. 買物 **KAIMONO**, buy-things, means **shopping**.

| 330 | ON READING: **KA** | 通貨 **tsūka** *currency*<br>金貨 **kinka** *gold coin* |
|---|---|---|
| 貨 | *money, goods* | 雑貨 **zakka** *general merchandise,*<br>*sundry goods* |
| 11 strokes | `ノ  イ  イ  化  化  化  貨  貨  貨  貨`<br>`貨` | |

The element for **change** 化 was added to the element for **shell** 貝 (in its meaning "money") to make the new composite kanji 貨 symbolizing that which can be exchanged for money. The meaning of 貨 is **money** or **goods which are exchanged for money**. It is not used as a word by itself. In compound words it is pronounced **KA**. 貨物 **KAMOTSU**, goods-things, means **freight** or **cargo**. A 貨物船 **KAMOTSUSEN**, goods-things-ship, is a **freighter** or **cargo ship**. 外貨 **GAIKA**, outside-money, means **foreign currency**.

| 331 | ON READINGS: **KIN, KON** | 純金 **junkin** *fine gold* |
| | KUN READINGS: **kane, kana** | 金色 (の) **kin-iro** *gold, (golden)* |
| 金 | *gold, metal, money* | 針金 **harigane** *wire* |
| | | 金具 **kanagu** *clasp* |
| 8 strokes | ノ 人 스 쇼 仐 仐 爺 金 |

The Chinese drew a pictograph of a hill containing a mine strewn with nuggets to symbolize a mine of gold. They simplified it first to 金 and then removed some of the nuggets and wrote the final form 金, meaning **gold** or **metal** or **money**. Used as a word by itself it is pronounced **KANE** or **KANA**. In compound words it is pronounced **KIN** or **KON**. A 金貨 **KINKA**, gold-money, is a **gold coin**. A 金持 **KANEMOCHI**, gold-hold, is a **rich person**. A 金庫 **KINKŌ**, gold-storehouse, is a **SAFE**. 金曜日 **KINYŌBI**, gold-week-day, is **Friday**.

The kanji for most metals are composed of the element 金 in its meaning of **metal** with another element which describes the metal.

| 332 | ON READING: **GIN** | 銀色 **gin-iro** *silver* |
| | | 銀河系 **Gingakei** *the Milky Way* |
| 銀 | *silver* | 銀座 **Ginza** *Ginza district (in Tokyo)* |
| | | 銀製品 **ginseihin** *silverware* |
| | ノ 人 厶 厶 牟 牟 爺 金 釒 釘 |
| 14 strokes | 釘 釘 釘 銀 |

For example, **silver** is a composite of the element 金 and a pictograph of the heating of a substance over a **fire** 火 until it turns white 白. The Chinese simplified the pictograph first to 鎴 and wrote the final form 銀, meaning **silver**. Used as a word by itself it is pronounced **SHIROGANE** (literally "white metal"). In compound words it is pronounced **GIN**. A 銀貨 **GINKA**, silver-money, is a **silver coin**. A 銀行 **GINKŌ**, silver-go, is a **bank**. 水銀 **SUIGIN**, water-silver, is **mercury**.

| 333 | ON READING: **ZA** | 座席 **zaseki** *seat* |
|---|---|---|
| | KUN READING: **suwa(ru)** | 口座 **kōza** *one's account* |
| 座 | *seat; to sit down* | 歌舞伎座 **Kabukiza** *the Kabuki theater (in Tokyo)* |
| 10 strokes | | 座る **suwaru** *to sit down* |

`丶` `亠` `广` `广` `庀` `庀` `庀` `座` `座` `座`

The Chinese drew a pictograph of people 从 seated on the ground 土 under a roof 广 to symbolize sitting or the seat. They wrote the final form 座, meaning **seat** or **sit down** or **have a sit-down meeting**. Used as a word by itself (generally as the verb to **sit down**) it is pronounced **SUWA-RU**. In compound words it is pronounced **ZA**. The 銀座 **GINZA**, silver-seat, is the name of a famous street in Tokyo. 星座 **SEIZA**, star-seat, means a **constellation of stars**, for example Orion. 中座 **CHŪZA**, middle-meeting, means **leave a meeting without an excuse**.

| 334 | ON READING: **EN** | 園芸 **engei** *gardening* |
|---|---|---|
| | KUN READING: **sono** | 学園 **gakuen** *school* |
| 園 | *yard, garden* | 遊園地 **yūenchi** *amusement park* |
| 13 strokes | | 花園 **hanazono** *flower garden* |

`丨` `冂` `冂` `冃` `甲` `閁` `閁` `周` `閁` `閁` `閁` `園` `園`

The Chinese drew a pictograph of a man in mandarin clothes 𡴎 seated on the **ground** 土 in his refuge 囗 to symbolize a garden where one goes for peaceful contemplation. They simplified the pictograph first to 袁, then wrote the final kanji 園, meaning **yard** or **garden**. Used as a word by itself it is pronounced **SONO**. In compound words it is pronounced **EN**. A 公園 **KŌEN**, public-garden, is a **public park**. A 動物園 **DŌBUTSU-EN**, animal-park, is **a zoo**.

| 335 | ON READING: **TOKU** | 特別な **tokubetsu na** *special*<br>特技 **tokugi** *skill* |
|---|---|---|
| 特 | *special* | 独特な **dokutoku na** *unique*<br>特注 **tokuchū** *custom-built* |
| 10 strokes | ノ　ト　キ　牛　牛　牜　牜　牜　特　特 | |

The element for **bull** 牛, modified slightly 牜 to fit into a kanji square was combined with the element for **temple** 寺 to symbolize something special, the same way we say in English "a bull in a china shop." The Chinese wrote the kanji 特, meaning **special**. Used either as a word by itself or in compound words it is pronounced **TOKU**. 特産 **TOKUSAN**, special-produce, is a **specialty product**, generally referring to a product for which a particular geographical area is noted. A 特売 **TOKUBAI**, special-sell, is a **sale at discount prices**. A 特集 **TOKUSHŪ**, special-gather, is a **special edition**, of a newspaper or magazine. 特急 **TOKKYŪ** (**TOKUKYŪ** pronounced euphonically), special-fast, means **special-express train**.

| 336 | ON READING: **YŌ**<br>KUN READING: **hitsuji** | 羊毛 **yōmō** *wool*<br>牧羊犬 **bokuyōken** *sheep dog* |
|---|---|---|
| 羊 | *sheep* | 羊雲 **hitsujigumo** *altocumulus cloud,*<br>*sheep cloud* |
| 6 strokes | 丶　丷　兰　兰　兰　羊 | |

The kanji for a **sheep** also started from a picture of its head 𦍌. The Chinese drew the pictograph 𦍌 then simplified it to 𦍌. They wrote the final kanji 羊, meaning **sheep**. Used as a word by itself it is pronounced **HITSUJI**. In compound words, 羊 is pronounced **YŌ**. A 子羊 **KOHITSUJI**, child-sheep, is a **lamb**. 羊肉 **YŌNIKU**, sheep-meat, is **mutton**.

| 337 | ON READING: **YŌ** | 洋楽 **yōgaku** *western music*<br>洋風 **yōfū** *western style* |
|---|---|---|
| 洋 | *ocean; foreign, western* | 洋食 **yōshoku** *western food* |
| 9 strokes | 丶　丶　氵　氵　氵　沣　洋　洋　洋 | |

Sheep were not native to China and came from "the land across the ocean," so the Chinese drew the kanji for **ocean** by combining the element for **sheep** 羊

with the element for **water** 水, modified to シ to fit the square. They wrote the kanji 洋, meaning **ocean**. It was extended to mean **foreign**, particularly Western, as well. It is not used as a word by itself. In compound words it is pronounced **YŌ**. 西洋 **SEIYŌ**, west-ocean, means **the West**, the Occident. A 西洋人 **SEIYŌJIN**, west-ocean-person, is a **Westerner**. The 大西洋 **TAISEIYŌ**, great-west-ocean, is the **Atlantic Ocean**. 東洋 **TŌYŌ**, east-ocean, means **the East**, the Orient. 洋菓子 **YŌGASHI**, western-pastries, are **Western-style cakes**.

| 338 | ON READING: **BI**<br>KUN READING: **utsuku(shi'i)**<br><br>*beautiful* | 美術館 **bijutsukan** *art museum*<br>賛美歌 **sanbika** *carol*<br>美男子 **bidanshi, binanshi**<br>*good-looking guy* |
|---|---|---|
| 美<br>9 strokes | ` ʼ ⺍ ⺑ 半 𦍌 美 美 美 | |

To express the meaning **beautiful** the Chinese combined the element for **sheep** 羊, which they must have thought were beautiful, with the element for **big** 大 and formed the new kanji 美, meaning **beautiful**. Used as a word by itself it is pronounced **UTSUKU-SHI'I**. In compound words it is pronounced **BI**. A 美人 **BIJIN**, beautiful-person, is a **beautiful woman**.

| 339 | ON READING: **YŌ**<br>KUN READING: **sama**<br><br>*scene, appearance, way, manner, method; condition; (polite suffix) Mr./Ms.* | 様式 **yōshiki** *design, style*<br>様子 **yōsu** *atmosphere, condition*<br>模様 **moyō** *pattern*<br>様々な **samazama na** *various, a lot of* |
|---|---|---|
| 様<br>14 strokes | 一 十 才 木 朾 栟 样 栏 栏 样<br>样 様 様 様 | |

A pictograph of a sheep 羊 grazing under a tree 木 beside a stream 水 symbolized a scene in a pastoral painting. The Chinese combined these elements into a new composite kanji 様 meaning **a scene**, **the appearance**, **the way things are or are done**. It is also a suffix attached to words to express politeness and respect. It is not used as a word by itself. In compound words it is pronounced **SAMA** or **YŌ**. 竹田様 **TAKEDA-SAMA**, is a very polite way of saying Mr./Ms. Takeda. 皆様 **MINA-SAMA**, all-respectfully, means **everyone**. 仕様 **SHIYŌ**, work-way, means **a way to do it**.

| 340 毛 4 strokes | ON READING: **MŌ**<br>KUN READING: **ke**<br><br>*hair, fur* | 毛布 **mōfu** *blanket*<br>毛細管 **mōsaikan** *capillary*<br>毛糸 **keito** *woolen yarn, wool*<br>枝毛 **edage** *split ends (hair)* |
|---|---|---|
| | 一 二 三 毛 | |

A pictograph of a mandarin's wispy beard 𣯿 was the symbol the Chinese drew for hair. They simplified the pictograph to 毛 then wrote the final kanji 毛, meaning **human hair** or **animal fur**. Used as a word by itself it is pronounced **KE**. In compound words it is pronounced **MŌ**. 羊毛 **YŌMŌ**, sheep-hair, means **wool**.

| 341 形 7 strokes | ON READINGS: **KEI, GYŌ**<br>KUN READINGS: **kata,**<br>**katachi**<br><br>*form, pattern, shape* | 形式 **keishiki** *format, form*<br>図形 **zukei** *diagram; graphic*<br>形相 **gyōsō** *(a fierce) look*<br>手形 **tegata** *handprint* |
|---|---|---|
| | 一 二 于 开 开 形 形 | |

The Chinese drew a pictograph showing a wooden frame 井 beside the element for **hair** 毛 (here representing a writing brush made of hair) to symbolize a form or pattern drawn by a person. The element for hair was modified to 彡 to fit the kanji square. The pictograph for frame was simplified to 开, and the final form was written 形, meaning **form** or **pattern** or **shape**. Used as a word by itself it is pronounced **KATA** or **KATACHI**. In compound words it is pronounced **KEI** or **GYŌ**. A 人形, **NINGYŌ**, person-form, is a **doll**. A 形見 **KATAMI**, shape-see, is a **remembrance**, usually very sentimental, of a deceased friend or family member. 円形 **ENKEI**, coin-shape, means **a circle**.

| 342 刑 6 strokes | ON READING: **KEI**<br><br>*punishment* | 刑法 **keihō** *penal code/law*<br>処刑 **shokei** *execution*<br>死刑 **shikei** *death penalty*<br>刑務所 **keimusho** *prison, jail* |
|---|---|---|
| | 一 二 于 开 刑 刑 | |

They took the element for a frame 井 used to hold a prisoner and added the element for a **sword** 刂 to guard him, and formed a new composite kanji symbolizing punishment. They wrote the kanji 刑, meaning **punishment**. It is not used as a word by itself. In compound words it is pronounced **KEI**. 刑期 **KEIKI**, punishment-term, means **prison sentence**. A 刑事 **KEIJI**, punish-event, is a **detective**.

| 343 | ON READINGS: **HEI, BYŌ** <br> KUN READINGS: **taira, hira** | 公平 **kōhei** *fairmindedness* <br> 平凡 **heibon** *common, ordinary* |
|---|---|---|
| 平 | *flat, level, peace* | 平らな **taira na** *even, flat, level* <br> 平社員 **hirashain** *(lowly) employee* |
| 5 strokes | 一　乛　丆　立　平 | |

The Chinese drew a pictograph of a waterweed floating flat upon a pond 𠀐 to symbolize the idea of flat or level. They simplified it to 𠀎, then drew the kanji 平, meaning **flat** or **level**. Used as a word by itself it is pronounced **TAIRA** or **HIRA**. In compound words it is pronounced **HEI** or **BYŌ**. 水平線 **SUIHEI-SEN**, water-level-line, means **horizontal**, or **horizon**, if you are looking out over water. 平等 **BYŌDŌ**, level-class, means **equality**. 平日 **HEIJITSU**, level-day, means **weekday**. 平和 **HEIWA**, level-harmony, means **peace**.

| 344 | ON READING: **TON** <br> KUN READING: **buta** | 養豚 **yōton** *pig farming* <br> 豚カツ **tonkatsu** *pork cutlet* |
|---|---|---|
| 豚 | *pig* | 子豚 **kobuta** *piglet, piggy* <br> 豚汁 **tonjiru, butajiru** *miso soup with pork and vegetables* |
| 11 strokes | 丿 几 几 月 犳 犳 肜 豚 豚 豚 豚 | |

A picture of a **pig** was drawn, then simplified at first and later. The Chinese combined this pictograph with the element for **meat**, modified to fit the square 豕, and wrote the kanji 豚, meaning **pig**. Used as a word by itself it is pronounced **BUTA**. In compound words it is pronounced **TON**. 豚肉 **BUTAN-IKU**, pig-meat, is **pork**.

| 345 家 10 strokes | ON READINGS: **KA, KE** KUN READINGS: **ie, ya** *house* | 家庭 **katei** *household* 家来 **kerai** *servant* 家出 **iede** *runaway* 借家 **shakuya** *rented house* |
| --- | --- | --- |

`丶 宀 宀 宀 宀 宁 宁 家 家 家`

They put the pictograph for pig 豕 under the pictograph for roof ⌒ to make a new kanji 家 meaning **a person's house**, which is where in ancient days the family lived beside their livestock. Used as a word by itself it is pronounced **IE**. In compound words it is pronounced **KA, KE** or **YA**. 家具 **KAGU**, house-utensils, means **furniture**. 大家 **ŌYA**, big-house, means **landlord**.

| 346 安 6 strokes | ON READING: **AN** KUN READING: **yasu(i)** *restfulness, peace; inexpensive* | 安全 **anzen** *safety, security* 安静 **ansei** *rest* 安価 **anka** *cheap price, a low price* 安売り **yasu-uri** *discount, sale* |
| --- | --- | --- |

`丶 丷 宀 宀 安 安`

The Chinese put a **woman** 女 under a **roof** 宀 and drew a new kanji 安 meaning **restfulness** or **peace**. In early China, women controlled the household and the budget so the woman in the house 安 also came to mean **parsimonius**. Used as a word by itself, usually as an adjective meaning **inexpensive**, it is pronounced **YASU-I**. In compound words it is pronounced **AN**. 不安 **FU'AN**, not-restful, means **restless** or **uneasy**. 安心 **ANSHIN**, restful-heart, means **feel relieved, be reassured, be confident**. 安物 **YASUMONO**, inexpensive-goods, means **bargain items**, usually of shoddy quality. 平安 **HEI'AN**, Level-peace, is the name of one of the early Japanese Imperial Dynasties.

| 347 案 10 strokes | ON READING: **AN** *plan, idea* | 新案 **shin'an** *new proposal* 案の定 **an-no-jō** *as expected* 草案 **sōan** *draft, sketch* |
| --- | --- | --- |

`丶 宀 宀 宀 安 安 宰 宰 案 案`

The element for **roof** 宀 was combined with the elements for **woman** 女 and **tree** 木 to symbolize a woman planning her garden. They wrote the kanji 案,

meaning **plan** or **idea**. Used either as a word by itself or in compound words it is pronounced **AN**. A 名案 **MEI'AN**, name-plan, is **a good idea**. 案外 **ANGAI**, plan-outside, means **unexpected**. 案内 **AN'NAI**, plan-inside, means **guide** or **show around**. An 案内書 **AN'NAISHO**, guide-writing, is **a guide-book**.

| 348 字 6 strokes | ON READING: **JI** KUN READING: **aza** *letter, character, symbol* | 字体 **jitai** *character style, font* 文字 **moji** *character, letter* 活字 **katsuji** *printing type* |
|---|---|---|

| ` | ハ | 宀 | 宁 | 宁 | 字 |
|---|---|---|---|---|---|

They put a **child** 子 under a **roof** 宀 to form a new kanji 字 symbolizing a child in a classroom learning his letters. 字 means **letter** or **character** or **a symbol**, like a hieroglyph. Used either as a word by itself or in compound words, it is pronounced **JI**. A 文字 **MOJI**, text-letter, means a **letter of the alphabet**. 字体 **JITAI**, character-body, means **the form of a character**. For example, 學 and 学 are both the same character and both mean **learn**, but the forms of the character are different, one being an abbreviation of the other. 名字 **MYŌJI**, name-character, means a **person's surname**. 十字 **JŪJI**, ten-symbol, means a **cross**. 十字路 **JŪJIRŌ**, cross-road, means **crossroads**. 十字軍 **JŪJIGUN**, Cross-army, means **the Army of the Crusades**.

| 349 漢 13 strokes | ON READING: **KAN** *China, Chinese; man* | 大食漢 **taishokukan** *big eater, gourmand* 漢方薬 **kanpōyaku** *oriental medicine* 漢数字 **kansūji** *Chinese numeral* |
|---|---|---|

| ` | 冫 | 氵 | 汀 | 汁 | 汁 | 泄 | 淸 | 渲 |
|---|---|---|---|---|---|---|---|---|
| 渲 | 漢 | 漢 | | | | | | |

To symbolize the word for China or Chinese, the Chinese combined the elements for **earth** 土, **water** 氵, **plants** 艹 and **person** 人 and grouped them into a kanji centered on the element for **center** 中. They drew the final form 漢, meaning **China** or **Chinese**. Used either as a word by itself or in compound words, it is pronounced **KAN**. A 漢字 **KANJI**, Chinese-character, is a **kanji**. 漢文 **KANBUN**, Chinese-text, means **Chinese classic literature**. 漢詩 **KANSHI**, Chinese-poem, means **Chinese poetry**.

| 350<br><br>魚<br><br>11 strokes | ON READING: **GYO**<br>KUN READINGS: **sakana, uo**<br><br>*fish* | 金魚 **kingyo** *goldfish*<br>魚市場 **uoichiba** *fish market*<br>魚釣り **sakanatsuri** *fishing* |
|---|---|---|
| | ノ　ク　ケ　ク　肏　角　角　角　魚　魚 | |
| | 魚 | |

The Chinese drew a picture of a fish 🐟 to mean a **fish**. They stylized it to 🐟, then wrote the final form 魚. Used as a word by itself it is pronounced **SAKANA** or **UO**. In compound words it is pronounced **GYO**. A 魚屋 **SAKANA-YA**, fish-store, is a **fishmonger**. A 人魚 **NINGYO**, person-fish, is a **mermaid**.

| 351<br><br>漁<br><br>14 strokes | ON READINGS: **GYO, RYŌ**<br><br>*fishing* | 漁村 **gyoson** *fishing village*<br>漁師 **ryōshi** *fisherman*<br>大漁 **tairyō** *good catch* |
|---|---|---|
| | 丶　冫　氵　氵　沪　沪　浀　漁　漁 | |
| | 漁　漁　漁　漁 | |

To distinguish **fishing** from a **fish**, the Chinese put the **fish** 魚 in **water** 氵, and drew the kanji for **fishing** 漁. It is not used as a word by itself. In compound words it is pronounced **GYO** or **RYŌ**. A 漁船 **GYOSEN**, fishing-ship, is a **fishing boat**. 漁業 **GYOGYŌ**, fishing-industry, means **fishery**, or **the fishing industry**.

| 352<br><br>糸<br><br>6 strokes | ON READING: **SHI**<br>KUN READING: **ito**<br><br>*thread* | 綿糸 **menshi** *cotton yarn*<br>製糸 **seishi** *filature, spinning*<br>糸巻き **itomaki** *bobbin, peg* |
|---|---|---|
| | く　幺　幺　糸　糸　糸 | |

The Chinese drew a pictograph of raw silk as it comes out of a cocoon 🧵 to mean a **thread**. They simplified it to 糸, then drew the final kanji 糸. Used as a word by itself, it is pronounced **ITO**. Used in compound words it is pronounced **SHI**. 毛糸 **KE'ITO**, hair-thread, means **woolen yarn**. 生糸 **KI'ITO**, raw-silk, is **raw silk**. 糸口 **ITOGUCHI**, thread-opening, means **a clue** or **the beginning**, **the first step**.

| 353 | ON READING: **KEI** KUN READINGS: **kakari, kaka(ru)** | 係数 **keisū** *coefficient* 係争 **keisō** *disputed, pending* 案内係 **an'naigakari** *attendant* 客室係 **kyakushitsu** *room clerk* 係留 **keiryū** *mooring* |
| --- | --- | --- |
| 係 | *relation; person in charge of* | |
| 9 strokes | ノ　イ　仁　仁　伭　伭　伭　係　係 | |

They combined the element for **thread** 糸 (with a knot tied at the top 系 to indi-cate the tying) with the element for **person** 人 to form the new kanji 係, mean-ing **be tied to**, or **have a relationship with**, or **be in charge of**. Used as a word by itself it is pronounced **KAKARI** or **KAKA-RU**. Used in compound words it is pronounced **KEI**. The 係員 **KAKARI'IN**, in-charge-clerk, is the **person in charge** of the work crew, the business office or other group. 関係 **KANKEI**, barrier-thread, means **connection, relationship**.

| 354 | ON READING: **KI** KUN READING: **iku, iku(ra)** | 幾何学 **kikagaku** *geometry* 幾つ **ikutsu** *how many* 幾ら **ikura** *how much* 幾日 **ikunichi** *how many days* |
| --- | --- | --- |
| 幾 | *how many, how much* | |
| 12 strokes | く　乞　幺　幺ぐ　幺ら　幺幺　丝　华　华　幾 幾　幾 | |

To protect silk thread production, developed in China over 5,000 years ago, from foreign competition the Chinese closely controlled the secret of raising silk-worms. The authorities sent armed guards to everyone in the silkworm trade to ask how many silkworms each farmer had. To draw the pictograph meaning **how many**, the Chinese scholars drew a scene by taking the element for **silk thread** 糸 and doubling it 絲, then modifying it to fit into the kanji square by remov-ing the stems 丝, then adding at the bottom right a broad-bladed halberd 戈, the weapon carried by the guards, and confronting the silkworm grower represented by the element for **person** 人 at the bottom left. The scholars wrote the new kanji 幾, meaning **how many** or **how much**. As a word by itself, it is pronounced **IKU**, meaning **how many**, or 幾ら **IKU-RA**, meaning **how much** (either pro-nunciation requires a kana to show the correct ending). In compound words it is pronounced **KI**.

| 355 | ON READING: **KI** | 機器 **kiki** *device, hardware* |
| | KUN READING: **hata** | 機械 **kikai** *machine* |
| 機 | *loom, device, engine* | 機会 **kikai** *chance, opportunity* |
| | | 機織り **hataori** *weaving* |

| 一 | 十 | 才 | 木 | 朮 | 栌 | 柊 | 桜 | 樵 | 樵 |
|---|---|---|---|---|---|---|---|---|---|
| 樵 | 桦 | 桦 | 機 | 機 | 機 | | | | |

16 strokes

The Chinese added the element for **wood** 木 to the element for **how many silk-worms** 幾 to symbolize the wooden loom that spins the silk into thread. They wrote the final kanji 機, meaning a **loom**, **device**, or **engine**. Used as a word by itself it is pronounced **HATA**. In compound words it is pronounced **KI**. A 機関 **KIKAN**, engine-connector, is an **engine** that connects an energy source to a machine. A 水力機関 **SUIRYOKU KIKAN**, water-power-engine, is a **water turbine**. 危機 **KIKI**, dangerous-device, means a **crisis**. A 動機 **DŌKI**, move-device, is a **motive**.

| 356 | ON READING: **KAI** | 戒心 **kaishin** *caution, care* |
| | KUN READING: | 警戒 **keikai** *vigilance, alertness* |
| 戒 | **imashi(meru)** | 戒める **imashimeru** *to admonish, to rebuke* |
| | *to admonish, to rebuke* | 戒め **imashime** *morality, rebuke* |

| 一 | 二 | 干 | 开 | 戒 | 戒 | 戒 | | | |
|---|---|---|---|---|---|---|---|---|---|

7 strokes

The Chinese drew a pictograph of two hands ㄐㄋ holding a broad-blade halberd 戈 in a posture ㄐㄋ戈 that threatens a transgressor. They drew the final form of the kanji 戒, meaning **admonish** or **rebuke**. Used as a word by itself it is pronounced **IMASHI-MERU**. In compound words it is pronounced **KAI**. 戒名 **KAIMYŌ**, rebuke-name, is a **name adopted by Buddha's acolytes**.

| 357 | ON READING: **KAI** | 機械式 **kikaishiki** *mechanical* |
|---|---|---|
| 械 | *device* | 精密機械 **seimitsukikai** *precision mechanical equipment* 器械 **kikai** *instrument, device* |
| 11 strokes | 一 十 才 木 杁 杙 杙 杤 械 械 械 | |

The Chinese added the element for **wood** 木 to the element for **rebuke** 戒 , to symbolize the device they used to rebuke those who step out of line. They wrote the new kanji 械, meaning **device**. It is not used as a word by itself. In compound words it is pronounced **KAI**. A 機械 **KIKAI**, device (for making things)-device (for keeping order), is a **machine**.

| 358 | ON READING: **SEN** KUN READING: **izumi** | 源泉 **gensen** *source, origin, quarry* 温泉 **onsen** *hot spring* 冷泉 **reisen** *cold spring* 平泉 **Hiraizumi** *Hiraizumi City* |
|---|---|---|
| 泉 | *natural spring* | |
| 9 strokes | ′ ′′ 宀 白 白 宀 泉 泉 泉 | |

To form the kanji for a natural spring, clear water flowing from the ground, the Chinese combined the element for **water** 水 and the element for **white** 白 . They wrote the kanji 泉, meaning **natural spring**. Used as a word by itself it is pronounced **IZUMI**. Used in compound words it is pronounced **SEN**. 泉水 **SENSUI**, spring-water, is a **spring**.

| 359 | ON READING: **SEN** | 線路 **senro** *rail track* <br> 点線 **tensen** *dotted line* |
|---|---|---|
| 線 | *line* | 線香 **senkō** *incense stick* <br> 曲線 **kyokusen** *curved line* |

| | | | | | | | | | |
|---|---|---|---|---|---|---|---|---|---|
| ⟨ | 幺 | 幺 | 乡 | 糸 | 糸 | 糸 | 糹 | 紉 | 紉 |

| | | | | | | | | | |
|---|---|---|---|---|---|---|---|---|---|
| 糸 | 紣 | 綿 | 緽 | 線 | | | | | |

15 strokes

They combined the element for **thread** 糸 with the element for **spring** 泉 to symbolize the way the water flows in a long thin line like a thread. They wrote the kanji 線, meaning **line**, as in telephone line, railroad line, airplane flight, or anything long and thin and continuous. Used either as a word by itself or in compound words it is pronounced **SEN**. A 内線 **NAISEN**, inside-line, is a **telephone extension**. The 山手線 **YAMATESEN**, Yamate-line, is the **Yamate Rail Line** which circles central Tokyo. A 光線 **KŌSEN**, ray-line, is a **light ray**.

| 360 | ON READING: **MEN** <br> KUN READING: **wata** | 綿あめ **wata-ame** *cotton candy* <br> 綿花 **menko** *cotton* |
|---|---|---|
| 綿 | *cotton* | 真綿 **mawata** *floss silk* <br> 綿毛 **watage** *fluff, down* |

| | | | | | | | | | |
|---|---|---|---|---|---|---|---|---|---|
| ⟨ | 幺 | 幺 | 乡 | 糸 | 糸 | 糸 | 糹 | 紉 | 紉 |

| | | | | | | | | | |
|---|---|---|---|---|---|---|---|---|---|
| 綿 | 綿 | 綿 | 綿 | | | | | | |

14 strokes

The element for **white** 白 was combined with the element for **thread** 糸 to indicate white thread, then the element for **cloth** 巾 was added to show what the thread would be used for, and a new composite kanji 綿 was formed, meaning **cotton**. Used as a word by itself it is pronounced either **MEN**, where it means **finished cotton**, or **WATA**, where it means **raw cotton**. In compound words it is pronounced **MEN**. 木綿 **MOMEN** (using a very special pronunciation of 木, meaning **tree** or **bush**), bush-cotton, is the generic word for **cotton**. A 海綿 **KAIMEN**, ocean-cotton, is a **naturally-formed sponge**. 綿菓子 **WATAKASHI**, cotton-sweets, are **cotton candy**, as you find at fairs and festivals.

| 361 | ON READING: **TŌ** <br> KUN READING: **fuyu** | 冬季 **tōki** *winter season* <br> 春夏秋冬 **shunkashūtō** *the four seasons* |
|---|---|---|
| 冬 | *winter* | 真冬 **mafuyu** *mid winter* <br> 冬支度 **fuyujitaku** *preparation for winter* |
| 5 strokes | ノ　ク　夂　冬　冬 | |

Icicles hanging from roof eaves ❄ was the pictograph the Chinese drew to symbolize the winter. They first simplified it to 夂, then wrote the final kanji 冬, meaning **winter**. Used as a word by itself it is pronounced **FUYU**. In compound words it is pronounced **TŌ**. 冬物 **FUYUMONO**, winter-things, means **items used in winter**, like winter clothes and heavy blankets.

| 362 | ON READING: **SHŪ** <br> KUN READINGS: **owa(ru)**, **owa(ri)** | 終了 **shūryō** *close, ending, stop* <br> 終日 **shūjitsu** *all day long, whole day* <br> 最終 **saishū** *final, end* |
|---|---|---|
| 終 | *to end, to finish; the end* | 終わる **owaru** *to finish, to close* |
| | く　幺　幺　糸　糸　糸　糸　糸　終　終 | |
| 11 strokes | 終 | |

They combined the element for **winter** 冬 with the element for **thread** 糸 to symbolize the ending of the thread, and formed the new kanji 終, meaning **end** or **finish**. Used as a word by itself it is pronounced **OWA-RU** as a verb, and **OWA-RI** as a noun (with a kana in both cases to show the grammar). In compound words it is pronounced **SHŪ**. The kanji 終 is usually found on the last line of the last page of a novel, and flashed after the last scene of a movie.

| 363 氏 4 strokes | ON READING: **SHI** KUN READING: **uji** <br> *clan, family, family name* | 諸氏 **shoshi** *you all, gentleman* <br> 源氏物語 **Genji monogatari** *The Tale of Genji* <br> 彼氏 **kareshi** *boyfriend* <br> 氏神様 **ujigami-sama** *guardian god* |
|---|---|---|
| | ノ　　く　　モ　　氏 | |

To symbolize the clan or family the Chinese drew a picture of a bow with an arrow drawn and ready to protect the family land ⼅. They simplified it first to 氐, then wrote the final kanji 氏, meaning **clan** or **family** or **family name**. Used as a word by itself it is pronounced either **SHI** or **UJI**. In compound words it is pronounced **SHI**. 氏名 **SHIMEI**, family-name, means a **person's full name**, including family name and first name. 氏 **SHI**, family name, is also used after a person's family name to signify Mister, Miss, or Mrs.

| 364 紙 10 strokes | ON READING: **SHI** KUN READING: **kami** <br> *paper* | 紙面 **shimen** *plane of paper* <br> 用紙 **yōshi** *form, blank (paper)* <br> 新聞紙 **shinbunshi** *newspaper* <br> 紙くず **kamikuzu** *waste paper* |
|---|---|---|
| | く　　乡　　幺　　乍　　糸　　糸　　紅　　紅　　紙　　紙 | |

To symbolize the meaning **paper**, the Chinese combined the element for **thread** 糸, symbolizing cloth, the material on which they wrote before they invented paper, with the element for **clan and family** 氏, the clan history being the first thing anyone wrote down. The final form of the kanji was written 紙, meaning **paper**. Used as a word by itself it is pronounced **KAMI**. In compound words it is pronounced **SHI**. A 手紙 **TEGAMI**, hand-paper, is a **letter** sent to someone.

# SECTION TEN

## Kanji List

| | | | | | |
|---|---|---|---|---|---|
| 365 皿 | 366 温 | 367 血 | 368 貧 | 369 犬 | 370 器 |
| 371 虫 | 372 凡 | 373 風 | 374 独 | 375 番 | 376 第 |
| 377 百 | 378 宿 | 379 千 | 380 万 | 381 弓 | 382 引 |
| 383 矢 | 384 知 | 385 医 | 386 酒 | 387 利 | 388 別 |
| 389 所 | 390 場 | 391 元 | 392 完 | 393 院 | 394 病 |
| 395 折 | 396 近 | 397 新 | 398 質 | 399 代 | 400 貸 |
| 401 作 | 402 式 | 403 試 | 404 会 | 405 社 | |

| 365 | KUN READING: **sara** | 灰皿 **haizara** *ashtray*<br>紙皿 **kamizawa** *paper plate*<br>受け皿 **ukezara** *saucer, container for things*<br>深皿 **fukazawa** *deep dish, bowl* |
|---|---|---|
| 皿 | *plate, dish, bowl* | |
| 5 strokes | ＼　冂　冊　皿　皿 | |

The Chinese drew a pictograph of a bowl 盉 to symbolize a plate or bowl. They simplified it to 盉, then wrote the final form of the kanji 皿, meaning **plate** or **bowl**. Used either as a word by itself or in compound words it is pronounced **SARA**. An 大皿 **ŌZARA**, is a **big plate**. A 皿洗い機 **SARA-ARAI-KI** (written with one kana, pronounced **I**, after **ARA** to give the grammatical ending to the verb **ARAU**, meaning **wash**), dish-wash-machine, is a **dishwasher**.

| 366 | ON READING: **ON**<br>KUN READINGS:<br>**atata(kai), atata(maru), atata(meru)** | 気温 **kion** *temperature*<br>温度計 **ondokei** *thermometer*<br>温かい **atatakai** *warm*<br>温める **atatameru** *to heat, to warm*<br>温暖化 **ondanka** *(global) warming* |
|---|---|---|
| 温 | *warm; to warm, to heat, to get warm* | |
| | ＼　＼　氵　氵　沪　沪　沪　沪　沪　温 | |
| 12 strokes | 温　温 | |

To form the kanji meaning to warm, the Chinese put the element for **water** 水 with the element for **plate** 皿 and warmed it with the element for **sun** 日. They wrote the kanji 温. By itself as an adjective, it is pronounced **ATATA-KAI** (adjective), **ATATA-MARU** (intransitive) or **ATATA-MERU** (transitive), often shortened euphonically to **ATTA-KAI**, **ATTA-MARU** or **ATTA-MERU**. In compound words it is pronounced **ON**. An 温泉 **ONSEN**, warm-spring, is a **spa** or **hot spring**. An 温室 **ONSHITSU**, warm-room, is a **hothouse**. 体温 **TAI-ON**, body-warmth, is **body temperature**. A 体温計 **TAI-ONKEI**, body-warmth-measure, is a **thermometer**.

| 367 | ON READING: **KETSU** | 血液型 **ketsuekigata** *blood type* |
| | KUN READING: **chi** | 止血 **shiketsu** *hemostasis; stop* |
| 血 | | *bleeding* |
| | *blood* | 採血 **saiketsu** *blood draw* |
| | | 血眼 **chimanako** *frenzy* |
| 6 strokes | ノ イ 冎 冋 血 血 | |

On top of the element for **plate** 皿 the Chinese put a drop ノ of the most
important liquid of all, blood, to form the kanji for **blood** 血. Used as a word
by itself it is pronounced **CHI**. In compound words it is pronounced **KETSU**.
出血 **SHUKKETSU** (**SHUTSU-KETSU** pronounced euphonically), emerge-
blood, means **bleeding**. 血圧 **KETSU-ATSU**, blood-pressure, means **blood
pressure**. A 鼻血 **HANAJI** (**HANA-CHI** pronounced euphonically), is a **nose-
bleed**.

| 368 | ON READINGS: **HIN, BIN** | 貧富 **hinpu** *rich and poor* |
| | KUN READING: **mazu(shi'i)** | 貧弱 **hinjaku** *meagerness* |
| 貧 | | 貧乏 **binbō** *poor, poverty* |
| | *poor, impoverished* | 貧しい **mazushi'i** *poor* |
| | ノ 八 分 分 分 谷 谷 谷 谷 貧 | |
| 11 strokes | 貧 | |

The Chinese put the element for **cut up into parts** 分 with the element for **shell**
(in its meaning **money**) 貝 , making a new kanji to symbolize reduction of a
person's money by cutting off some parts. They wrote the new kanji 貧 , meaning **poor** or **impoverished**. Used as a word by itself, usually as an adjective, it is
pronounced **MAZU-SHI'I**. In compound words it is pronounced **HIN** or **BIN**.
貧血 **HINKETSU**, impoverished-blood, means **anemia**.

| 369 犬 4 strokes | ON READING: **KEN** KUN READING: **inu** *dog* | 犬種 **kenshu** *types of dog* 警察犬 **keisatsu-ken** *police dog* 飼い犬 **kai'inu** *house dog, one's dog* 野良犬 **norainu** *stray dog* |
|---|---|---|

一　ナ　大　犬

The Chinese pictograph for dog was ✗. They simplified it first to 犬 then wrote the final kanji 犬, which resembles the kanji for big 大 with an ear. Used as a word by itself it is pronounced **INU**. In compound words it is pronounced **KEN**. A 子犬 **KO-INU**, child-dog, is a **puppy**. An 犬小屋 **INUGOYA**, dog-small-house, is a **doghouse**. An 愛犬 **AIKEN**, love-dog, is a **pet dog**.

| 370 器 15 strokes | ON READING: **KI** KUN READING: **utsuwa** *vessel, utensil* | 器量 **kiryō** *looks, features; capability* 器用 **kiyō** *skillfulness, dexterity* 楽器 **gakki** *musical instrument* 機器 **kiki** *device, hardware* |
|---|---|---|

丶　丷　口　吅　吅　吅　吅　罗　哭　哭

罗　哭　器　器　器

The Chinese put four **mouths** 吅 around a **dog** 犬 (without its ear) to symbolize the plates and tools they used in making and eating a meal. They wrote the kanji 器, meaning **vessel** or **utensil**. Used as a word by itself it is pronounced **UTSUWA**. In compound words it is pronounced **KI**. 器物 **KIBUTSU**, utensil-things, are **kitchenware**. 土器 **DOKI**, earth-utensils, are **earthenware** or **ceramic plates and bowls**.

| 371 | ON READING: **CHŪ** | は 虫 類 **hachūrui** *reptile* |
|---|---|---|
| 虫 | KUN READING: **mushi** | 幼 虫 **yōchū** *larva* |
| | *worm, insect, bug* | 害 虫 **gaichū** *vermin, pest, bug* |
| | | 虫 か ご **mushikago** *insect cage* |
| 6 strokes | ヽ 　 冂 　 口 　 中 　 虫 　 虫 | |

The Chinese drew a pictograph of a worm or viper ꙮ to mean a **worm** or **bug**. They simplified it first to 𢀖, then drew the kanji 虫. Used as a word by itself it is pronounced **MUSHI**. In compound words it is pronounced **CHŪ**. A 毛 虫 **KEMUSHI**, hair-bug, is a **caterpillar**. A 虫 歯 **MUSHIBA**, bug-tooth, is a **decayed tooth** or a **cavity**.

| 372 | ON READINGS: **BON, HAN** | 凡 才 **bonsai** *ordinary ability* |
|---|---|---|
| 凡 | KUN READINGS: **oyoso** | 凡 例 **hanrei** *explanatory note, key* |
| | *ordinary, common, in general; nearly, about, around* | 凡 そ **ōyoso** *about, around, roughly* |
| 3 strokes | ノ 　 几 　 凡 | |

They drew a pictograph of the opened sky with just one dot beneath it 冖丶 to symbolize that everything beneath the sky is all the same. They simplified it to 冂丶, then drew the final kanji 凡. It means **ordinary**, **common**, **featureless**, and was extended to mean **in general**, **nearly** or **about**. Used as a word by itself it is pronounced **OYO-SO**, where it means **about**, **nearly**, **roughly**. In compound words it is usually pronounced **BON** or **HAN**. A 凡 人 **BONJIN**, ordinary-person, is the **common man**. 平 凡 **HEIBON**, flat-featureless, means **monotonous** or **ordinary**. 非 凡 **HIBON**, un-common, means **extraordinary**, **unusual**, **uncommon**.

| 373 | ON READINGS: **FŪ, FU** | 風力 **fūryoku** *wind power* |
|---|---|---|
| 風 | KUN READINGS: **kaze, kaza** | 風情 **fuzei** *taste, flavor, mood* |
| | *wind, style* | そよ風 **soyokaze** *breeze* |
| 9 strokes | | 風上 **kazakami** *windward* |

丿 几 几 凡 凧 凮 風 風 風

Under the opened sky with just one dot 几 the Chinese added a **locust** 虫 to symbolize the **wind** that brings the locusts. They wrote the kanji 風, meaning the **wind**. It was extended to means **the way the wind blows**, or a **style**. Used as a word by itself it is pronounced **KAZE** or **KAZA**, meaning **wind**. In compound words it is pronounced **FŪ** or **FU**, meaning **wind** or **style**. 東風 **TŌFŪ**, east-wind, means **east wind**. 風船 **FŪSEN**, wind-boat, means **balloons** that children play with. 風車 **FŪSHA**, wind-wheel, is a **windmill**. It also means a **pinwheel**, a toy for children. The same two kanji can also be pronounced **KAZAGURUMA**, in which case it means only **pinwheel**. 和風 **WAFŪ**, Japan-style, means **Japanese style**. 洋風 **YŌFŪ**, foreign-style, means **Western style**.

| 374 | ON READING: **DOKU** | 独身 **dokushin** *single, unmarried* |
|---|---|---|
| 独 | KUN READING: **hito(ri)** | 単独 **tandoku** *alone, solo* |
| | *independent, all alone* | 独り者 **hitorimono** *single person* |
| 9 strokes | | 独特 **dokutoku** *unique, unusual* |

丿 犭 犭 犭 犯 犯 独 独 独

To symbolize the condition of being alone without the need to depend on any-one else, the Chinese combined the elements for two species that have no need for each other, a **dog** 犬 and a **locust** 虫. They modified the element for dog to fit the square by using an earlier simplification 犭 and wrote the new compos-ite kanji 独, meaning **independent**, **all alone**, **without anyone else**. Used as a word by itself it is pronounced **HITO-RI**. In compound words it is pronounced **DOKU**. 独立 **DOKURITSU**, alone-stand, means **independence**. 独り語 **HI-TORIGOTO** (**HITORI** needs a kana to show the grammar), alone-speak, means a **soliloquy**. 独語 **DOKUGO**, alone-talk, means **talking to yourself**. The same two kanji, 独語, also means the **German language**, since the Chinese use the kanji 独, **independent**, to stand for **Germany**. 独学 **DOKUGAKU**, alone-learn, means **self-taught**. 独力 **DOKURYOKU**, alone-strength, means **done by your own efforts**, **single-handed**, **self-made**.

| 375 | ON READING: **BAN** | 番組 **bangumi** *program (TV, etc.)*<br>順番 **junban** *order, turn* |
|---|---|---|
| 番<br><br>12 strokes | *number, one's turn; to guard* | 番号 **bangō** *number*<br>番人 **ban-nin** *keeper, guard* |

一 ⺊ ⺁ ㄇ 亚 平 乎 釆 釆 番 番

番 番

The elements for **harvested rice, stacked and bundled** 米, still waiting in the **paddy** 田 to be tallied, and a counting stick ╱ for marking bundles, were all combined to make the new kanji 番, meaning **number** or **one's turn**. It was extended to also mean **keep watch over** or **guard the harvest**. Used either as a word by itself or in compound words it is pronounced **BAN**. 一番 **ICHIBAN**, one-number, means **number one**, and also means **the most** or **very**. 二番目 **NIBANME**, two-number-ordinal, means **second in turn**, or **second in line**. A 番 人 **BANNIN**, guard-person, is a **watchman**. 交番 **KŌBAN**, cross-guard, means a **police box**. 番外 **BANGAI**, turn-outside, means **unexpected**.

| 376 | ON READING: **DAI** | 第一人者 **dai'ichi-ninsha** *authority*<br>第一声 **dai'issei** *first word* |
|---|---|---|
| 第<br><br>11 strokes | *order, numerical order* | 落第 **rakudai** *flunk, dropout* |

ノ ⺊ ᅡ ⺊ ⺮ ⺮ 竺 竺 笞 第

第

While **BAN** is the generic term for **number**, a separate kanji acts as a prefix to indicate an ordinal number, translating as **-irst, -nd, -rd, -th**, depending on the number that follows it. The Chinese drew this kanji from a pictograph of a row of bamboo slats tied together with string to make a crude abacus used as a primitive counting machine 畕. They first simplified the pictograph to 弗 and then to 弔, and drew the final form 弔. Then they added the element for **bamboo** ⺮ to form the final kanji 第, meaning **order**, particularly **numerical order**. Used either as a word by itself or in compound words, it is pronounced **DAI**. 第一 **DAI'ICHI**, order-one, means **first**. 第一歩 **DAI'IPPO** (DAI-ICHI-HO pronounced euphonically), order-one-step, means the **first step**. 第三者 **DAISAN-SHA**, order-three-person, means a **third person, a disinterested party**.

| 377 | ON READING: **HYAKU** | 百貨店 **hyakkaten** *department store* |
|---|---|---|
| 百 | *hundred* | 百科事典 **hyakka-jiten** *encyclopedia* |
| 6 strokes | 一 ー ア 丆 百 百 | |

The Chinese combined the element for **one** 一 with the element for a grain of rice 白 (which they also used to represent the meaning white) to symbolize one bag of rice, which weighs one hundred pounds. They wrote the kanji 百, meaning **hundred**. Used either as a word by itself or in compound words it is pronounced **HYAKU**. 五百 **GOHYAKU**, five-hundred, means **five-hundred**. 九百円 **KYŪHYAKU-EN**, nine-hundred-yen, means **900 Yen**.

| 378 | ON READING: **SHUKU** KUN READINGS: **yado, yado(ru)** | 宿泊 **shukuhaku** *visit, staying* 宿題 **shukudai** *homework* 雨宿り **amayadori** *to take shelter* |
|---|---|---|
| 宿 | *hotel, lodging; to reside* | 宿る **yadoru** *to dwell, to reside* |
| 11 strokes | ， 宀 宀 宀 宀 宀 宀 宿 宿 宿 | |

The Chinese put **one hundred** 百 **people** 人 under a **roof** 宀 to form a new kanji 宿 meaning a **hotel**. Used as a word by itself, generally as a verb meaning **to lodge**, it is pronounced **YADO** or **YADO-RU** (with a kana to show the verb ending). In compound wods it is pronounced **SHUKU**. A 宿屋 **YADOYA**, hotel-building, is an **inn** or a **lodging house**.

| 379 | ON READING: **SEN** <br> KUN READING: **chi** | 千円 **sen-en** *one thousand yen* <br> 千切り **sengiri** *fine/thin strips* <br> 千差万別 **sensa-banbetsu** <br> *be infinite in variety* <br> 千代紙 **chiyogami** *patterned paper* |
| 千 | *thousand* | |
| 3 strokes | ノ 二 千 | |

To symbolize **one-thousand**, they combined the element for **one** 一 with the element for **person** 人 to represent a phalanx of 1,000 troops. They modified the element for **person** to 丁, and wrote the kanji 千. In olden days, the Chinese wrote two-thousand with the element for **two** 二 to represent 2,000 troops 秊, and wrote three-thousand with the element for three 三 to represent 3,000 troops 秂. 千, **thousand**, is rarely used as a word by itself, except in several proper names where it is pronounced **CHI**. In compound words it is pronounced **SEN**. 一千 **ISSEN** (**ICHISEN** pronounced euphonically), one-thousand, means **one thousand**. 三千 **SANZEN** (**SANSEN** pronounced euphonically), three-thousand, is **three thousand**.

| 380 | ON READINGS: **MAN, BAN** | 万年 **man-nen** *perpetual* <br> 万国 **bankoku** *international* <br> 万全 **banzen** *absolute, perfect* <br> 万歳 **Banzai** *Hurrah!* |
| 万 | *ten thousand* | |
| 3 strokes | 一 フ 万 | |

To symbolize the kanji for **ten thousand**, the Chinese borrowed the ancient Indian religious symbol 卍, which meant ten-thousand gods. The Chinese first simplified it to 丆, then wrote the final form 万. It is not used as a word by itself. In compound words it is pronounced **MAN** or **BAN**. 一万 **ICHIMAN**, one-ten thousand, means **ten thousand**. 万一 **MAN-ICHI**, ten thousand-one (a ten-thousand to one chance), means **in case such-and-such a thing happens**. 百万 **HYAKUMAN**, hundred-ten thousand (one hundred times ten-thousand), means **one million**.

| 381 | ON READING: **KYŪ** | 洋弓 **yōkyū** *archery* |
|---|---|---|
| 弓 | KUN READING: **yumi** | 弓矢 **yumiya** *bow and arrow* |
| | *archer's bow* | 弓なり **yuminari** *curved, arched* |
| 3 strokes | ⼍  ⼕  弓 | |

The Chinese drew a picture of an archer's bow without the string 𝌂 to mean an **archer's bow**. They squared it slightly and wrote the kanji 弓. Used as a word by itself it is pronounced **YUMI**. In compound words it is pronounced **KYŪ**. A 弓取 **YUMITORI**, bow-take, is an **archer**. 弓道 **KYŪDŌ**, bow-way, is **archery**.

| 382 | ON READING: **IN** | 引退 **intai** *retirement* |
|---|---|---|
| 引 | KUN READING: **hi(ku)** | さく引 **sakuin** *index* |
| | *to pull* | 引き出し **hikidashi** *drawer* |
| 4 strokes | ⼍  ⼕  弓  引 | |

To the **archer's bow** 弓 they added a string | and wrote a new kanji 引 meaning **to pull**. Used as a word by itself, generally as a verb, it is pronounced **HI-KU**. In compound words it is pronounced **IN**. 引 usually appears on all the doors you should pull to open. (The doors you push to open will use the kanji 押 **OSU**, meaning **push**.) 引力 **INRYOKU**, pull-power, means **gravitation**. 引用 **INYŌ**, pull-use, means **a quotation** or **to quote the words of someone else**. A 字引き **JIBI-KI** (**JI-HI-KI** pronounced euphonically; with a kana to show the grammatical ending **KI** for the verb **HIKU**), word-pull, is a **dictionary**.

| 383 | ON READING: **SHI** | 一矢 **isshi** *one arrow* |
|---|---|---|
| | KUN READING: **ya** | 矢印 **yajirushi** *arrow* |
| 矢 | | 矢継ぎ早に **yatsugibaya ni** *fast-breaking* |
| | *arrow* | 矢尻 **yajiri** *arrow-head* |
| 5 strokes | ノ ト ニ チ 矢 | |

They drew a pictograph of an arrow ↟ to mean **arrow**. They simplified it first to ↟ and then to 𠂉. They wrote the final form 矢, meaning **arrow**. Used as a word by itself it is pronounced **YA**. In compound words it is pronounced **SHI**. A 矢先 **YASAKI**, arrow-tip, is **an arrowhead**.

| 384 | ON READING: **CHI** | 知識 **chishiki** *knowledge* |
|---|---|---|
| | KUN READINGS: **shi(ru),** | 通知 **tsūchi** *notice* |
| | **shi(raseru)** | 知る **shiru** *to know, to receive, to learn* |
| 知 | *to know, to make known, to inform* | 物知り **monoshiri** *knowledgeable* |
| 8 strokes | ノ ト ニ チ 矢 知 知 知 | |

The Chinese combined the element for **arrow** 矢 with the element for **mouth** 口 into a new kanji 知 to symbolize knowing enough to speak as fast and straight as an arrow. It means **to know** or **to make known** or **to inform**. Used as a word by itself, generally as a verb, it is pronounced **SHI-RU** (intransitive, **to know**) or **SHI-RASERU** (transitive, **to make known** or **to inform**). In compound words it is pronounced **CHI**. A 知人 **CHIJIN**, know-person, is an **acquaintance**. A 知事 **CHIJI**, know-things, is a **state governor**.

| 385<br><br>医<br><br>7 strokes | ON READING: **I**<br><br>*medicine, healing* | 医師 **ishi** *medical doctor*<br>名医 **mei'i** *famous doctor*<br>医院 **i'in** *doctor's office* |
|---|---|---|
| | 一 　一 　一 　三 　弄 　矢 　医 | |

A pictograph of an **arrow** 矢 in the chest, the human chest 匚, symbolized the pulling out of arrows from a wounded soldier's chest. The final form of the kanji was 医, meaning **medicine** or **healing**. Used either as a word by itself or in compound words it is pronounced **I**. An 医者 **ISHA**, medicine-person, is a **doctor**. A 歯医者 **HA-ISHA**, tooth-medicine-person, is a **dentist**. 医学 **IGAKU**, medicine-learning, means **medical science**.

The kanji 医, meaning **medicine** or **healing**, was adapted from an earlier version (still used from time to time) by taking from it only the element for an arrow in the chest. The older version contained the arrow in the chest 医 and also pictographs of a hand holding a medical instrument 殳 and of a bottle containing antiseptic alcohol 酉.

The hand holding the medical instrument was first simplified to 殳 and then to 殳. The bottle containing medicine was first simplified to 酉 and then to 酉. The Chinese put them all together and formed the kanji 醫. This kanji was recently modernized and simplified 医 by using only the element of the arrow in the chest. Both forms are pronounced the same, **I**, and mean the same. The modern form is just easier and quicker to write so it is the version now most often used.

| 386<br><br>酒<br><br>10 strokes | ON READING: **SHU**<br>KUN READINGS: **sake, saka**<br><br>*rice wine, liquor* | 飲酒 **inshu** *(alcohol) drinking*<br>梅酒 **umeshu** *plum wine*<br>甘酒 **amazake** *amazake (sweet fermented rice drink)*<br>酒場 **sakaba** *bar* |
|---|---|---|
| | 丶　冫　氵　汀　汀　沔　洒　洒　酒　酒 | |

The Chinese added the modified element for **water** 氵 to the element for a bottle of antiseptic alcohol and formed the new kanji 酒, meaning **rice wine** or **hard liquor**. Used as a word by itself it is pronounced **SAKE** or **SAKA**. In compound words it is pronounced **SHU**. 日本酒 **NIHONSHU**, Japan-sake, is **Japanese rice-wine** or **sake**. A 酒屋 **SAKA-YA** (**SAKE-YA** pronounced euphonically), is a **liquor store**, selling packaged liquor to consume off-premises.

| 387 | ON READING: **RI** | 利息 **risoku** *interest* |
|---|---|---|
| 利 | KUN READING: **ki(ku)** | 勝利 **shōri** *victory* |
| | *profit, benefit* | 利き酒 **kikizake** *blind tasting* |
| | | 利き腕 **kikiude** *one's better arm* |
| 7 strokes | ノ 二 千 矛 禾 利 利 | |

The element for **sword** 刀 and the element for a ripened rice plant ready to harvest 禾 were combined to draw the pictograph 初, which symbolizes the cutting of the rice harvest. The sword was modified to 刂 to fit the square and the final form of the composite kanji was written 利, meaning **profit** or **benefit**. Used as a word by itself, it is pronounced **KI-KU**. In compound words it is pronounced **RI**. 利子 **RISHI**, profit-child, is the **interest paid on a loan**. 利用 **RIYŌ**, profit-use, means **to use** or **utilization**. 利回り **RI-MAWA-RI** (with a kana to show the grammatical ending of the verb **MAWARU**, go-around), profit-go-round, is the **yearly interest** or **dividends** paid on stocks or bonds. 利口 **RIKŌ**, profit-mouth, means **clever**, **shrewd** or **smart**.

| 388 | ON READING: **BETSU** | 区別 **kubetsu** *difference* |
|---|---|---|
| 別 | KUN READING: **waka(reru)** | 別々 **betsubetsu** *separately, individually* |
| | *to separate, to diverge* | 分別 **bunbetsu, funbetsu** *segregation; discrimination* |
| | | 別れる **wakareru** *to break up, to divorce* |
| 7 strokes | 丶 冂 口 号 另 别 別 | |

The Chinese drew a picture of a skeleton 冎, which they simplified first to 咼 and then to 另, combined it with the element for sword 刀 modified to 刂 to symbolize separating flesh from bones. They wrote the new kanji 別, meaning **separate** or **diverge**. Used as a word by itself, usually as a verb, it is pronounced **WAKA-RERU**. In compound words it is pronounced **BETSU**. A 別名 **BETSU-MEI**, separate-name, is an **alias**. 特別 **TOKUBETSU**, special-separate, means **special**.

| 389 | ON READING: **SHO** | 住所 **jūsho** *address* |
|---|---|---|
| | KUN READING: **tokoro** | 近所 **kinjo** *neighborhood* |
| 所 | *place* | 台所 **daidokoro** *kitchen* |
| | | 洗面所 **senmenjo** *bathroom* |
| 8 strokes | 一　フ　ヲ　戸　戸　所　所　所 | |

A pictograph of a hacksaw 𠂉 was added to the element for door 戸 to symbolize the building of a structure. The hacksaw was simplified first to 𠂊 then to 斤. The new composite kanji was written 所, meaning a **place**. Used as a word by itself it is pronounced **TOKORO**. In compound words it is pronounced **SHO**. 所有 **SHOYŪ**, place-have, means **possession** or **ownership**.

| 390 | ON READING: **JŌ** | 会場 **kaijō** *hall, meeting place* |
|---|---|---|
| | KUN READING: **ba** | 式場 **shikijō** *ceremonial hall* |
| 場 | *place* | 広場 **hiroba** *open space, square* |
| | | 場面 **bamen** *scene* |
| 12 strokes | 一　十　土　圹　圹　圹　坦　坦　場　場　場 | |

To write another kanji meaning **place**, the Chinese drew a pictograph of the flags they used to signal people to assemble 𠃌 (simplified first to 刁 then to 勿) then put it together with the elements for **land** 土 and **sun** 日 above the horizon line 一. They drew the new kanji 場, meaning **a place**. 場 is not often used as a word by itself. Used in compound words it is pronounced **BA** or **JŌ**. 場所 **BASHO**, place-place, is a common word for **place**. A 工場 **KŌJŌ**, work-place, is a **factory**. A 刑場 **KEIJŌ**, punish-place, is an **execution ground**. A 戦場, **SENJŌ**, war-ground, is a **battlefield**. 立場 **TACHIBA**, stand-place, means **one's standpoint** or **position**. A 道場 **DŌJŌ**, way-place ("way" in the philosophical sense of "following a Way" such as Taoism or a disciplined sport such as judo or fencing), is a **training site** or a **gymnasium**.

| 391 | ON READINGS: **GEN, GAN** | 元旦 **gantan** *New Year's Day* |
| | KUN READING: **moto** | 元素 **genso** *chemical element* |
| 元 | *origin, source* | 家元 **iemoto** *master* |
| | | 元払い **motobarai** *shipping prepayment* |
| 4 strokes | 一 二 テ 元 | |

The Chinese drew a pictograph of a human being with its head in prominence 𠘧 to symbolize the concept that the human brain is the origin or source of everything on earth. They simplified it first to 𠘧, then to 兒. They drew the final form of the new kanji 元, meaning **origin** or **source**. Used as a word by itself it is pronounced **MOTO**. In compound words it is pronounced **GEN** or **GAN**. 元日 **GANJITSU**, origin-day, is **New Year's day**. 元手 **MOTODE**, source-hand, means **capital funds**. The same two kanji in reverse order, 手元 **TEMOTO**, hand-source, means **at hand** or **in hand**.

| 392 | ON READING: **KAN** | 完全な **kanzen na** *complete, perfect* |
| | | 完成する **kansei suru** *to complete* |
| 完 | *finish, completion* | 未完成 **mikansei** *unfinished* |
| | | 完了 **kanryō** *finish, completion* |
| 7 strokes | ' 宀 宀 宀 宀 宀 完 | |

The Chinese wrapped the element for **frame** 冂, modified to 宀 to fit the square, around the element for **source** or **origin** 元 to symbolize the finish or completion of a project. They wrote the new kanji 完, meaning **finish** or **completion**. It is not used as a word by itself. In compound words it is pronounced **KAN**. 完工 **KANKŌ**, completion-work, means **to finish a construction project**. 未完 **MIKAN**, not yet-completion, means **incomplete**.

| 393 | ON READING: **IN** | 病院 **byōin** *hospital* |
|---|---|---|
| 院 | building (for temple, palace, hospital, school), institution | 退院 **tai'in** *discharge from the hospital* |
| | | 院長 **inchō** *hospital director* |
| | | 上院 **jō-in** *Senate* |
| 10 strokes | ７　３　阝　阝'　阝'　阝宀　阝宀　阝宀　阝宀　院 | |

To the kanji meaning **finish** or **completion of a project** 完 the Chinese added the
element for **terraced hillside** 阝 to symbolize a completed building of importance
set high up on the terraced hillside. They wrote the kanji 院, meaning a **building
used for important projects,** such as a research institute or other institution, a
hospital, a temple or a parliament. It is not used as a word by itself. In compound
words it is pronounced **IN**. A 大学院 **DAIGAKU-IN**, university-institute, is a
**graduate school**. A 寺院 **JI'IN**, temple-institution, is a **temple**. 入院 **NYŪ-IN**,
enter-institution, means **be hospitalized**.

| 394 | ON READINGS: **BYŌ, HEI** | 病気 **byōki** *illness, sickness* |
|---|---|---|
| 病 | KUN READINGS: **ya(mu), yamai** | 看病 **kanbyō** *nursing* |
| | | 疾病 **shippei** *disease, illness* |
| | illness; to be ill | 病み付き **yamitsuki** *addict* |
| 10 strokes | '　宀　广　广　疒　疒　疒　病　病　病 | |

The Chinese drew a pictograph of a stretcher 广 transporting patients 人 to a
surgical table 冂 to symbolize a person under care. They stood the stretcher up
on end 疒 to roll the patient onto the table. They wrote the new composite kanji
病 meaning **illness**. Used as a word by itself, usually as a verb meaning **to be ill**,
it is pronounced **YA-MU** or **YAMAI**. In compound words it is pronounced **BYŌ**
or **HEI**. A 病院 **BYŌ-IN**, illness-institution, is a **hospital**. A 病人 **BYŌNIN**,
illness-person, is a **patient**. 急病 **KYŪBYŌ**, sudden-illness, means a **sudden
attack** or a **medical emergency**. A 重病 **JŪBYŌ**, heavy-illness, means a **serious
illness**.

| 395 | ON READING: **SETSU** <br> KUN READING: **o(ru)** | 屈折 **kussetsu** *inflection, refraction* <br> 折る **oru** *to break, to bend, to fold* <br> 折れ曲がる **oremagaru** *to bend* <br> 折り返し **orikaeshi** *without delay; repetition, shuttle service* |
|---|---|---|
| 折 | *to break, to bend, to fold* | |
| 7 strokes | 一　才　扌　扩　扩　折　折 | |

They put the element for **hacksaw** 斤 with the element for **hand** 手, modified to fit the square 扌, and made the new kanji 折, meaning **break** or **bend** or **fold**. When used as a word by itself, usually as a verb, it is pronounced **O-RU**. In compound words it is pronounced **SETSU**. 折り紙 **ORIGAMI** (written with a kana to show the grammatical ending of **O-RU**), fold-paper, is **the art of folding paper into figures**. 右折 **USETSU**, right-bend, means **a right-turn**. 左折 **SASETSU**, left-bend, means **a left-turn**. 折半 **SEPPAN** (**SETSU-BAN** pronounced euphonically), break-half, means **divide 50-50**.

| 396 | ON READING: **KIN** <br> KUN READING: **chika(i)** | 近代 **kindai** *modern age* <br> 接近 **sekkin** *access, approximation* <br> 近づく **chikazuku** *to come close* <br> 近道 **chikamichi** *shortcut* |
|---|---|---|
| 近 | *close by, near* | |
| 7 strokes | ノ　ｆ　斤　斤　沂　沂　近 | |

The element for **hacksaw** 斤 was put atop the element for **forward movement** 辶 to cut off the advance and symbolize the concept close by or near. The Chinese wrote the final kanji 近, meaning **close by** or **near**. Used as a word by itself as an adjective, it is pronounced **CHIKA-I**. In compound words it is pronounced **KIN**. 近所 **KINJO**, near-place, means **neighborhood**. 近東 **KINTŌ**, near-east, means **the Near East**, referring to the countries at the east end of the Mediterranean Sea. A 近道 **CHIKAMICHI**, close-road, is a **shortcut**.

| 397 新 13 strokes | ON READING: **SHIN** KUN READINGS: **atara(shi'i), arata, ni'i** | 最新の **saishin no** *current, latest* 新しい **atarashi'i** *new* 新たに **arata ni** *newly; to refresh* 新潟 **Ni'igata** *Ni'igata Prefecture* |
|---|---|---|
| | *new* | |
| | ` 亠 亠 产 立 立 辛 辛 亲 亲 | |
| | 新 新 新 | |

The element for hacksaw 斤 was put beside the elements for a **stand** 立 of **trees** 木 to symbolize a new stand of trees ready for cutting. They wrote the new kanji 新, meaning **new**. Used as a word by itself as an adjective, it is pronounced **ATARA-SHI'I**, **ARATA** or **NI'I**. In compound words it is pronounced **SHIN**. A 新聞 **SHINBUN**, new-hearing, is a **newspaper**. 新年, **SHIN-NEN**, New-year, is the **New Year holiday**. 新人 **SHINJIN**, new-person, is a **newcomer**.

| 398 質 15 strokes | ON READINGS: **SHITSU, SHICHI, CHI** | 実質 **jisshitsu** *real term* 本質 **honshitsu** *essential, substance* 質素な **shisso na** *plain, simple* 人質 **hitojichi** *hostage* |
|---|---|---|
| | *character, nature, quality; to pawn* | |
| | ´ 厂 斤 斤 斤´ 斤´ 斤´ 斤´ 斦 斦 | |
| | 斦 斦 斦 斦 質 | |

The Chinese put the elements for two hacksaws 斦 above the element for **shell**, meaning **money** 貝, to symbolize dissecting something valuable to see what is inside. They wrote the new kanji 質, meaning **character** or **nature** or **quality**. It was extended to mean **to pawn**, which is temporarily exchanging goods for a sum of money dependent on the quality of the goods. It is not used as a word by itself. In compound words it is pronounced **SHITSU**, **SHICHI** or **CHI**. 品質 **HINSHI-TSU**, goods-quality, means **quality**. A 質屋 **SHICHI-YA**, pawn-shop, is a **pawn shop**. 質問 **SHITSUMON**, nature-ask, means **question**.

| 399 | ON READINGS: **DAI, TAI** | 世代 **sedai** *generation* |
|---|---|---|
| 代 | KUN READINGS: **ka(waru), ka(eru), yo** | 現代 **gendai** *nowadays, modern era*<br>交代 **kōtai** *rotation, replacement* |
| | *fee, generation; charge;*<br>*to substitute, to replace* | 身代わり **migawari** *dummy,*<br>*scapegoat, substitution* |
| 5 strokes | ノ イ 仁 代 代 | |

As described earlier, the Chinese drew a pictograph of a **lance** with a wide handle so the warrior could still hold and control it after it pierced the target 弌. This was simplified to 弌, and written in final form 戈. They then drew a pictograph of a short lance without the handle 㐅 and wrote the kanji 弋. Neither kanji now stand alone but both are often used as elements in other kanji, 戈 bringing the meaning **long lance** and 弋 bringing the meaning **short lance**.

The Chinese combined the element for **short lance** 弋 with the element for **person** 人, to symbolize the substitution of a weapon for a person to strengthen total military force. They wrote the new kanji 代, meaning **to substitute one thing for another**. It means a **fee** or **charge** when money is substituted for goods or services, and it means a **generation** when one generation is substituted for the previous one. Used as a word by itself, generally as a verb meaning **substitute** or **replace**, it is pronounced **KA-WARU, KA-ERU** or **YO**. In compound words it is pronounced **DAI** or **TAI**. It also has the special pronunciation of **YO** when it is used in proper names, as in 代代木 **YOYOGI**, the name of a popular district in Tokyo. Incidentally, when a kanji is duplicated in succession in a word, the second rendition is usually written with the kanji ditto mark 々, so **YOYOGI** is properly written 代々木.

部屋代 **HEYADAI**, room-fee, is **room rent**. 代理 **DAIRI**, substitute-manage, means **represent** or **proxy** or **agency**. A 校長代理 **KŌCHŌDAIRI**, school-principal-proxy is the **acting principal**. A 時代 **JIDAI**, time-substitute, is an **epoch**.

| 400 | ON READING: **TAI**<br>KUN READING: **ka(su)** | 貸与 **taiyo** *lease*<br>賃貸 **chintai** *rental, rent*<br>貸す **kasu** *to lend*<br>貸し出し **kashidashi** *circulation* |
|---|---|---|
| 貸<br><br>12 strokes | *loan; to lend* | |

ノ　イ　イ　代　代　代　代　伐　貸　貸

貸　貸

The Chinese put the element for **substitute** 代 atop the element for **shell** (signifying **money**) 貝 and wrote a new kanji 貸 symbolizing the substitution of security for money in a loan transaction. 貸 means **a loan** or **to lend**. Used as a word by itself, generally as a verb, it is pronounced **KA-SU**. In compound words it is pronounced **TAI**. A 貸家 **KASHIYA** (usually written with a kana to show the grammatical ending of the verb **KASU**), means **house for rent**.

| 401 | ON READINGS: **SAKU, SA**<br>KUN READING: **tsuku(ru)** | 作詞家 **sakushika** *songwriter*<br>作成 **sakusei** *development, making*<br>作業 **sagyō** *operation, work*<br>動作 **dōsa** *motion, action, performance* |
|---|---|---|
| 作<br><br>7 strokes | *to make, to construct, to compose* | |

ノ　イ　イ　伫　作　作　作

Instead of the element for hacksaw 斤, which was used for finer work, the Chinese drew a pictograph of an ordinary saw 𠂇, which they first simplified to 乍 then to 乍 and drew the final element 乍. They put this element with the element for **person** 人 and wrote a new composite kanji 作, meaning **to make** or **to construct**. Used as a word by itself, usually as a verb, it is pronounced **TSUKU-RU**. In compound words it is pronounced **SAKU** or **SA**. A 作品 **SAKUHIN**, make-thing, is **a work**, **a production**, or **an opus**. A 作家 **SAKKA** (**SAKUKA** pronounced phonetically), make-person, is **an author** or **a writer** (occasionally the kanji 家 meaning **house** is extended, as in this case, to mean the **house of a specialist**).

| 402 | ON READING: **SHIKI** | 形式 **keishiki** *form, format* |
|---|---|---|
| 式 | *ceremony, style* | 数式 **sūshiki** *mathematical formula* <br> 一式 **isshiki** *kit, set* |
| 6 strokes | 一 二 丁 王 式 式 | |

They put the element for **tool** 工 with the element for **short lance** 弋 to symbolize the construction and the guarding of the stage where ceremonies took place. They wrote the new kanji 式, meaning **ceremony**. It was extended to mean the way things are done, or the **style**. Used either as a word by itself or in compound words 式 is pronounced **SHIKI**. 日本式, **NIHONSHIKI**, Japan-style, means **Japanese style** or **the Japanese way**. 洋式 **YŌSHIKI**, foreign-style, means **Western style**. 入学式 **NYŪGAKUSHIKI**, enter-school-ceremony, means **matriculation ceremony**.

| 403 | ON READING: **SHI** <br> KUN READINGS: **tame(su), kokoro(miru)** | 試験 **shiken** *exam, test, trial* <br> 試合 **shiai** *match, game* <br> 試みる **kokoromiru** *to try, to make an attempt* |
|---|---|---|
| 試 | *test, trial; to test, to try* | 運試し **undameshi** *to take one's chance* |
| | 丶 亠 亖 言 言 言 言 言 訂 | |
| 13 strokes | 訂 試 試 | |

The element for **speak** 言 was added to the element for **ceremony** 式 to symbolize making a person speak on a ceremonial stage and be evaluated. They wrote the new kanji 試, meaning **test** or **trial**. Used as a word by itself, usually as a verb, it is pronounced **TAME-SU** or **KOKORO-MIRU**. Used in compound words it is pronounced **SHI**. 試運転 **SHI-UNTEN**, test-drive, means **test drive**.

| 404<br><br>会<br><br>6 strokes | ON READINGS: **KAI, E**<br>KUN READING: **a(u)**<br><br>*meeting, society; to meet* | 会計 **kaisei** *accounting*<br>社会 **shakai** *society, community*<br>会得する **etoku suru** *to learn, to digest*<br>会う **au** *to meet* |
|---|---|---|

ノ 人 人 合 会 会

The kanji for **meet** came from a pictograph of **two** 二 **noses** ム, signifying people, meeting under a roof 𠆢. It was put together as 会, meaning **meet**. Used as a word by itself it is pronounced **A-U**. In compound words it is pronounced **KAI** or **E**. A 会館 **KAIKAN**, meet-building, is a **hall** or an **assembly hall** or a **grand building**. 会食 **KAISHOKU**, meet-eat, is a **banquet** or a **dinner party**. A 会話 **KAIWA**, meet-speak, is a **conversation**. A 協会 **KYŌKAI**, cooperate-association, is a **society** or an **association**. The 日米協会 **NICHIBEI KYŌKAI** is the Japan-America Society.

| 405<br><br>社<br><br>7 strokes | ON READING: **SHA**<br>KUN READING: **yashiro**<br><br>*shrine, society, business institution, company* | 社員 **shain** *company staff, employee*<br>社会人 **shakaijin** *member of society*<br>社交的 **shakōteki** *outgoing, sociable*<br>支社 **shisha** affiliate, branch office |
|---|---|---|

` ラ ラ ネ ネ 社 社

The element of a sacrificial altar with the sacrifice atop it 示, modified to ネ to fit the left side of a kanji square, was combined with the element for **earth** 土 to symbolize a place where people gather to undertake a social project. They wrote the final form 社, meaning a **shrine** or a **society** or a **business institution**. Used as a word by itself it is pronounced **YASHIRO**. In compound words it is pronounced **SHA**. A 会社 **KAISHA**, meet-business, is a **company**. The same two kanji in reverse order 社会 **SHAKAI**, society-meet, means **society in general**. A 本社 **HONSHA**, root-business, is the **head office of a company**. 神社 **JINJA** (**JINSHA** pronounced euphonically), God-shrine, is a **shrine**.

# AFTERWORD

In reading this book, you will have learned more than 400 kanji, and more than half of the pictographs the Chinese used to compose all of their kanji. With this knowledge you will already know the pictographic meanings of many hundreds more kanji that the Chinese formed from different combinations of the pictographs you have learned.

You will not, of course, know the pronunciation of a new kanji, nor its dictionary meaning, but knowing how the Chinese constructed the kanji will allow you to make a good guess at its meaning. Looking up the kanji in a dictionary should be enough in most cases to connect the meanings of the individual pictographs with the kanji's dictionary meaning. Flashcards and workbooks are available to help cement hard-to-remember kanji in your memory.

For example, the kanji 鳴 is composed of the pictographs for **mouth** 口 and **bird** 鳥. A good guess might be that it means the **singing of a bird**, and that would be correct. Looking 鳴 up in a dictionary would show that it also means the **chirping of an insect** like a cricket or the **cries of other animals.**

The kanji 岸 is composed of the pictographs for **mountain** 山, **cliff** 厂, and **dry** (the clothesline pole) 干. There are many possible guesses that you could make about the meaning of 岸. All of them would have some basis, but the Chinese saw 岸 as the cliffs between the mountains and the water, on the dry side of the dividing line, and meant a **riverbank** or **shore** or **coast.**

To learn the approximately 2,000 kanji that appear in Japanese newspapers you will have to learn the meanings of less than 100 additional pictographs, since not all existing pictographs are used in those 2,000 kanji. Mastering the Japanese language will of course require full knowledge of grammar, vocabulary, and pronunciation, for which there are many excellent texts and study guides available, but your present knowledge of the kanji and how they are put together will give you a strong headstart down that road.

# APPENDIX A

## The Kana Syllabaries

The Japanese writing system includes two sets of kana, each containing 46 characters. One set is called *Hiragana* and the other is called *Katakana*, and each set contains the same sounds as the other. As a general practice, the Hiragana are used to form grammatical word endings and the Katakana are used to write in Japanese the foreign loan words that the Japanese have borrowed.

Each kana is a syllable rather than a single letter, and most kana are combinations of one consonant and one vowel. These syllables are formed basically by adding each of the vowels **A**, **I**, **U**, **E**, and **O** to each of the consonants **K**, **S**, **T**, **N**, **H**, **M**, **Y**, **R**, and **W**. The **A**, **I**, **U**, **E**, and **O** sounds themselves and the **N** sound complete each set of kana.

Exceptions to this pattern are that the syllable **SI** is replaced by **SHI**, the syllable **TI** is replaced by **CHI**, and the syllable **TU** is replaced by **TSU** (the sounds **SI**, **TI**, and **TU** do not exist in Japanese). Also, the syllables **YI**, **YE**, **WI**, **WU**, and **WE** are no longer used.

In addition to the sounds that appear in the accompanying charts, other sounds are formed in one of two ways: by combining two or more kana to form one syllable, or by adding two small lines (called *nigori*) or a small circle (called *maru*) to certain of the kana to change their pronunciation slightly.

Examples of the first method are the adding of any of the single vowels to the end of a kana to form the long vowels, or the adding of the **Y**-syllables や, ゆ, or よ to the **I** column syllables to form new syllables in the pattern **KYA**, **KYU**, or **KYO**. The syllable **TŌ** is written と う, and the syllable **KYŌ** is written き ょ う.

An example of the second method is the forming of the syllables beginning with the consonants **G**, **Z**, **D**, **B**, and **P**.

Adding *nigori* to the **K**-row かきくけこ the **G**-row:

| が | ぎ | ぐ | げ | ご |
|----|----|----|----|----|
| **GA** | **GI** | **GU** | **GE** | **GO** |

Adding *nigori* to the **S**-row forms the **Z**-row:

| ざ | じ | ず | ぜ | ぞ |
|----|----|----|----|----|
| **ZA** | **JI** | **ZU** | **ZE** | **ZO** |

Adding *nigori* to the **T**-row forms the **D**-row:

| だ | ぢ | づ | で | ど |
|----|----|----|----|----|
| **DA** | **JI** | **ZU** | **DE** | **DO** |

Adding *nigori* to the **H**-row forms the **B**-row:

| ば | び | ぶ | べ | ぼ |
|----|----|----|----|----|
| **BA** | **BI** | **BU** | **BE** | **BO** |

Adding *maru* to the **H**-row forms the **P**-row:

| ぱ | ぴ | ぷ | ぺ | ぽ |
|----|----|----|----|----|
| **PA** | **PI** | **PU** | **PE** | **PO** |

To form the sounds JI and ZU, じ and ず are much more commonly used than ぢ or づ. The latter are used mainly in certain compound words.

Except for the formation of the long vowels, where a line is generally used rather than an extra vowel, these rules apply to *katakana* as well. In *katakana*, **TŌ** is written ト ウ.

This is the Hiragana/Katakana chart:

| | A | I | U | E | O | YA | YU | YO |
|---|---|---|---|---|---|---|---|---|
| **Single vowel** | あア<br>**A** | いイ<br>**I** | うウ<br>**U** | えエ<br>**E** | おオ<br>**O** | | | |
| **K** | かカ<br>**KA** | きキ<br>**KI** | くク<br>**KU** | けケ<br>**KE** | こコ<br>**KO** | きゃキャ<br>**KYA** | きゅキュ<br>**KYU** | きょキョ<br>**KYO** |
| **G** | がガ<br>**GA** | ぎギ<br>**GI** | ぐグ<br>**GU** | げゲ<br>**GE** | ごゴ<br>**GO** | ぎゃギャ<br>**GYA** | ぎゅギュ<br>**GYU** | ぎょギョ<br>**GYO** |
| **S** | さサ<br>**SA** | しシ<br>**SHI** | すス<br>**SU** | せセ<br>**SE** | そソ<br>**SO** | しゃシャ<br>**SHA** | しゅシュ<br>**SHU** | しょショ<br>**SHO** |
| **Z** | ざザ<br>**ZA** | じジ<br>**ZI** | ずズ<br>**ZU** | ぜゼ<br>**ZE** | ぞゾ<br>**ZO** | じゃジャ<br>**JA** | じゅジュ<br>**JU** | じょジョ<br>**JO** |
| **T** | たタ<br>**TA** | ちチ<br>**CHI** | つツ<br>**TSU** | てテ<br>**TE** | とト<br>**TO** | ちゃチャ<br>**CHA** | ちゅチュ<br>**CHU** | ちょチョ<br>**CHO** |
| **D** | だダ<br>**DA** | ぢヂ<br>**ZI** | づヅ<br>**ZU** | でデ<br>**DE** | どド<br>**DO** | ぢゃヂャ<br>**JA** | ぢゅヂュ<br>**JU** | ぢょヂョ<br>**JO** |
| **N** | なナ<br>**NA** | にニ<br>**NI** | ぬヌ<br>**NU** | ねネ<br>**NE** | のノ<br>**NO** | にゃニャ<br>**NYA** | にゅニュ<br>**NYU** | にょニョ<br>**NYO** |

| | A | I | U | E | O | YA | YU | YO |
|---|---|---|---|---|---|---|---|---|
| **H** | はハ<br>**HA** | ひヒ<br>**HI** | ふフ<br>**FU** | へヘ<br>**HE** | ほホ<br>**HO** | ひゃヒャ<br>**HYA** | ひゅヒュ<br>**HYU** | ひょヒョ<br>**HYO** |
| **B** | ばバ<br>**BA** | びビ<br>**BI** | ぶブ<br>**BU** | べベ<br>**BE** | ぼボ<br>**BO** | びゃビャ<br>**BYA** | びゅビュ<br>**BYU** | びょビョ<br>**BYO** |
| **P** | ぱパ<br>**PA** | ぴピ<br>**PI** | ぷプ<br>**PU** | ぺペ<br>**PE** | ぽポ<br>**PO** | ぴゃピャ<br>**PYA** | ぴゅピュ<br>**PYU** | ぴょピョ<br>**PYO** |
| **M** | まマ<br>**MA** | みミ<br>**MI** | むム<br>**MU** | めメ<br>**ME** | もモ<br>**MO** | みゃミャ<br>**MYA** | みゅミュ<br>**MYU** | みょミョ<br>**MYO** |
| **Y** | やヤ<br>**YA** | | ゆユ<br>**YU** | | よヨ<br>**YO** | | | |
| **R** | らラ<br>**RA** | りリ<br>**RI** | るル<br>**RU** | れレ<br>**RE** | ろロ<br>**RO** | りゃリャ<br>**RYA** | りゅリュ<br>**RYU** | りょリョ<br>**RYO** |
| **W** | わワ<br>**WA** | | んン<br>**N** | | をヲ<br>**O** | | | |

# APPENDIX B

## Kanji Summary Table

| KANJI NO. | KANJI | PAGE NO. | ON READING | KUN READING | ENGLISH MEANING |
|---|---|---|---|---|---|
| 1 | 日 | 19 | **NICHI, JITSU** | **hi, bi, ka** | Sun, a day |
| 2 | 木 | 19 | **MOKU** | **ki** | Tree, wood |
| 3 | 本 | 20 | **HON** | **moto** | Origin, source, book |
| 4 | 未 | 20 | **MI** | **mada** | Immature, not yet there |
| 5 | 末 | 21 | **MATSU** | **sue** | The end, extremity, tip |
| 6 | 東 | 21 | **TŌ** | **higashi** | East |
| 7 | 京 | 22 | **KYŌ, KEI** | | Capital |
| 8 | 田 | 22 | **DEN** | **ta, da** | Rice field, rice-paddy |
| 9 | 力 | 23 | **RIKI, RYOKU** | **chikara** | Strength, power |
| 10 | 男 | 23 | **DAN, NAN** | **otoko** | Man, male |
| 11 | 女 | 23 | **JO, NYO, NYŌ** | **onna, me** | Woman |
| 12 | 妹 | 24 | **MAI** | **imōto** | Younger sister |
| 13 | 母 | 24 | **BO** | **haha** | Mother |
| 14 | 人 | 24 | **NIN, JIN** | **hito** | Person |

| KANJI NO. | KANJI | PAGE NO. | ON READING | KUN READING | ENGLISH MEANING |
|---|---|---|---|---|---|
| 15 | 毎 | 25 | MAI, GOTO | | Every |
| 16 | 休 | 26 | KYŪ | yasu(mu) | To take a break, to take a holiday, to rest |
| 17 | 体 | 26 | TAI, TEI | karada | Body |
| 18 | 子 | 27 | SHI, SU | ko | Child |
| 19 | 好 | 28 | KŌ | su(ku), konomu | Love, like, goodness |
| 20 | 大 | 28 | TAI, DAI | ō, ō(ki'i) | Big, large |
| 21 | 天 | 29 | TEN | ama, ame | Heaven, sky |
| 22 | 王 | 29 | Ō | | King |
| 23 | 全 | 30 | ZEN | matta(ku), subete | The whole, complete; completely, totally |
| 24 | 太 | 30 | TAI, TA | futoi, futo(ru) | Fat, very big |
| 25 | 小 | 30 | SHŌ | chi'i(sai), ko, o | Small |
| 26 | 少 | 31 | SHŌ | suko(shi), suku(nai) | Few, little |
| 27 | 立 | 31 | RITSU, RYŪ | ta(tsu), ta(teru), tachi | To stand, to rise up |
| 28 | 一 | 32 | ICHI | hito, hito(tsu) | One |
| 29 | 二 | 32 | NI | futa, futa(tsu) | Two |
| 30 | 三 | 32 | SAN | mi, mit(tsu) | Three |
| 31 | 五 | 33 | GO | itsu(tsu) | Five |
| 32 | 四 | 33 | SHI | yo, yon, yot(tsu) | Four |
| 33 | 十 | 34 | JŪ | tō, to | Ten |
| 34 | 世 | 34 | SE, SEI | yo | Generation |
| 35 | 協 | 35 | KYŌ | | To unite, to join in cooperation |
| 36 | 九 | 35 | KYŪ, KU | kokono(tsu) | Nine |
| 37 | 八 | 36 | HACHI | ya, yat(tsu), yō | Eight |
| 38 | 六 | 36 | ROKU | mu, mui, mut(tsu) | Six |
| 39 | 刀 | 38 | TŌ | katana | Sword |
| 40 | 刃 | 38 | JIN | ha | Blade |
| 41 | 分 | 39 | BUN, BU, FUN (PUN) | wa(keru), wa(karu) | To cut and divide, to understand; piece, a part, share, minute |
| 42 | 七 | 40 | SHICHI | nana, nano, nana(tsu) | Seven |
| 43 | 切 | 40 | SETSU | ki(ru) | To cut |
| 44 | 川 | 40 | SEN | kawa (gawa) | River |
| 45 | 州 | 41 | SHŪ | su | Sandbank, state, province |
| 46 | 水 | 41 | SUI | mizu | Water |
| 47 | 海 | 42 | KAI | umi | Ocean |
| 48 | 氷 | 42 | HYŌ | kōri, hi | Ice |

| KANJI NO. | KANJI | PAGE NO. | ON READING | KUN READING | ENGLISH MEANING |
|---|---|---|---|---|---|
| 49 | 入 | 43 | NYŪ | i(reru), hai(ru) | To insert, to put in, to enter, to go in |
| 50 | 口 | 43 | KŌ, KU | kuchi (guchi) | Mouth, opening |
| 51 | 中 | 44 | CHŪ (JŪ) | naka | Middle, inside |
| 52 | 仲 | 44 | CHŪ | naka | Relationship |
| 53 | 介 | 45 | KAI | | To mediate |
| 54 | 界 | 45 | KAI | | Boundary |
| 55 | 央 | 46 | Ō | | The exact middle |
| 56 | 映 | 46 | EI | utsu(su), utsu(ru), ha(eru) | To reflect, to stand out; refrection |
| 57 | 画 | 46 | GA, KAKU | | Picture, painting, drawing |
| 58 | 古 | 47 | KO | furu(i) | Old |
| 59 | 品 | 47 | HIN | shina | Goods, things |
| 60 | 区 | 48 | KU | | Ward, district, section |
| 61 | 町 | 48 | CHŌ | machi | Town, section of a ward |
| 62 | 丁 | 49 | CHŌ, TEI | | Unit of measure, counter of things (tofu, etc.), block |
| 63 | 言 | 49 | GEN, GON | i(u), koto | To say, to speak |
| 64 | 信 | 49 | SHIN | | To believe, to trust |
| 65 | 己 | 50 | KO, KI | ono(re) | Self; from start to finish |
| 66 | 記 | 50 | KI | shiru(su) | To say it, to write it, to chronicle it |
| 67 | 計 | 50 | KEI | haka(ru) | Counting, measuring |
| 68 | 舌 | 51 | ZETSU | shita | Tongue |
| 69 | 話 | 51 | WA | hanashi, hana(su) | To talk |
| 70 | 活 | 52 | KATSU | | Life, activity |
| 71 | 語 | 52 | GO | kata(ru) | Word, language |
| 72 | 英 | 53 | EI | | Brilliant, superior, talented, England |
| 73 | 上 | 53 | JŌ | ue, uwa, nobo(ru), a(garu), a(geru), kami | Up, over, on top of; to climb up, to rise up |
| 74 | 下 | 54 | KA, GE | shita, shimo, moto, sa(garu), kuda(ru), kuda(saru), o(riru) | Down, under, below; to climb down, to drop down, to give down |
| 75 | 山 | 55 | SAN | yama | Mountain |
| 76 | 火 | 55 | KA | hi | Fire |
| 77 | 炎 | 56 | EN | hono-o | Flame |
| 78 | 谷 | 56 | KOKU | tani, ya | Valley, gorge |
| 79 | 穴 | 58 | KETSU | ana | Hole, open space |
| 80 | 工 | 58 | KŌ, KU | | To fabricate, to make |

| KANJI NO. | KANJI | PAGE NO. | ON READING | KUN READING | ENGLISH MEANING |
|---|---|---|---|---|---|
| 81 | 空 | 59 | KŪ | sora, kara, a(ku) | Sky, empty; vacant |
| 82 | 石 | 59 | SEKI, SHAKU | ishi | Stone |
| 83 | 由 | 59 | YU, YŪ | | The path out, the way, the means |
| 84 | 油 | 60 | YU | abura | Oil |
| 85 | 井 | 60 | SEI, SHŌ | i | Well, frame |
| 86 | 月 | 60 | GETSU, GATSU | tsuki | Moon, month |
| 87 | 夕 | 61 | SEKI | yu | Evening |
| 88 | 外 | 61 | GAI, GE | soto, hoka, hazu(su) | Other, outside of |
| 89 | 名 | 62 | MEI, MYŌ | na | A name |
| 90 | 多 | 62 | TA | ō(i) | Many |
| 91 | 期 | 63 | KI, GO | | Period of time, term, periodic |
| 92 | 棋 | 63 | KI, GI | | Japanese chess |
| 93 | 碁 | 64 | GO | | Go (game) |
| 94 | 明 | 64 | MEI, MYŌ | aka(ri), aka(rui), aki(raka), a(keru), a(ku) | Bright |
| 95 | 光 | 65 | KŌ | hikari, hika(ru) | Light; to shine, to sparkle |
| 96 | 早 | 65 | SŌ, SA | haya(i), haya(maru) | Early, fast, quick |
| 97 | 草 | 66 | SŌ | kusa | Grass |
| 98 | 朝 | 66 | CHŌ | asa | Morning |
| 99 | 土 | 67 | DO, TO | tsuchi | Earth, soil |
| 100 | 出 | 67 | SHUTSU | de(ru), da(su) | To come out, to go out, to take out, to send out, to depart |
| 101 | 生 | 68 | SEI, SHŌ | iki(ru,) u(mu), u(mareru), o(u), ha(eru), ki, nama | To live, to be born, to give birth; life, raw, uncooked |
| 102 | 星 | 68 | SEI, SHŌ | hoshi | Star |
| 103 | 者 | 69 | SHA | mono | Person |
| 104 | 圧 | 69 | ATSU | | Pressure |
| 105 | 里 | 70 | RI | sato | Village |
| 106 | 黒 | 70 | KOKU | kuro(i) | Black |
| 107 | 玉 | 70 | GYOKU | tama | Jewel, ball |
| 108 | 宝 | 71 | HŌ | takara | Treasure |
| 109 | 国 | 71 | KOKU | kuni | Country, state |
| 110 | 内 | 72 | NAI | uchi | Inside |
| 111 | 理 | 72 | RI | | To manage, to supervise; reason, rationality |
| 112 | 米 | 73 | BEI, MAI | kome | Rice |

| KANJI NO. | KANJI | PAGE NO. | ON READING | KUN READING | ENGLISH MEANING |
|---|---|---|---|---|---|
| 113 | 斗 | 73 | **TO** | | Ladle, unit of measure |
| 114 | 料 | 74 | **RYŌ** | | Charge, rate, fee, materials measured |
| 115 | 無 | 74 | **MU, BU** | **na(i)** | To cease to exist, none, no |
| 116 | 科 | 75 | **KA** | | Category, department, branch |
| 117 | 年 | 75 | **NEN** | **toshi** | Year, age |
| 118 | 白 | 77 | **HAKU, BYAKU** | **shiro, shiro(i), shira** | White |
| 119 | 食 | 77 | **SHOKU, JIKI** | **tabe(ru), ku(u)** | To eat |
| 120 | 欠 | 78 | **KETSU** | **ka(ku), ka(keru)** | Lack, absence; to lack, to decline |
| 121 | 飲 | 78 | **IN** | **no(mu)** | To drink |
| 122 | 数 | 79 | **SŪ** | **kazu, kazo(eru)** | To count; counting, number |
| 123 | 林 | 79 | **RIN** | **hayashi** | Woods |
| 124 | 森 | 80 | **SHIN** | **mori** | Forest |
| 125 | 果 | 80 | **KA** | **ha(tasu), ha(te)** | Fruit; to carry out; end |
| 126 | 汁 | 80 | **JU** | **shiru** | Liquid, juice |
| 127 | 菓 | 81 | **KA** | | Confection, refreshment, sweets |
| 128 | 茶 | 81 | **CHA, SA** | | Tea, brown |
| 129 | 手 | 82 | **SHU, ZU** | **te, ta** | Hand |
| 130 | 友 | 82 | **YŪ** | **tomo** | Friend |
| 131 | 左 | 82 | **SA** | **hidari** | Left |
| 132 | 右 | 83 | **U, YŪ** | **migi** | Right |
| 133 | 肉 | 83 | **NIKU** | | Meat |
| 134 | 焼 | 84 | **SHŌ** | **ya(ku), ya(keru)** | To singe, to burn, to roast |
| 135 | 有 | 84 | **YŪ, U** | **aru** | To have, to exist |
| 136 | 寸 | 85 | **SUN** | | Unit of measurement, just a tiny bit |
| 137 | 村 | 85 | **SON** | **mura** | Village |
| 138 | 守 | 86 | **SHU, SU** | **mamo(ru), mori** | To protect, to guard, to defend; amulet |
| 139 | 寺 | 86 | **JI** | **tera** | Temple |
| 140 | 竹 | 87 | **CHIKU** | **take** | Bamboo |
| 141 | 等 | 87 | **TŌ** | **hito(shi'i), nado** | Class, grade; equal, similar; and so on |
| 142 | 詩 | 88 | **SHI** | | Poetry, poem |
| 143 | 時 | 88 | **JI** | **toki** | Time, hour |
| 144 | 持 | 88 | **JI** | **mo(tsu)** | To have, to hold, to possess |
| 145 | 主 | 89 | **SHU** | **nushi, omo** | Master, owner, chief; main, major |

| KANJI NO. | KANJI | PAGE NO. | ON READING | KUN READING | ENGLISH MEANING |
|---|---|---|---|---|---|
| 146 | 住 | 89 | JŪ | su(mu) | To reside, to live |
| 147 | 付 | 90 | FU | tsu(keru), tsu(ku) | to attach, to stick to, be attached to, to come with; with |
| 148 | 府 | 90 | FU | | Seat of government; prefecture (Kyoto and Osaka) |
| 149 | 受 | 91 | JU | u(keru), u(karu) | To receive, to pass (an exam) |
| 150 | 争 | 91 | SŌ | araso(u) | To quarrel, to dispute, to conflict, to struggle |
| 151 | 甲 | 92 | KŌ, KAN | | Armor |
| 152 | 押 | 92 | Ō | o(su) | To push |
| 153 | 単 | 92 | TAN | | Sole, simple, single; basic unit |
| 154 | 戦 | 93 | SEN | tataka(u), ikusa | To fight, to make war; battle, war |
| 155 | 共 | 93 | KYŌ | tomo | Together |
| 156 | 交 | 94 | KŌ | ma(jiru), ma(zeru), maji(waru), ka(wasu) | Intersection, exchange, mixing; to mix, to blend, to intersect, to exchange |
| 157 | 校 | 94 | KŌ | | School |
| 158 | 学 | 94 | GAKU | mana(bu) | To learn, to study |
| 159 | 文 | 95 | BUN, MON | fumi | Writing, text, culture |
| 160 | 支 | 97 | SHI | sasa(eru) | Branch; to hold up, to support |
| 161 | 枝 | 97 | SHI | eda | Branch of a tree |
| 162 | 書 | 97 | SHO | ka(ku) | To write, to compose; writing, book |
| 163 | 筆 | 98 | HITSU | fude | Writing brush |
| 164 | 事 | 98 | JI | koto | Thing, affair, happening, matter, event |
| 165 | 史 | 99 | SHI | | History |
| 166 | 吏 | 99 | RI | | Government official |
| 167 | 使 | 100 | SHI | tsuka(u) | Servant, messenger, use; to use |
| 168 | 士 | 100 | SHI | | Warrior, scholar |
| 169 | 仕 | 101 | SHI | tsuka(eru) | Servant; to work, to serve |
| 170 | 化 | 101 | KA, KE | ba(keru) | To change, to transform; ~-ization |
| 171 | 花 | 101 | KA | hana | Flower |
| 172 | 粧 | 102 | SHŌ | | Makeup |
| 173 | 比 | 102 | HI | kura(beru) | Comparison; to compare |
| 174 | 皆 | 103 | KAI | mina, minna | All, everyone |
| 175 | 階 | 103 | KAI | | Step, floor, rank |
| 176 | 官 | 104 | KAN | | Government bureaucrat |
| 177 | 館 | 104 | KAN | yakata | Official building |

| KANJI NO. | KANJI | PAGE NO. | ON READING | KUN READING | ENGLISH MEANING |
|---|---|---|---|---|---|
| 178 | 反 | 105 | **HAN, TAN** | **so(ru), so(rasu)** | To oppose; reverse, anti-; to be against |
| 179 | 坂 | 105 | **HAN** | **saka** | Slope, hill |
| 180 | 止 | 106 | **SHI** | **to(meru), to(maru)** | To stop |
| 181 | 先 | 106 | **SEN** | **saki** | Already been there; precedent, leading edge; previous |
| 182 | 洗 | 107 | **SEN** | **ara(u)** | Washing; to wash |
| 183 | 足 | 107 | **SOKU** | **ashi, ta(riru), ta(su)** | Leg, foot; to be satisfied, to add to; enough |
| 184 | 禁 | 108 | **KIN** | | To forbid; ban, prohibition |
| 185 | 祭 | 108 | **SAI** | **matsu(ru), matsuri** | To deify; worship, festival |
| 186 | 際 | 109 | **SAI** | **kiwa** | To interact, to come into contact |
| 187 | 各 | 109 | **KAKU** | **ono-ono** | Each and every |
| 188 | 路 | 110 | **RO** | **ji** | Road |
| 189 | 客 | 110 | **KYAKU, KAKU** | | Guest, customer |
| 190 | 正 | 111 | **SEI, SHŌ** | **masa, tada(su), tada(shi'i)** | To correct; proper, right, righteous, reasonable, legitimate |
| 191 | 証 | 111 | **SHŌ** | | Proof |
| 192 | 政 | 112 | **SEI, SHŌ** | **matsurigoto** | Government |
| 193 | 行 | 112 | **KŌ, GYŌ** | **i(ku), yu(ku), okona(u)** | Line, row; to go, to do, to act, to hold |
| 194 | 歩 | 113 | **HO, BU** | **aru(ku), ayu(mu)** | To walk |
| 195 | 渉 | 113 | **SHŌ** | | To cross over carefully, to cross, to liaison with |
| 196 | 渋 | 114 | **JŪ** | **shibu, shibu(i), shibu(ru)** | To hesitate, to be reluctant; quiet, sober, tasteful |
| 197 | 街 | 114 | **GAI, KAI** | **machi** | Street, avenue |
| 198 | 待 | 115 | **TAI** | **ma(tsu)** | To wait |
| 199 | 心 | 115 | **SHIN** | **kokoro** | Heart |
| 200 | 羽 | 117 | **U** | **ha, hane, wa (ba, pa)** | Wing |
| 201 | 非 | 117 | **HI** | | Not, non-, un- |
| 202 | 不 | 117 | **FU, BU** | | Negative, wrong, false, unjust; dis-, in-, mis- |
| 203 | 悲 | 118 | **HI** | **kana(shi'i), kana(shimu)** | Sad |
| 204 | 愛 | 118 | **AI** | | Love |
| 205 | 急 | 119 | **KYŪ** | **iso(gu)** | Sudden, urgent; in a hurry |
| 206 | 音 | 119 | **ON, IN** | **oto, ne** | Sound |
| 207 | 意 | 120 | **I** | | Thoughts, intentions, the mind |
| 208 | 味 | 120 | **MI** | **aji, aji(wau)** | To taste |

| KANJI NO. | KANJI | PAGE NO. | ON READING | KUN READING | ENGLISH MEANING |
|---|---|---|---|---|---|
| 209 | 目 | 121 | **MOKU, BOKU** | **me, ma** | Eye |
| 210 | 注 | 121 | **CHŪ** | **soso(gu)** | To pour, to be careful, to pay attention |
| 211 | 相 | 122 | **SŌ, SHŌ** | **ai** | To observe closely; mutual |
| 212 | 省 | 122 | **SHŌ, SEI** | **habu(ku), kaeri(miru)** | Government ministry; to omit, to save |
| 213 | 直 | 123 | **CHOKU, JIKI** | **nao(ru), nao(su), su(gu), tada(chi-ni)** | Honest, straight; immediately, at once, proper; to make straight, to fix |
| 214 | 亡 | 123 | **BŌ, MŌ** | **na(ki)** | To die, to escape, to lose |
| 215 | 盲 | 124 | **MŌ** | **mekura** | Blind |
| 216 | 忘 | 124 | **BŌ** | **wasu(reru)** | To forget |
| 217 | 帽 | 125 | **BŌ** | | Hat |
| 218 | 市 | 125 | **SHI** | **ichi** | City, central marketplace |
| 219 | 見 | 126 | **KEN** | **mi(ru), mi(eru), mi(seru)** | To see |
| 220 | 自 | 126 | **JI, SHI** | **mizuka(ra)** | Self |
| 221 | 習 | 127 | **SHŪ** | **nara(u)** | To learn |
| 222 | 具 | 127 | **GU** | | Utensil, tool |
| 223 | 貝 | 128 | **KAI** | | Shell, shellfish |
| 224 | 費 | 128 | **HI** | **tsui(yasu)** | Expense, expenditure; to spend |
| 225 | 算 | 129 | **SAN** | | To calculate |
| 226 | 首 | 129 | **SHU** | **kubi** | Neck, head |
| 227 | 県 | 130 | **KEN** | | Prefecture, state |
| 228 | 耳 | 130 | **JI** | **mimi** | Ear |
| 229 | 聖 | 131 | **SEI** | | Holy, sacred |
| 230 | 取 | 131 | **SHU** | **to(ru)** | To take |
| 231 | 最 | 132 | **SAI** | **motto(mo)** | The most, the highest degree |
| 232 | 歯 | 132 | **SHI** | **ha** | Tooth, teeth |
| 233 | 鼻 | 133 | **BI** | **hana** | Nose |
| 234 | 公 | 133 | **KŌ** | **ōyake** | Public |
| 235 | 松 | 134 | **SHŌ** | **matsu** | Pine tree |
| 236 | 私 | 134 | **SHI** | **watakushi, watashi** | I, my, me, mine |
| 237 | 和 | 135 | **WA** | **nago(mu), yawa(ragu)** | Peace, harmony; to moderate, to ameliorate, to abate, to lessen; Japanese style |
| 238 | 秋 | 135 | **SHŪ** | **aki** | Autumn |
| 239 | 兄 | 137 | **KEI, KYŌ** | **ani** | Elder brother |
| 240 | 税 | 137 | **ZEI** | | Taxes |
| 241 | 説 | 138 | **SETSU, ZEI** | **to(ku)** | Opinion, theory; to preach, to explain |

| KANJI NO. | KANJI | PAGE NO. | ON READING | KUN READING | ENGLISH MEANING |
|---|---|---|---|---|---|
| 242 | 競 | 138 | **KYŌ, KEI** | **se(ru), kiso(u)** | To compete |
| 243 | 険 | 139 | **KEN** | **kewa(shi'i)** | Risky, steep, dangerous |
| 244 | 保 | 139 | **HO** | **tamo(tsu)** | To preserve, to maintain, to protect, to keep |
| 245 | 厄 | 140 | **YAKU** | | Bad luck, misfortune, disaster |
| 246 | 危 | 140 | **KI** | **abuna(i), a(yaui)** | Dangerous |
| 247 | 回 | 140 | **KAI** | **mawa(su), mawa(ru)** | To rotate, to revolve, to go around, to circulate |
| 248 | 同 | 141 | **DŌ** | **ona(ji)** | Same |
| 249 | 尚 | 141 | **SHŌ** | **nao** | Further, furthermore, still more |
| 250 | 常 | 142 | **JŌ** | **tsune, toko** | Always, usual |
| 251 | 堂 | 142 | **DŌ** | | Hall, building (temple, chapel, etc.) |
| 252 | 高 | 143 | **KŌ** | **taka(i), taka, taka-(maru), taka(meru)** | Tall, high, expensive |
| 253 | 宮 | 143 | **KYŪ, GŪ** | **miya** | Palace, temple, shrine |
| 254 | 党 | 144 | **TŌ** | | Faction, party (political), bloc, caucus |
| 255 | 車 | 144 | **SHA** | **kuruma** | Car, cart |
| 256 | 庫 | 144 | **KO** | | Storage shed, storehouse |
| 257 | 転 | 145 | **TEN** | **koro(bu), koro(garu)** | To tumble, to turn, to roll |
| 258 | 軍 | 145 | **GUN** | | Armed forces, military |
| 259 | 運 | 146 | **UN** | **hako(bu)** | To transport, to carry |
| 260 | 送 | 146 | **SŌ** | **oku(ru)** | To send |
| 261 | 用 | 147 | **YŌ** | **mochi(iru)** | To use, to put to use |
| 262 | 通 | 147 | **TSŪ** | **tō(ru), tō(su), kayo(u)** | To go through, to commute |
| 263 | 道 | 148 | **DŌ, TŌ** | **michi** | Way, road |
| 264 | 雨 | 148 | **U** | **ame, ama** | Rain |
| 265 | 傘 | 149 | **SAN** | **kasa** | Umbrella |
| 266 | 雪 | 149 | **SETSU** | **yuki** | Snow |
| 267 | 申 | 150 | **SHIN** | **mō(su)** | To expound |
| 268 | 神 | 150 | **SHIN, JIN** | **kami** | God |
| 269 | 電 | 151 | **DEN** | | Electricity |
| 270 | 汽 | 151 | **KI** | | Steam |
| 271 | 気 | 152 | **KI, KE** | | Spirit, unseen force |
| 272 | 周 | 152 | **SHŪ** | **mawa(ri)** | Circumference; around |
| 273 | 週 | 153 | **SHŪ** | | Week |
| 274 | 干 | 153 | **KAN** | **ho(su), hi(ru)** | Dry |
| 275 | 刊 | 154 | **KAN** | | To publish |

| KANJI NO. | KANJI | PAGE NO. | ON READING | KUN READING | ENGLISH MEANING |
|---|---|---|---|---|---|
| 276 | 舟 | 154 | SHŪ | fune, funa | Small ship, boat |
| 277 | 船 | 154 | SEN | fune, funa | Boat, ship |
| 278 | 机 | 155 | KI | tsukue | Desk |
| 279 | 航 | 155 | KŌ | | Voyage |
| 280 | 重 | 157 | JŪ, CHŌ | omo(i), e, kasa(neru) | Heavy, grave, layered |
| 281 | 動 | 157 | DŌ | ugo(ku) | To move |
| 282 | 働 | 158 | DŌ | hatara(ku) | Work; to work |
| 283 | 罪 | 158 | ZAI | tsumi | Crime, sin |
| 284 | 買 | 159 | BAI | ka(u) | To buy |
| 285 | 売 | 159 | BAI | u(ru) | To sell |
| 286 | 商 | 160 | SHŌ | akina(u) | Trading, doing business |
| 287 | 読 | 160 | DOKU, TŌ | yo(mu) | To read |
| 288 | 員 | 161 | IN | | Member, employee, staff |
| 289 | 円 | 161 | EN | maru(i) | Yen, circle, round |
| 290 | 門 | 162 | MON | kado | Gate |
| 291 | 聞 | 162 | BUN, MON | ki(ku) | To hear, to ask |
| 292 | 問 | 163 | MON | to(u), to(i), ton | To ask, to inquire |
| 293 | 間 | 163 | KAN, KEN (GEN) | aida, ma | Between (time or space), space |
| 294 | 関 | 164 | KAN | seki, kaka(waru) | Barrier |
| 295 | 開 | 164 | KAI | hira(ku), a(ku), a(keru) | To open |
| 296 | 閉 | 165 | HEI | shi(meru), to(jiru) | To close |
| 297 | 戸 | 165 | KO | to | Door |
| 298 | 是 | 166 | ZE | kore | Right, proper; this |
| 299 | 頁 | 166 | PĒJI | | Page |
| 300 | 題 | 167 | DAI | | Subject, theme, title |
| 301 | 豆 | 167 | TŌ, ZU | mame | Beans; very small, miniature |
| 302 | 腐 | 168 | FU | kusa(ru) | To rot, to decay, to spoil |
| 303 | 頭 | 168 | TŌ, ZU | atama | Head, leader |
| 304 | 馬 | 169 | BA | uma, ma | Horse |
| 305 | 尺 | 169 | SHAKU | | Foot (unit of length), scale |
| 306 | 駅 | 170 | EKI | | A station |
| 307 | 駐 | 170 | CHŪ | | To stop, to stay, to reside |
| 308 | 長 | 171 | CHŌ | naga(i) | Long, senior, the boss |
| 309 | 帳 | 171 | CHŌ | | Notebook, register |
| 310 | 鳥 | 172 | CHŌ | tori | Bird |
| 311 | 島 | 172 | TŌ | shima | Island |
| 312 | 西 | 173 | SAI, SEI | nishi | West |

| KANJI NO. | KANJI | PAGE NO. | ON READING | KUN READING | ENGLISH MEANING |
|---|---|---|---|---|---|
| 313 | 煙 | 173 | EN | kemuri, kemu(i) | Smoke |
| 314 | 集 | 174 | SHŪ | atsu(maru), atsu-(meru), tsudo(u) | To gather together, to collect |
| 315 | 曜 | 175 | YŌ | | Day of the week |
| 316 | 至 | 176 | SHI | ita(ru) | To reach, to arrive at |
| 317 | 室 | 176 | SHITSU | | Room (in a house) |
| 318 | 屋 | 177 | OKU | ya | Shop, building, house |
| 319 | 店 | 177 | TEN | mise | Shop, store |
| 320 | 局 | 178 | KYOKU | | Office, department |
| 321 | 部 | 178 | BU | | Part, department, division |
| 322 | 産 | 179 | SAN | u(mu), u(mareru), ubu | To give birth, produce; naive |
| 323 | 業 | 179 | GYŌ, GO | waza | Profession, occupation |
| 324 | 楽 | 181 | RAKU, GAKU | tano(shi'i), tano(shimu) | Music, pleasure |
| 325 | 薬 | 181 | YAKU | kusuri | Medicine, drugs |
| 326 | 牛 | 182 | GYŪ | ushi | Cow, bull |
| 327 | 乳 | 182 | NYŪ | chichi, chi | Milk |
| 328 | 半 | 182 | HAN | naka(ba) | Half |
| 329 | 物 | 183 | BUTSU, MOTSU | mono | Things |
| 330 | 貨 | 183 | KA | | Money, goods |
| 331 | 金 | 184 | KIN, KON | kane | Gold, metal, money |
| 332 | 銀 | 184 | GIN | | Silver |
| 333 | 座 | 185 | ZA | suwa(ru) | Seat; to sit down |
| 334 | 園 | 185 | EN | sono | Yard, garden |
| 335 | 特 | 186 | TOKU | | Special |
| 336 | 羊 | 186 | YŌ | hitsuji | Sheep |
| 337 | 洋 | 186 | YŌ | | Ocean; foreign, Western |
| 338 | 美 | 187 | BI | utsuku(shi'i) | Beautiful |
| 339 | 様 | 187 | YŌ | sama | Scene, appearance, way, manner, method; condision; (polite suffix) Mr./Ms. |
| 340 | 毛 | 188 | MŌ | ke | Hair, fur |
| 341 | 形 | 188 | KEI, GYŌ | kata, katachi | Form, pattern, shape |
| 342 | 刑 | 188 | KEI | | Punishment |
| 343 | 平 | 189 | HEI, BYŌ | taira | Flat, level, peace |
| 344 | 豚 | 189 | TON | buta | Pig |
| 345 | 家 | 190 | KA, KE | ie, ya | House |
| 346 | 安 | 190 | AN | yasu(i) | Restfulness, peace, inexpensive |
| 347 | 案 | 190 | AN | | Plan, idea |

| KANJI NO. | KANJI | PAGE NO. | ON READING | KUN READING | ENGLISH MEANING |
|---|---|---|---|---|---|
| 348 | 字 | 191 | JI | | Letter, character, symbol |
| 349 | 漢 | 191 | KAN | | China, Chinese; man |
| 350 | 魚 | 192 | GYO | sakana | Fish |
| 351 | 漁 | 192 | GYO RYŌ | | Fishing |
| 352 | 糸 | 192 | SHI | ito | Thread |
| 353 | 係 | 193 | KEI | kakari, kaka(ru) | Relation, person in charge of |
| 354 | 幾 | 193 | KI | iku(tsu), iku(ra) | How many, how much |
| 355 | 機 | 194 | KI | hata | Loom, device, engine |
| 356 | 戒 | 194 | KAI | imashi(meru) | To admonish, to rebuke |
| 357 | 械 | 195 | KAI | | Device |
| 358 | 泉 | 195 | SEN | izumi | Natural spring |
| 359 | 線 | 196 | SEN | | Line |
| 360 | 綿 | 196 | MEN | wata | Cotton |
| 361 | 冬 | 197 | TŌ | fuyu | Winter |
| 362 | 終 | 197 | SHŪ | owa(ru), owa(ri) | End, finish |
| 363 | 氏 | 198 | SHI | uji | Clan, family, family name |
| 364 | 紙 | 198 | SHI | kami | Paper |
| 365 | 皿 | 200 | SARA | | Plate, dish, bowl |
| 366 | 温 | 200 | ON | atata(kai), atata(maru), atata(meru) | Warm; to warm, to heat, to get warm |
| 367 | 血 | 201 | KETSU | chi | Blood |
| 368 | 貧 | 201 | HIN, BIN | mazu(shi'i) | Poor, impoverished |
| 369 | 犬 | 202 | KEN | inu | Dog |
| 370 | 器 | 202 | KI | utsuwa | Vessel, utensil |
| 371 | 虫 | 203 | CHŪ | mushi | Worm, insect, bug |
| 372 | 凡 | 203 | BON, HAN | oyo(so) | Ordinary, common, in general, nearly, about |
| 373 | 風 | 204 | FŪ, FU | kaze, kaza | Wind, style |
| 374 | 独 | 204 | DOKU | hito(ri) | Independent, all alone |
| 375 | 番 | 205 | BAN | | Number, one's turn; to guard |
| 376 | 第 | 205 | DAI | | Order, numerical order |
| 377 | 百 | 206 | HYAKU | | Hundred |
| 378 | 宿 | 206 | SHUKU | yado, yado(ru) | Hotel, lodge; to reside |
| 379 | 千 | 207 | SEN | chi | Thousand |
| 380 | 万 | 207 | MAN, BAN | | Ten thousand |
| 381 | 弓 | 208 | KYŪ | yumi | Archer's bow |
| 382 | 引 | 208 | IN | hi(ku) | To pull |
| 383 | 矢 | 209 | SHI | ya | Arrow |

| KANJI NO. | KANJI | PAGE NO. | ON READING | KUN READING | ENGLISH MEANING |
|---|---|---|---|---|---|
| 384 | 知 | 209 | CHI | shi(ru), shi(raseru) | To know, to make known, to inform |
| 385 | 医 | 210 | I | | Medicine, healing |
| 386 | 酒 | 210 | SHU | sake, saka | Rice wine, liquor |
| 387 | 利 | 211 | RI | ki(ku) | Profit, benefit |
| 388 | 別 | 211 | BETSU | waka(reru) | To separate, to diverge |
| 389 | 所 | 212 | SHO | tokoro | Place |
| 390 | 場 | 212 | JŌ | ba | Place |
| 391 | 元 | 213 | GEN, GAN | moto | Origin, source |
| 392 | 完 | 213 | KAN | | Finish, completion |
| 393 | 院 | 214 | IN | | Building for temple, palace, hospital, school, institution |
| 394 | 病 | 214 | BYŌ, HEI | ya(mu), yamai | Illness; to be ill |
| 395 | 折 | 215 | SETSU | o(ru) | To break, to bend, to fold |
| 396 | 近 | 215 | KIN | chika(i) | Close by, near |
| 397 | 新 | 216 | SHIN | atara(shi'i), arata, ni'i | New |
| 398 | 質 | 216 | SHITSU, SHI-CHI, CHI | | Character, nature, quality; to pawn |
| 399 | 代 | 217 | DAI, TAI | ka(waru), ka(eru), yo | Fee, generation; to substitute, to replace |
| 400 | 貸 | 218 | TAI | ka(su) | Loan; to lend |
| 401 | 作 | 218 | SAKU, SA | tsuku(ru) | To make, to construct, to compose |
| 402 | 式 | 219 | SHIKI | | Ceremony, style |
| 403 | 試 | 219 | SHI | tame(su), kokoro-(miru) | Test, trial; to test, to try |
| 404 | 会 | 220 | KAI, E | a(u) | Meeting, society; to meet |
| 405 | 社 | 220 | SHA | yashiro | Shrine, society, business institution, company |

# APPENDIX C

## Index To English Meanings (the number after each kanji refers to the page it is found)

expensive 高 143
explain 説 138
expound 申 150
extremity 末 21
eye 目 121

fabricate 工 57
faction 党 144
false 不 117
family, family name
 氏 198
fast 早 65
fat 太 30
fee 料 74, 代 217
festival 祭 108
few 少 31
fight 戦 93
finish 終 197, 完 213
fire 火 55
fish 魚 192
fishing 漁 192
five 五 33
flame 炎 56
flat 平 189
floor 階 103
flower 花 101
fold 折 215
foot 足 107
foot (unit of length)
 尺 169
forbid 禁 108
foreign 洋 186
forest 森 80
forget 忘 124
form 形 188
four 四 33
frame 井 60
friend 友 82
from start to finish
 己 50
fruit 果 80
fur 毛 188
further, furthermore
 尚 141

garden 園 185
gate 門 162
gather together 集 174
generation 世 34, 代
 217

get warm 温 200
give birth 生 68, 産
 179
go 行 112
Go (game) 碁 64
go around 回 140
go in 入 43
go out 出 67
go through 通 147
God 神 150
gold 金 184
goodness 好 28
goods 品 47, 貨 183
gorge 谷 56
government 政 112
government bureau-
 crat 官 104
government ministry
 省 122
government official
 吏 99
grade 等 87
grass 草 66
grave 重 157
guard 守 86, 番 205
guest 客 110

hair 毛 188
half 半 182
hall 堂 142
hand 手 82
happening 事 98
harmony 和 135
hat 帽 125
have 有 84, 持 88
head 首 129, 頭 168
healing 医 210
hear 聞 162
heart 心 115
heat 温 200
heaven 天 29
heavy 重 157
hesitate 渋 114
high 高 143
highest degree 最
 132
hill 坂 105
history 史 99
hold 持 88, 行 112
hold up 支 97

hole 穴 58
holy 聖 131
honest 直 123
horse 馬 169
hotel 宿 206
hour 時 88
house 屋 176, 家 190
how many, how
 much 幾 193
hundred 百 206

I 私 134
ice 氷 42
idea 案 190
illness 病 214
immature 未 20
immediately 直 123
impoverished 貧 201
in a hurry 急 119
in charge of 係 193
in general 凡 203
independent 独 204
inexpensive 安 190
inform 知 209
inquire 問 163
insect 虫 203
insert 入 43
inside 中 44, 内 72
institution 院 213
intentions 意 120
interact 際 109
intersect 交 94
intersection 交 94
island 島 172
~-ization 化 101

Japanese chess 棋 63
Japanese style 和 135
jewel 玉 70
join in cooperation
 協 35
juice 汁 80
just a tiny bit 寸 85

keep 保 139
king 王 29
know 知 209

lack 欠 78
ladle 斗 73

language 語 52
large 大 28
layered 重 157
leader 頭 168
leading edge 先 106
learn 学 94, 習 127
left 左 82
leg 足 107
legitimate 正 111
lend 貸 218
lessen 和 135
letter 字 191
level 平 189
liaison with 渉 113
life 活 52, 生 68
light 光 65
like 好 28
line 行 112, 線 196
liquid 汁 80
liquor 酒 210
little 少 31
live 生 68, 住 89
loan 貸 218
lodge 宿 206
long 長 171
loom 機 194
lose 亡 123
love 好 28, 愛 118

main 主 89
maintain 保 139
major 主 89
make 工 57, 作 218
make known 知 209
make straight 直 124
make war 戦 93
makeup 粧 102
male 男 23
man 男 23, 漢 191
manage 理 72
manner 様 187
many 多 62
master 主 89
materials measured
 料 74
matter 事 98
means, the 由 59
measuring 計 50
meat 肉 83
mediate 介 45

medicine 薬 181, 医 210
meeting; meet 会 220
member 員 161
messenger 使 100
metal 金 184
method 様 187
middle 中 44, 央 46
military 軍 145
milk 乳 182
mind, the 意 120
miniature 豆 167
minute 分 39
misfortune 厄 140
mixing; mix 交 94
moderate 和 135
money 貨 183, 金 184
month, moon 月 60
morning 朝 66
most, the 最 132
mother 母 24
mountain 山 55
mouth 口 43
move 動 157
Mr./Ms. (polite suffix) 様 187
music 楽 181
mutual 相 122
my, me, mine 私 134

naive 産 179
name 名 62
natural spring 泉 195
nature 質 216
near 近 215
nearly 凡 203
neck 首 129
negative 不 117
new 新 216
nine 九 35
none, no 無 74
nose 鼻 133
not yet there 未 20
not, non-, un- 非 117
notebook 帳 171
number 数 79, 番 205
numerical order 第 205

observe closely 相 122
occupation 業 179
ocean 海 42, 洋 186
office 局 178
official building 館 104
oil 油 60
old 古 47
omit 省 122
on top of 上 53
one 一 32
one's turn 番 205
open 開 164
open space 穴 58
opening 口 43
opinion 説 138
oppose 反 105
order 第 205
ordinary 凡 203
origin 本 20, 元 213
other 外 61
outside of 外 61
over 上 53
owner 主 89

page 頁 166
painting 画 46
palace 宮 143
paper 紙 198
part 分 39, 部 178
party (political) 党 144
pass (an exam) 受 91
path out, the 由 59
pattern 形 188
pawn 質 216
pay attention 注 121
peace 和 135, 平 189, 安 190
period of time, periodic 期 63
person 人 24, 者 69
picture 画 46
piece 分 39
pig 豚 189
pine tree 松 134
place 所 212, 場 212
plan 案 190
plate 皿 200

pleasure 楽 181
poem, poetry 詩 88
poor 貧 201
possess 持 88
pour 注 121
power 力 23
preach 説 138
prefecture 県 130
prefecture (Kyoto and Osaka) 府 90
preserve 保 139
pressure 圧 69
previous 先 106
produce 産 179
profession 業 179
profit 利 211
prohibition 禁 108
proof 証 111
proper 正 111, 直 123, 是 166
protect 守 86, 保 139
province 州 41
public 公 133
publish 刊 154
pull 引 208
punishment 刑 188
push 押 92
put in 入 43
put to use 用 147

quality 質 216
quarrel 争 91
quick 早 65
quiet 渋 114

rain 雨 148
rank 階 103
rate 料 74
rationality 理 72
raw 生 68
reach 至 175
read 読 160
reason 理 72
reasonable 正 111
rebuke 戒 194
receive 受 91
reflect, reflection 映 46
refreshment 菓 81

register 帳 171
relation 係 193
relationship 仲 44
replace 代 217
reside 住 89, 駐 170, 宿 206
rest 休 26
restfulness 安 190
reverse 反 105
revolve 回 140
rice 米 73
rice field, rice-paddy 田 22
rice wine 酒 210
right 右 83, 正 111, 是 166
righteous 正 111
rise up 立 31, 上 53
risky 険 139
river 川 40
road 路 110, 道 148
roast 焼 84
roll 転 145
room (in a house) 室 176
rot 腐 168
rotate 回 140
round 円 161
row 行 112

sacred 聖 131
sad 悲 118
same 同 141
sandbank 州 41
save 省 122
say 言 49
say it 記 50
scene 様 187
scholar 士 100
school 校 94
seat 座 185
seat of government 府 90
section 区 48
section of a ward 町 48
see 見 126
self 己 50, 自 126
sell 売 159
send 送 146